MY GLORIOUS DEFEATS

MY GLORIOUS DEFEATS

HACKTIVIST, NARCISSIST, ANONYMOUS: A MEMOIR

BARRETT BROWN

MCD
Farrar, Straus and Giroux
New York

MCD
Farrar, Straus and Giroux
120 Broadway, New York, NY 10271

Printed in the United States of America
First edition, 2024

Library of Congress Cataloging-in-Publication Data
Names: Brown, Barrett, author.
Title: My glorious defeats : hacktivist, narcissist, anonymous: a memoir / Barrett Brown.
Description: First edition. | New York : MCD / Farrar, Straus and Giroux, 2024.
Identifiers: LCCN 2019054793 | ISBN 9780374217013 (hardcover)
Subjects: LCSH: Brown, Barrett. | Journalists—United States—Biography.
Classification: LCC PN4874.B767 A3 2019 | DDC 070.92 [B]—dc23
LC record available at https://lccn.loc.gov/2019054793

www.mcdbooks.com • www.fsgbooks.com
Follow us on social media at @mcdbooks and @fsgbooks

10 9 8 7 6 5 4 3 2 1

In memory of Michael Hastings

In a rare moment of self-pity Lenin wrote to Inessa Armand in 1916: "Since 1893 on, one struggle after another, against political stupidity, vileness, and so on." He did not reflect that most of those struggles were of his own making and that he enjoyed them.

—ADAM B. ULAM, *The Bolsheviks*

CONTENTS

HUBRIS

1

Microverse

Summer 2014

The old brick building to which we were being led had served as an internment center for German nationals during World War II. Now it mostly held Americans. I wondered briefly whether I should write this down the next time I managed to get hold of a pencil.

There were eight of us being escorted across the compound of Federal Correctional Institution Seagoville, which had been put on lockdown as a result of our actions; prison inmates, confined to whatever building they'd happened to be in when the incident began, stared at us through the windows. I'd never seen the yard before, having spent the preceding months in the prison's jail unit along with others who were awaiting trial or sentencing or transfer. Our own building had been modern, purpose-built for incarceration, and we never really saw it from the outside. Out here, on the other side of the tall barbed-wire fence that bisected the compound and divided the jail from the prison proper, the whole place had the look of a college campus—albeit a third-rate college in a second-tier state, never producing any really successful graduates who might be inclined to write an endowment check.

When we arrived at the brick metaphor for American decline, situated at the other end of the yard from the jail unit that had lately made up my universe, we were taken through the main door and then down a stairwell to the receiving area, where we were divided into pairs. As our turn came, two of us were placed in one of the holding cells at the foot of the stairs. The cell gate was locked behind us, and my companion and I took turns backing up to the bars so that the guards could remove our handcuffs through a little rectangular gap.

"What's got you so mad, white boy?" an intake guard asked me. I declined to respond. I wasn't mad anymore; the regret had already begun to set in. Also the guard himself was white, which I found confusing.

We stripped and threw out our jail uniforms. In exchange we were handed bright yellow spandex pants, flimsy boxer shorts, white T-shirts, and blue slip-on shoes, and then left to wait. The corridor was made of concrete. All the light came from naked bulbs.

There was a light switch in the cell, and I turned it on. "Leave it dark," drawled my companion. "That bulb's gonna make it hotter."

"We're gonna have to get used to that," I retorted.

"Oh, that's right!" He said this with great cheerfulness, and I liked him for it. I'd barely known him back in the unit, where we'd played chess a couple of times. Now we would be living together for twenty-three to twenty-four hours a day in a small concrete room for at least a month or two over the course of a Texas summer, with no air-conditioning and little to occupy our time. He had already accepted this.

I hadn't. The adrenaline rush I always get from confrontations with unjust authority had played itself out, and now I regretted the loss of my books, the spacious corner cell I'd shared with the old Vietnam vet, my phone calls, my little radio. I'd been held in the Special Housing Unit once before, upon arriving at another prison, but only for a few days while I waited for space to open up in the jail unit. That time, I'd been able to bring books into the hole, along with paper and pens. Now I had nothing. And so I went over the events of the last few hours, wondering if it had been worth it and deciding that it hadn't. Nothing had really been accomplished by what we'd done; the elderly man we'd been trying to defend had been brought to the SHU along with us, which was the very outcome we'd set out to prevent. Probably he'd be in more trouble now. And I wouldn't have any coffee for days and days and days.

My new friend and I were cuffed back up and taken to a cell about halfway down the corridor. The door was already open; we walked in; the door was closed and locked; we backed up against it to be uncuffed through the rectangular slot located at hip level, which was then closed and locked from the outside. We dropped our blankets on our mattresses and appraised our quarters. The bulk of it was taken up by the bunk bed, a stainless-steel sink-and-toilet unit, and a metal desk affixed to the wall. A window with a tightly laced metal grille sat in the wall opposite the door; it had a rotating lever that could be used to draw the glass in, which I knew to be an unusual feature, representative of the more easygoing approach to prison design that marked mid-twentieth-century facilities. The window looked out upon a courtyard, and a tree.

Regret gnawed upon my soul, as it does each time it occurs to me that my past self has sold out my present self, depriving him of later comfort in exchange for momentary satisfaction. Previously this had taken the form of heroin addiction. Now it was the impulse to defy authority without clear strategic advantage.

"Is that you, Brown?!" someone shouted from down the hall.

I went back to the steel door, which featured a metal lattice grille over a rectangular gap, situated vertically and at face level, two feet above the horizontal chute. I pressed my cheek against the grille and shouted out confirmation that I was myself and could be no other.

"I'll send you some coffee tonight! You're awesome, Brown!"

It was a Hispanic fellow I'd vaguely known from the jail unit, where newspaper and magazine articles about my adventures on the outside had circulated for some time before my arrival. Now he was offering tribute.

Julian the Apostate, raised to Caesar but not yet Augustus, and wavering in the face of necessary civil war, must have been likewise affected when a Gaulic auxiliary shouted out from the ranks that he must follow his star. Even Emma Goldman had had her moment of doubt and pain, only to be rallied back to her natural strength through the stray words of some admiring fellow prisoner. I had no idea how this fellow proposed to give me coffee from his cell down the corridor, but that was rather secondary.

For was it not I myself who had decided, from adolescence on, that there could be no middle ground? Had I not filled teenage journals with inane yet consistent juvenilia to the effect that I would be Caesar or nothing? Had I not since taken a thousand conscious steps away from the sordid path of the postwar Westerner, in revolt against the passive mediocrity of our age? Had I not pledged myself to the life of the revolutionary adventurer, and to the unfinished work of the Enlightenment?

Each of the great men who had formed my psychological pantheon from childhood on had suffered for his efforts. And the road to the palace often winds through the prison. Yes, I had been cast into the crevasse. So had any number of those giants who once roamed the earth; they emerged, cast now in bronze.

But it wasn't the example of my personal deities that drove me on. There are lives, and fragments of lives, that we may look to for direction as the faithful look to saints. Two girls, as later reported by Solzhenitsyn, were held in an early Soviet prison where talking was forbidden; they sang songs on the subject of lilacs, and continued singing as guards pulled them down the hall by their hair. These accounts merely shame me, as they should shame you. But shame is not sufficient groundwork for the things that I would have to do if I were to prevail in a cause that was not only just but entirely compatible with my own eternal cause, which is me. Duty is enough for some. I require glory. And now I saw the way forward, once again.

Yes, I was in the crevasse. But my soft power, cultivated over several high-stakes years, extended even here, in the form of an inmate's deference. Someday it would extend everywhere and take other forms.

I had miscalculated today. But I'd miscalculated before

while still managing to make many such failures the foundation of some future victory. This situation, too, could be turned to my ultimate advantage. And if the guards dragged me down the hall by the hair, I would take the opportunity to sing my own praises.

That night, a guard came by, opened the chute, and passed through a blank envelope. It was sealed. I opened it. It was filled with instant coffee.

One is awoken by the clang of the metal door slot as it's unlocked and falls into its resting position. A breakfast tray is slid onto the now-horizontal slot, to be taken up by one of the inmates and replaced by a second tray, which is also taken up, followed by four plastic bags of milk and two apples or bananas or, if you're unlucky, pears. As long as the guard is there, one might ask him to hit the light switch that sits outside one's door. It's about 5:30 a.m. They return after some ten or fifteen minutes to take back up the trays, and, if it's a weekday, to ask who wants to go outside for their allotted hour of recreation later that morning. They must know this in advance so that the duty officer can plan things such that incompatible inmates who may be inclined to attack each other on sight aren't placed in the same recreation cage.

I already knew all these basics from my original three-day stint in the hole at the Fort Worth Federal Correctional Institution, which, like all institutions run by the Bureau of Prisons, operates under a series of program statements composed out of the national office and officially applicable to federal facilities from California to Maine.

But rules have no importance in a country such as ours. It's quite enough to know the whims of those they've placed in charge.

"Get that cup off my windowsill!" shouted some sort of fascist.

I stood up and glanced through the door grate. It was a pig I'd never seen before. His name tag read *Mack*. He was in charge here.

After I removed the offending foam cup from the fascist's windowsill, he explained to me, in somewhat less aggressive tones, that no objects must be placed on the windowsill, which was his.

The next day my cellie and I decided to go out for morning rec. When the guard came back at the appointed time, he took a look through the door grate and informed us that we'd need to make our beds before we could go out; he'd return for us in a bit, after he'd taken the others.

The institution of bed-makery was among the first clues I'd encountered as a child that the society I'd been born into was a haphazard and psychotic thing against which I must wage eternal war. There was no reason, and could be none, that a set of sheets must be ritually configured each morning before the affairs of man can truly begin. It does not appease the spirits of hearth and home; it pays no homage to Pythagoras and sacred geometry. If it truly served some benefit to one's character, then the U.S. military, among which this tradition reaches its deranged pinnacle, would be pumping out brigade after brigade of hyper-enlightened scholar-knights rather than the sort of people who scream at me about where I put my cup. But I also knew full well that if I were to someday strike major blows against bed-making and eating at tables, I would first have to concentrate on the larger issues. Pick your battles; start with the hard ones. I made my bed, and my cellie did likewise.

The guard came back and opened the slot to cuff us up. In the SHU, a door must never be opened until all occupants are cuffed, and an inmate must remain cuffed whenever he is not in a cell or a cage. This is one of the few policies that is almost universally adhered to by the cops—thereby providing inmates with a rare point of strategic certainty on which to base some of their own tactics, as we shall see.

We were taken down the corridor and out a door leading onto the fire escape, and down the steps to a fenced-off space where some of our comrades had already been placed. Mack walked up to us.

"Why are these men just now coming down?" he asked the guards escorting us.

"They had to make their beds," replied one.

"Uh-uh. No rec. You gentlemen want rec, you have your cells ready for rec when we call rec. Take 'em back. Wastin' my time," he concluded inexplicably.

I spent an hour most mornings pacing around in a large cage and talking to whichever other SHU inmates had been thrown in with me or placed in an adjacent cage. I'd spent about a year and a half incarcerated in three different facilities, but there was still much I didn't know, and here I would have less to distract me from learning. And I had much to learn about the SHU in particular, especially if I was to be the first journalist in American history to report from inside it.

Among my regular recreation partners were two middle-aged Hispanics who lived in a cell a bit down and across the hall from ours, well within shouting distance. My only exchange with either of these fellows had been with the older, bearded one, whom I'd asked what he'd done to be put in the hole.

"I can't walk here," he'd shouted back.

This had confused me at the time. To not be able to "walk" a "yard" meant that one had been banned by some sufficiently powerful faction of inmates from doing time at that particular prison. Generally the inmate is simply informed that he will be beaten down unless he "checks in," which entails asking to be placed in the SHU. In most cases, the inmate will eventually be shipped to some other prison where it's believed that he'll face less opposition. I knew of only two reasons why someone would be barred from walking a yard: one is thought to be a snitch, or one is thought to be a child molester.

This fellow didn't strike me as a child molester, though I knew by now that not all of them fit a particular type. It was quite possible that he was a snitch, though; I'd also been around long enough to know that it's often the fellows who look toughest who end up folding the quickest (indeed, I'd learned this the hard way, well before I ended up behind bars). So I didn't inquire further.

The bearded Hispanic turned out to be neither snitch nor pedophile; rather, I had simply been ignorant of a key aspect of prison life, having spent much of the last year or so of my own incarceration sitting off in my ivory bunk bed and pursuing my various ideological inquiries and anarchist revolutionary plans while the ebb and flow of incarceration politics had played out on the margins of my awareness. As it turned out, both this fellow and his cellie were banned from walking here because they were members of the Mexican Mafia.

Years ago, the Mexican Mafia and the Texas Syndicate held sway over the bulk of Hispanic prisoners in the region, whether American or immigrant; this was in addition to their status as the primary Hispanic drug operations in Texas. Under the dual reign of these two powers, Mexican nationals and other foreign Hispanics were routinely oppressed—forced to pay "taxes" and otherwise kowtow to their prison-savvy liege lords. The control of the Mexican Mafia in particular often extended over their fellow U.S. Hispanics as well, including small gangs composed mostly of younger drug dealers.

But one such vassal gang—made up largely of ambitious kids from Dallas, Houston, San Antonio, and Austin—eventually broke loose. These were the Tangos, further divided via assorted and mysterious honorifics into regional variants like Tango Puro and Tango Blast. After years of glorious struggle, they won control of a number of state and federal prisons and thereafter cast out the Mexican Mafia oppressors, forcing its members to check in to the SHU pending transfer to those yards the more established gang had been able to retain. What a victory to have been party to! Oh, to have merely seen it! In celebration, they declared their four primary cities to be the Four Horsemen and went about devising all manner of other gang propaganda and visual symbology—Dallas members, for instance, tended to get neck tattoos depicting the blue star of the Cowboys, the stylized *D* that is the city's official symbol, and the 214 area code. Today, these Tangos oversee the Hispanic affairs of many regional prisons alongside the Paisas—a more amorphous prison gang composed largely of day workers locked up for illegal reentry, which rose up against the Texas Syndicate in similar fashion, expelling them from a chain of prisons and thereby ensuring that their liberated territories would be beacons of relative safety and dignity for the countless immigrants whom the United States tosses into its broken prison system each day.

This is but one of those typhoon struggles that regularly occur within the sub-nation of 2.2 million people that the United States has insensibly created within itself and thereafter largely forgotten.

The first thing one learns upon being incarcerated in the United States is that race is central to prison life. The second thing one learns, more gradually, is that there are key exceptions. From a purely ethnic standpoint, the Tangos and Paisas are indistinguishable, as are the Northern and Southern Mexican gangs that perpetually wage war on each other in state and federal prisons across the American West. The same is true of Crips and Bloods, though as with other outfits that didn't originate as prison gangs, they're more likely to set aside their differences and coexist in those places where polity is defined by Blackness. Many prisons are divided into Black, Hispanic, and white groupings for purposes of mutual defense and community, to be sure; but many are not. In the federal system, one's home state may be the sole factor in determining what "car," or gang polity, one is pressured to join upon arrival. Race turns out to be simply the most basic of several overlapping organizing principles that have been implemented on a de facto basis by inmates—often with encouragement from prison administrators, who, like British colonial administrators in India, prefer their subjects to be divided against each other rather than united against them. The individual sensibilities and ideology of those who must survive within the system are irrelevant. But then one can say the same of the world outside, among the relatively free citizens whose own system has placed us here to begin with.

Much of my time in the rec cages was spent fucking around with a guy called Dank, whose large head and prison-issued glasses combined in such a way that he sort of looked like he was wearing a helmet. Dank was in on a couple of drug and gun charges. The extent of his sentence would depend largely on whether a decrepit building in which he'd stashed a pistol was designated as a residence, in which case he'd be hit with something called a "sentencing enhancement"—a piling-on of the time one faces when one's charge involves any of those particular practices that the federal government has determined to constitute some especially bad way to commit a crime. In his case, the enhancement would entail "burglary of a habitation," even though he hadn't entered the structure or taken anything out of it. As his lawyer had recently managed to determine, the building wasn't any sort of residence whatsoever, on the reasonable grounds that it had no residents; the prosecutor had simply claimed otherwise in his filings, knowing that defense lawyers don't always check up on all the angles and that prosecutors themselves face zero consequences for filing false statements and withholding evidence.

Aside from serving as a great lead-in to the various anti–Department of Justice themes I intend on throwing into this book, Dank was also a natural comedian specializing in impressions and off-the-cuff characters.

"This what Mexicans be like when they mad. They all runnin' out they front door like this," would go the establishing premise, after which Dank would suddenly rush from one end of the cage to the other with fists clenched and arms swinging in comical angry-Mexican-spouse speed and his mouth going, *"Cállate, cállate, cállate, cállate!"* which is Spanish for "shut up."

"They do that," confirmed Mack, who always stood outside whatever cage Dank was in so as to catch the free show.

Like me, Dank had developed his best character out of his own persona. His most popular act involved pretending that he had some ongoing dispute with whichever inmate was being led past our cages in handcuffs at any given moment.

"Yeah motherfucker you fucked now you thought i was playin' bitch imma beat yo ass shit gettin' real," he would declaim, accompanying himself with exaggerated aggressive prison posturing and banging against the chain-link fence. I regret being unable to do justice to this act, which invariably cracked up his target, the guards, and all who had the fortune of observing; to do so in print would be like trying to explain Jerry Lewis to an Anglo-Saxon. There was a variation on this in which, on mornings when he was uncuffed through the gate before anyone else who was in the cage with him, he would pretend to start to attack the cuffed inmate, though really this wasn't his bit but rather a well-established routine based on the actual attacks of opportunity that have traditionally occurred in those circumstances. Really I can think of at least two people who did this act at least as well as Dank.

For there were several of us among the usual morning SHU recreation crew with a mind for comedy. I myself began my writing career doing humor and even wrote a couple of pieces for *National Lampoon* in my early days, though not till after it'd already been bought by a bunch of Gulf princes or whatever the fuck happened to *National Lampoon*. Anyway, I'm very funny.

It was my idea, for instance, to do short skits based on the premise of one of those "scared straight" shows where troubled youth are presented with hardened convicts who belabor them with tales of prison adversity, except this one would involve minimum security inmates—minimum security being a designation universally known as a "camp." Seagoville happened to have a camp, and this was situated so as to actually surround our jail unit rec area. And so when the Fourth of July rolled around that summer, we had watched, mouths figuratively agape, as a long line of inmates formed to receive some sort of frozen summer bullshit treat. This was sufficient material for a professional such as myself.

> You wanna walk down this path right here? This real life! I went to go sign up for T-ball tryouts and they told me they already fill up! In here you a number! I waited in line twenty minutes to get me a sno-cone but when I got up front they tell me they out of cherry! Don't mean nothin' to them! This how we live up in here! They got more cherry flavoring a few minutes later and let me skip back up in line so I did get the flavor I originally wanted, but I prefer to avoid confrontation! This real life!

Again, this is funnier when I'm actually doing it in front of you, in a cage.

Dank was also rather adept at emotional assaults upon passing guards. One rather sleek-looking fellow, who one could tell was an asshole from ten meters away as he walked along the pavement beyond our cage, constituted a natural target due to his defined musculature, narrow frame, and overly well-fitting uniform.

"Damn, Tompkins, you lookin' cool as shit in those shades and yo tight-ass shorts," shouted Dank, thereby shifting every consciousness in earshot toward the fellow's unnecessarily visible and well-formed buttocks. The inmates laughed. So did our guards—and the dynamic here, I saw at the time, was of the We versus the Other, defined as makeshift alliances of the moment that transcended obvious divisions.

But of course the vast majority of each day was spent in our cells, and the major figure in one's life was one's cellie. D, the fellow I came in with, was an unusually good one. I'd known a few things about him from our sporadic chess matches, as well as prison gossip and my own scattered observations. He was a muscular redhead with a short beard and what appeared at first glance to be fairly typical prison tattoos peeking out from his neckline. Now that we were living together in perpetual hundred-degree heat that left us clad in boxers for much of each day, I saw the mural that covered his back: a baroque and apocalyptic combat scene, with AK-47s artfully arranged around it in a sort of frame, a caption running across his shoulders in Arabic script that translated to *Death rain down upon my enemies.*

D was a white Muslim—not the first I'd encountered, as

I'd actually dated two white Muslim women myself at various times (one a convert, one a Bosnian) and met another one in prison. But it was sufficiently rare to be considered impressive, particularly since he was fluent in classical Arabic and otherwise fairly observant (certainly more observant than the sort of women willing to date me). As Muslims often banded together into prison gangs at many yards—a "prison gang" being a broad and not always intuitive designation that will require more analysis later on—D tended to associate pretty heavily with other, more typical specimens of prison Islam, the great majority of whom are Black. But when held in those units where no Muslim gang has been formed, such as the J-2 jail unit from which the two of us came, he would just as happily count himself with the whites, known in their collective gang form as "Woods" at many prisons—but again, we are anticipating.

D's relative erudition melded oddly with his identity as a hoodlum from one of Dallas's more rundown suburbs; his lingo drew largely on Modern Thug English, developed both from the street and from the large portion of his adult life he had spent in the Texas state prison system before getting picked up on a federal weapons charge and thrown into the feds with high-caliber offenders such as myself. It is not entirely uncommon for Muslim converts to speak fondly of forties of malt liquor and hits of PCP, as D did, and even less uncommon for them to deal drugs to others; but the majority of prison Muslims have taken strides to abandon these habits, to litter their speech with Arabic paeans to Allah, and to otherwise be moderately irritating (and entirely unhelpful to those of us who need to buy drugs in prison). D still spoke very much like the twenty-first-century gangster he'd always been, and did so in an accent that mixed his semi-rural upbringing and hip-hoppity cadences in a manner that was distinctive and highly bizarre. I tried my best to capture his personality in my column, though I worried that I might be accused of simply making him up:

> On our second day in the SHU, a staff member came by to deliver paperwork to D, detailing the various alleged infractions that had sent him there. One sheet reported that "Inmate Lackey [his unfortunate real last name] was given an order to place his hands back on the wall during the control of the semi-disturbance. Inmate Lackey responded in an aggressive tone, 'I ain't going to do all that. Fuck no. If you going to lock me up then lock me up.' Inmate Lackey continued to keep his hands at waist level." D was charged, not unreasonably, with "Refusing an Order" and "Insolence Towards Staff."
>
> Presently he was allowed to read over the infraction documents through the door grille. Then the staff member asked if he had any preliminary comments for the disciplinary committee.
>
> "Tell 'em I don't recognize the authority of they court."
>
> "Sorry?"
>
> "I said, 'Tell 'em I don't recognize the authority of they court.'"
>
> "Oh, okay!" said the staff member, who had merely been having trouble understanding D's bizarre, semi-rural gangsta accent. He began to write: *I don't recognize . . . the authority . . .*
>
> "Of they court."
>
> "Of their court."

"Yeah."

"Okay, got it!"

The staff member left. D turned to me and said: "I got that shit from Saddam Hussein. That's what he told 'em when he was being tried for war crimes."

An hour later, he was back at the door grille, this time shouting some questionable legal advice to the guy in the cell across the hall who was going before a judge the next day: "Man, tell that bitch to suck yo dick!"

A couple of hours after that, he turned to me and said, apropos of nothing: "You know what was a good book, was that *Picture of Dorian Gray*."

D and I spent the first few days acclimating to the heat. In the federal prison system, there are regulations as to the temperatures in which inmates may be kept, but those are gotten around easily enough. The staff who periodically come by with a thermometer to ensure that the place that pays their salary is not holding people in inhumane conditions don't actually put the thermometer inside the cell, which could be easily done by having the guard unlock the chute; instead, they hold it up to the grille on the other side of the door—out in the hallway, where a giant fan blows cold air on the guards. I have no idea what temperature we were being kept in at Seagoville, and neither does the administration at Seagoville. But we were still better off than those Texas state prison inmates who have no air-conditioning at all, ever, despite a series of lawsuits in recent years over the deaths and illnesses that have resulted from being held in densely packed steel-and-concrete dungeons in a region where temperatures regularly creep above a hundred degrees.

For recreation, the two of us played chess with a board and pieces I'd made out of paper and envelopes (which, along with a few very short pencils and two foam cups, made up the bulk of our resources). His tendency to win, and my inability to lose games with any grace, mostly added to my frustrations. More commonly D occupied himself at the door after meals, when everyone tends to be awake and potential conversation partners are most readily available. As these exchanges must be shouted and are thus impossible to ignore, particularly when one participant is standing three feet away from you, I managed to pick up all manner of interesting cultural tidbits of the sort I would have otherwise had to obtain by doing actual interviews.

Aside from screaming pleasantries to other gangsters, D also liked to play a little game with Dank whereby he would blow air into one of the paper sacks we sometimes got meals in, twist the opening closed, and then pop it, creating an impressively obnoxious bang that could be heard throughout the building.

"I just shot yo ass, Dank!" D would explain.

Shortly afterward, another explosion would echo around the corridor, and Dank would announce that he, in turn, had shot D. Then they would laugh and laugh.

Dank, incidentally, had been thrown into the SHU on the not unreasonable grounds that he'd assaulted another inmate with a potentially deadly weapon right in the middle of the jail unit's dayroom, in plain view of the guards and cameras. Such incidents are common in prison, but the circumstances this time are well worth setting forth. You see, inmates maintain a vibrant economy—so vibrant that a full overview will have to wait until a later chapter, where this subject may be given its due. For now suffice it to say that Dank's role in this economy was to make and sell pies. These pies are created with the powdered coffee creamer sold in the commissary, crushed cookies molded into crusts, and various other ingredients thrown in for variety. The exact process by which this is done is a closely held secret that people actually sell to others, generally when they're about to be transferred elsewhere; all I can say for sure is that one major step entails putting Jolly Ranchers in a cup and melting them in a microwave.

Not having established any sort of pie cartel in our unit, Dank faced competition from a guy called LA (who was actually from Inglewood, but whatever). Conflict is hardly inevitable in such cases, but both of these fellows were so thoroughly accustomed to the enforced monopolies of the illegal drug trade that they were destined to fight. When the battle came, it was over which of them had the right to sell his pies from a particular table located near the black television (I'll explain what a black television is when I feel that you're ready). I wrote the following eyewitness account for my column a few weeks later:

> Harsh words were exchanged, and then the entrepreneurs went upstairs to an out-of-the-way cell on the second tier so that they might privately settle their commercial dispute through the custom of trial-by-combat. At the time, I happened to be taking my evening constitutional, during which I made about thirty circuits of the top-tier walkway, and so by stealthily glancing into the cell each time I passed, I

> was in a position to monitor the proceedings without attracting the attention of the guard. The first time I passed, the two of them were fighting. The second time, they were arguing. The third time, they were fighting again. The fourth time, they had once more resorted to words. Finally LA emerged from the cell and went to go watch TV, followed a few minutes later by Dank, who went over to where LA was sitting, apologized, and pointed out that in their rush to violence, they had both lost sight of what was really important, which was the making and selling of pies. Just kidding. What Dank actually did was go to where LA was sitting and hit him over the head with a sock stuffed with padlocks. Later, the guard found out about the fight and both combatants were taken to the hole, at which point the pie concession fell under the absolute control of a skinny white fraudster named Bobby whose pies are now universally acclaimed to be the best the jail has ever tasted. And so ends my tale of this Homeric pie fight, this blood-spattered Bake-Off.

Dank's antics continued in the hole, where he perpetrated so many bizarre and entertaining conflicts with the guards that D took to calling him "our TV." The two of us would watch through the door grate as the spirited fellow ran the gamut of SHU insurgency tactics from long-range sneak attacks to psychological warfare. Here follows an account of one of Dank's more picaresque assaults:

> One day, as our lunch trays were being passed through the door slots, Dank kind of just unilaterally decided

> that he and the guard were in some sort of conflict, repeatedly denounced the fellow as a "bitch-ass ho," and proceeded to "jack the trap," which is to say that he stuck his arm through the door slot so that it couldn't be closed and locked (or "secured," in the jargon of a federal correctional officer, to whom an unsecured slot is a very distressing affair indeed). Dank spent the next thirty minutes making declarations of his various grievances, real and imaginary, pausing now and again to engage other SHU inmates in shouted conversations concerning subjects entirely unrelated to the matter at hand, including that of an enjoyable evening he once spent at a local nightclub with his cousin and a couple of her friends, who, we were led to understand, were known to be very sexually promiscuous.

Most of Dank's efforts, like this one, began with the seizure of the door slot, a common first move that forces the hands of the guards; officers are compelled not just by irrelevant official policy that may be violated at will but also by de facto policy consisting of whatever their superior officers actually concern themselves over, to ensure that all door slots are closed and locked when not in official use. A jacked trap also serves as a beachhead for all manner of other direct actions, such as throwing things at guards. Dank generally contented himself with launching paper cups of water at the fan down the hall while D shouted out pointers (our door grille was better angled to see the fan than Dank's was), though on one occasion he was accused of throwing a cup of water at a notoriously irritating officer; the infraction charge was dropped after a review of the cameras showed that no such thing had occurred.

Despite all this, Dank was by no means the most disruptive of the inmates being held at Seagoville's SHU that summer; that honor went to a bizarre fellow by the name of Wolf. We were never sure exactly what his charge was, although many held suspicions that he was in on child porn or some such thing; he had a great deal of hair and a rather unkempt beard, but this provided no real clues. Wolf was held in a special cell at the end of the upper corridor, intended for problematic inmates; rather than the standard hip-level slot, his door was equipped with a more elaborate mechanism, a sort of box that could be pulled out by the guards and then pushed back in, thus allowing them to deliver an inmate's meals without giving the fellow a chance to throw cups of urine on them or what have you.

Wolf was the only inmate I ever came across who was not required to have a cellmate while housed in the SHU. Apparently, the fellow was in the habit of doing unorthodox things with his own feces, such as rubbing it on the face of whoever happened to be in the cell with him while they slept. Extrapolating from this, we may suppose he had other bad habits as well.

He was, naturally, a well-known figure at Seagoville. The jail unit I'd come from, known as J-2, had a walled-off corridor running into the side of it, entirely visible to us through plexiglass windows. The corridor held ten or so two-man cells that were mostly used to house inmates who were being transferred to other prisons, either originating from this area or stopping through from elsewhere via the Bureau of Prisons' transportation network that moves prisoners around the country on an ongoing basis. They had other uses as well; the twenty or so participants in our demonstration who had not been designated as actual leaders were being placed in those cells while we vanguard types were being led to the SHU. And they also functioned as suicide cells, which was fun for the rest of us, as we could all observe through the windows while whichever staff member had volunteered for time-and-a-half-pay suicide-watch duty dealt with the prospective self-snuffer from the other side of the door. In most cases, as I've been able to gather, these situations are pretty calm; an inmate who is suspected of wanting to off himself (usually because he's expressed this intention to staff) is placed in the cell with nothing other than underwear, and a staff member observes him while he lies on the bunk, enduring his own personal hell. The typical suicide watch doesn't make for much of a show, then. But the only instance I'd seen involved Wolf himself, who was not a typical inmate.

Aside from a proclivity toward feces and suicide, Wolf was a mystery to us. He was rumored to have makeshift lipstick made from Kool-Aid packets. This, incidentally, is a not infrequent practice at state jail institutions, where the phenomenon of "punks" is rather more widespread than it is in the federal system. *Punk* is a jailhouse term for a receptive homosexual. The modern usage itself is well over a century old, appearing for instance as common Northeastern prison slang in Alexander Berkman's *Prison Memoirs of an Anarchist*, which begins in 1892 (another contemporary term used to describe the practice itself, *kid business*, seems to have disappeared). Interestingly, Berkman himself was told by an unusually educated fellow inmate that the usage of *punk* for the sexually ambiguous derived from a stray line of Shakespeare. But we again risk considerable digression if we attempt to give this subject its full due here, other than to briefly note that, although certainly present, homosexuality is a far less universal aspect of American prison life than the public generally assumes; suffice to say that Wolf was a known punk and, having once been known as a punk, would almost certainly remain one in the eyes of his fellow prisoners forever after.

Wolf was less notable for his alleged punkitude than for his affinity for feces, as well as his tendency to act in such a way as to require more or less constant supervision by prison staff even when not on suicide watch. He rarely came out to shower, which was rather for the best since he was prone to seizing control of the stall by refusing to cuff up after he was done and thus forcing some manner of showdown before he could be subdued and taken back to his cell. This sort of thing made him unpopular in the corridor, as these incidents naturally led to delays in the thrice-weekly shower rotation.

Indeed, there was little about Wolf that fit neatly into the established rhythms of prison life. He bore inexplicable animosities toward inmates with whom he had no known history. Some days when we went out to the rec cages, Wolf—whom the staff would not dream of allowing to engage in recreation with other, more complete human beings, lest they kill him for his many crimes against decency—would often stand at his window, which happened to face the cages, and shout nonsense, usually at Dank.

"Daaaaaaaank . . . Daaaaaaaaaank . . . Daaaank . . . Daaaaaaaaaaaaaaank," he would scream, often for several minutes without pause (which is longer than it sounds).

Then, whenever he deduced that there was some lull in the conversation below, he would follow up with his perpetual thesis:

"I hear you got a big asshole, Dank."

Then he would resume the calls of "Daaaaaaank."

Occasionally Wolf's deranged chorus would be broken up by counter-insults shouted from the cages, with these naturally tending to dwell on Wolf's more or less documented history of ersatz lipstick application. On one occasion, an inmate vowed to kill Wolf's family. Wolf responded by providing his family's home address.

But the real problem with Wolf was his practice of attracting the prison tactical unit at inconvenient times. Based on some methodology that one could hardly credit, prison staff would occasionally determine that Wolf's behavior indicated suicidal ideation and conclude that he would get better if he were rushed in on by a pseudo-SWAT team and beaten down with clubs before being placed in some other cell. This would usually happen at night—and not during that early part of night when SHU inmates are still wide awake and shouting NBA scores at each other through their grates, but later, at two or three in the morning, when all respectable convicts are sound asleep. The process of slamming open a steel door, rushing into a tiny room filled with metal furniture while swinging batons, and beating up a noncompliant werewolf is rather hard to sleep through. Worse, after he'd been moved, a staffer would be posted at the door of Wolf's new cell for the next eighteen or so hours to ensure that this horrible monster did not destroy himself.

I know all the ins and outs of this because the last time Wolf was abducted and thrown into a new cell, it happened to be right next to my own. Wolf spent the rest of the night banging the desk-mounted metal stool into the wall, over and over again; as it happened, it was my wall, too.

By morning, many of the inmates on our corridor were shouting for Wolf to kill himself already.

"Guys, leave him alone!" squealed a child molester from down the hall.

"Shut your bitch mouth, pedo!" I retorted. I'm afraid I'm not quite as eloquent in person as I am in print.

Three weeks in, it was D's turn to revolt.

The two of us had just been placed back in the cell after our thrice-weekly shower and were still in the process of having our handcuffs removed by the guards when it occurred to us that something was awry. It didn't take long to figure out what was wrong: D's brown paper sack had been emptied of the snacks that were to serve as his morning meals on those days when the guards failed to bring his breakfast before sunrise, as they're supposed to do for Muslims during the ongoing Ramadan fast. Mack, we realized, had searched the cell while we were out and seized the offending foodstuffs, presumably on the grounds that D's possession of them constituted "hoarding," which is not permitted.

"I feel like buckin', cellie," D said to me in his odd, rumbling North Texas country-gangsta accent, using the universal prison term for insurrection. He grabbed a towel, and I knew what was coming. He was going to flood the corridor.

"I'll just get out of your way then."

I picked my papers and books off the floor and placed them on the top bunk, filled my cup with warm water from the sink and stirred in a shot of coffee, and then climbed up myself to wait out the conflict and whatever was to come of it. Even had I not been an anarchist revolutionary with a lust for insurgency, it wouldn't have crossed my mind to ask D to refrain from what he was about to do. To be cellmates in the SHU was to experience a partnership more intimate than most marriages, insomuch as we spent twenty-four hours a day with each other and tended to shower together more than most married couples. If my platonic prison husband felt the need to wage aqua-jihad against our captors, I was going to be supportive.

D began by stuffing one of his towels in the crack under our cell door so as to render it watertight. The other towel he used to clog up the toilet. Then he took his mattress and tore a hole on one end of it so that it would hang from the sprinkler head above the door; this would not only diminish the ability of the prison SWAT team to rush in on us with any real momentum, but also deny guards valuable intelligence via the door grille. Unfortunately the fabric was too flimsy to hold the weight and the mattress fell to the floor.

As D stood by the toilet hitting the flush button over and over again while muttering in classical Arabic, I reflected once again on the vagaries of fortune. Two years prior I'd been a respected sociopolitical commentator best known for my activism work in association with Anonymous, as well as for my articles for *Vanity Fair* and *The Guardian*. I'd appeared on *NBC Nightly News* and, shortly before my arrest, participated in a *Bloomberg Businessweek* panel alongside CEOs and retired government officials. I was quoted as an expert on something or other in one publication or another every few days, and my adventures were regularly chronicled in outlets like CNN, *Gawker*, and the *Daily Mail*, in descending order of accuracy.

But two years before that, I'd been living on a friend's couch in Brooklyn, selling the last of my personal items on Craigslist in order to buy heroin. This was actually a reassuring thought—that the path of my decline was more of a zigzag than a straight drop. Come to think of it, the vagaries of fortune had been awfully vague lately, even for vagaries. My position had always been ambiguous; this could be gleaned from the fact that, when I'd appeared on NBC, I'd been described by Brian Williams as "an underground commander in a new kind of war," whereas on the Bloomberg panel I'd merely been termed a "security expert," with nary a mention of my neo-warlike ways. In a hundred newspaper and magazine articles I was "the spokesperson for Anonymous"; in a hundred others, I was a journalist who simply reported on the activist collective. Elsewhere I was noted as the founder of a group called Project PM, which itself was variously listed as having been launched in 2009 or 2010 or 2011 to serve as a next-generation blogging platform, or perhaps as a "distributed think-tank" dedicated to researching private intelligence-contracting firms and publicizing our findings; or perhaps it was, in the words of the Department of Justice, a "criminal organization." There was also the question, still in some dispute at the time of my arrest, of whether I was a noble-minded revolutionary, or a demented charlatan, or a sly performance artist, or perhaps some ultramodern combination of all these things at once.

But things had improved since my arrest. In the wake of the Snowden revelations, my obsession with large-scale internet public-private espionage partnerships—which had previously struck some in the press as a bit crankish—was now being described as prescient. Publications that had once exaggerated my faults were now exaggerating my virtues.

Better yet, the dishonest and increasingly bizarre manner in which the DOJ had pursued its case against me had had the effect of convincing even staid outlets like *The New York Times* and *U.S. News & World Report* that the charges against me were simply retaliation for the work my team had done in detailing various state corporate plots against unfriendly activists and journalists, including one that had actually been set in motion by the DOJ itself. Now other revelations we'd put out only to have them largely ignored were getting a second, more appreciative look, and the media seemed to have settled on that "noble-minded revolutionary" angle, perhaps a bit hastily—for fortune comes and fortune goes, but the American press remains reliably haphazard.

Even more satisfied with myself than usual, I lay back on my bunk and watched as, slowly but surely, the water level rose below. Someday I'd get back out there and consolidate my gains. And I'd get one of those virtual reality headsets I was hearing about, too. In the meantime, I still had to contend with seventeen federal charges carrying a total of a hundred and five years in prison. But that was manageable, even necessary. Without peril there can be no glory.

2

The Accidental Insurrection

One pleasant afternoon in early 2007, I logged in to a virtual world called Second Life, changed my avatar to that of the Kool-Aid Man from the old television commercials, and teleported to a location I'd labeled on an overview map as *Fort Longcat*. The screen flashed; standing before me now were some dozen or so of my compatriots clad in all manner of surreal costumes. Some I would have known under different names, and on other accounts that had been banned along with the attached IP addresses and even the computers themselves (but with a certain software patch, these "hard bans" could be overcome; like the Tibetan mystics, we had transcended death). Others among them would be new reinforcements recently summoned to join our ranks by messages left on certain out-of-the-way message boards. If you asked each of these individuals who they were or what they represented, you'd get back a variety of answers: *imma /b/tard; anon here; /i/nsurgent lol; 7chan rulez u; /i/lluminati* . . . It was best to think of them as identifying with the largely inchoate online subculture known as Anonymous and to leave it at that, for now we were boarding our airship and setting off for other, more populated sections of the immense digital realm that we felt ourselves duty bound to terrorize in strange and beautiful ways.

Some of us appeared as Black men clad in stylish three-piece suits and Afros; some existed in the form of minor characters from Japanese cartoons; some looked relatively unremarkable aside from having the head of a cat. One fellow possessed a code that played the Soviet national anthem on a perpetual loop. Another kept typing out the phrase *We're going back to Potatos to get my fucking power glove!* Another: *Do you liek mudkipz?* Still another seemed to be dancing to the theme from *The Fresh Prince of Bel-Air*, and this melded into the Soviet anthem in a very ominous manner that I do not care to recall even a decade later. I myself was excitedly typing out exhortations, proclamations, incitements to war.

Each of us checked our gear. We had "Cosby bombs" that exploded into invisible little pieces of code that in turn bounced around the environment, playing audio clips taken from Jell-O pudding commercials of yore. We had rifles that took advantage of the world's virtual physics to knock a victim several in-game miles away before they could get a glimpse of your screen name and report you to the fascist moderators. These and other of our implements of high-concept chaos had been created by programmers who shared our urge to propagate the imagery by which the subculture defined itself.

Each element in this picture can actually be explained and traced back to some chance online exchange, some amusing story, some happy accident of translation that at some point found favor within our community and reached the threshold by which it would be remembered and reposted and attain the status of meme, to be cherished and perpetuated for its own sake. Even at this early point there were untold hundreds of distinct memes associated with Anonymous, usually deriving from the "random" or "/b/" message board at 4chan.org, 7chan.org, or one of the other popular websites where the young and disaffected spent their free time posting pictures and commentary (almost always without bothering to enter a screen name, and thus automatically listed, along with thousands of other users, under the default moniker of "Anonymous"). I happened to know many of these memes because I served as an editor and contributor at a wiki called Encyclopedia Dramatica, which documented such things for posterity; it was the only writing I did for free.

If we telescope in on just one of these elements, we can get a sense of how fractally baroque this culture was. Our spaceship—one of perhaps hundreds of thousands of scripted objects that Second Life players created for use in the world—was an exact replica of that used by a recurring set of characters from the postmodern animated series *Aqua Teen Hunger Force*: the alien Moonanites, themselves an homage to the aliens from the vintage *Space Invaders* video game. But rather than the bright primary colors in which the ship usually came, this one was papered over with what looked at first glimpse to be the Wikipedia logo. In fact, it was the rather similar logo for Encyclopedia Dramatica, which, in addition to its mission of documenting underground internet culture, also functioned as a living parody of Wikipedia's own editorial foibles. But this particular logo, repeated a dozen times across the surface of the ship in a manner similar to the "tile" option on your computer's wallpaper settings, had been altered even further, with Encyclopedia Dramatica replaced in this instance with the words *Faggery Daggery Doo.* This phrase in turn was an homage to something said about ED in a recent on-air exchange between a white supremacist radio host we'd been in conflict with at the time and one of his regular callers: "I wanna tell you that encyclopedia outfit you mentioned is a *fag* encyclopedia! They are faggery daggery doo!"

Getting fringe political commentators to make oddly phrased homophobic attacks on our websites was the sort of thing we lived for; hence the trophies in the form of commemorative images. But this particular incident also held deeper significance. The occasion for that radio conversation had been a still-ongoing conflict between a segment of Anonymous based out of 7chan on the one hand, and one of the nation's most prominent "white nationalist" personalities, Hal Turner, on the other. One night some months prior, a bunch of 7channers had amused themselves by calling in to Turner's show, ostensibly to provide accounts of how minorities were taking over the country, but really as part of a competition to see who could work as many internet memes as possible into a single rambling anecdote. Turner got wise to the act and posted some of the phone numbers on his website in revenge. During his next show he took a call from a teenage girl demanding that he remove the numbers. He refused. Had he searched YouTube for local news segments on the dread phenomenon of Anonymous, he might have just taken them down.

Turner soon found himself under attack via an array of methods that were in many cases so novel that names did not yet exist for them. Some of these techniques had been deployed in the prior two years, one or two at a time, against various parties who had crossed paths with Anonymous before. But never had these techniques been used all together, by perhaps a thousand people, against a single sustained target. A few were technical in nature, drawing upon obscure network protocols to allow internet users to temporarily knock out websites via sheer blunt force. Some methods were more sophisticated, involving outright hacking; a raid of Turner's email account yielded proof that he'd served as an FBI informant, confirmation of which cut him off from his white nationalist allies—as well as from the FBI itself, which now had no use for him. The campaign against Turner included many of the elements that would come into play on a more global stage in the years to come: the takeover and vandalism of enemy websites so as to prompt press attention to some issue; crowdsourced opposition research; the ability to mobilize huge numbers of people with a wide range of skills in short amounts of time and to provide opportunities for anyone with a good idea to get it aired and implemented within moments. It also left many with a taste for blood. And due to the accident of this unusually high-profile raid having targeted a white supremacist figure, quite a few outsiders got the impression that Anonymous was a sort of well-intentioned activist group. It wasn't. But there was little to stop it from becoming one as new participants flooded in with their mistaken impressions, which, in the absence of any organized opposition to the contrary, could quickly become reality. This was an age in which a loose network of gaming trolls could become a geopolitical force within a year or two, and largely by accident.

Five years on from the afternoon when we rode the skies on a spaceship of code on a mission to drop Mario bombs on a virtual nightclub, the National Security Agency director Michael Hayden gave a speech proclaiming that Anonymous would soon be capable of taking control of the nation's power plants. He was talking nonsense, of course, as intelligence professionals tend to do when budgets are at stake; by the time Hayden made that claim, Anonymous's power was already on the wane, and indeed some small but influential portion of it had recently come under partial control of the FBI, though that wouldn't be revealed until later.

For now, I was involved with all this because I had become obsessed with the question of what would happen when these people realized what they were capable of.

Like millions of other irreverent young men, I would find my way to 4chan.org, which, like Hegel, was to later give birth to two formidable yet opposing political currents, and which, also like Hegel, was filled with nonsense, though in this case the nonsense was fully intended.

I had stayed largely on the internet's surface from the time it became easily accessible in my early adolescence. I used it to find writing gigs, primarily, and to do research and pirate games and music; my life was given over to the world of bone and flesh. And then, in 2006, I happened upon an article about a guy in Seattle who had just ruined the lives of dozens of people with a few minutes of work. This fellow, it was reported, had posted a fake personals ad on

Craigslist claiming to be a female with submissive tendencies and desiring a strong male partner. Upon receiving the inevitable flood of responses, he posted them all—along with whatever names, pictures, email addresses, and phone numbers had been included. The material was kept on a website called Encyclopedia Dramatica, which had already achieved a considerably high Google rating; searches for these names would generally yield what the subject had intended to be a private communication to a compliant female, and, in some cases, a picture of his erect penis. The fellow's experiment was successful enough that he'd had to go into hiding immediately afterward.

ED was a revelation. It had the format of a wiki, whereby in theory anyone could contribute directly to its pages. In reality, it was maintained and largely written by a group of youngish hipsters based in San Francisco, mostly female or gay. The founding editors had developed a taste for internet drama from LiveJournal, an early blogging platform that brought together the sort of people each of us encounters through life, and whom we must normally content ourselves with merely describing to those who weren't there to meet them—it brought them all together and put them in a place where their exquisite nonsense would never be lost again.

I'm talking about the guy in your apartment complex who informs you, apropos of nothing, that he's good at naming new kinds of acid, and tells you of the time when, after a friend of his who had created a batch produced a sheet that was entirely white, this fellow called it, without hesitation, "Black Magic." The fat girl who reemerged in high school as a Goth, and pretended to conceal books on Wicca during lunch. All of those whose utterances became catchphrases in your circle of friends, even among those who'd never had a chance to meet them—all of them were on LiveJournal, and each was just a click away, if only you knew where to find them.

The purpose of ED, then, was to document the most ridiculous people the internet had to offer, to categorize and collate them, to develop new terminology by which to describe all of the new brands of social failings that online interaction had brought to the fore. Over time its mission expanded to cover the entirety of online phenomena, always with a satirical bent, eventually describing itself as a sort of postmodern version of Ambrose Bierce's *Devil's Dictionary.* In fact it was something very different, serving not merely as a satirical chronicle but also as many other things; it was, for instance, an incubator of language, lovingly adopting online malapropisms and incorporating them into its editorial voice, inventing phrases where none existed, and otherwise serving to catalog the evolving parlance of a world in which the output of previously unheard-from groups like fourteen-year-old boys was now readily accessible, and sometimes inescapable.

Deciphering either the tone or the content at ED took time; it made heavy use of memes, not all of which were readily identifiable as such, and referenced entities and sometimes entire concepts that were wholly alien to the uninitiated. But all of these phrases and identifiers were hyperlinked to other pages in which the background was explained with varying degrees of straightforwardness. Sometimes an example is given, as in the page on the postmodern text rejoinder *no u*:

> PRIMA: If you're just going to sit back and criticize the furry fandom without doing any research on the socio-political ramifications of the lifestyle or

culture, then you're nothing more than a prejudiced, narrow-minded homophobe.

SECUNDA: no u

Thus I learned that "internet disease" was the tendency for overweight people to use deceptive camera angles for their profile pictures, and was known more technically as "fat girl angle shots"; that a "Marie Sue" was a character, generally in fan fiction, that was clearly intended as an unrealistically perfect projection of the author; that there was such a thing as fan fiction; that lolicon was manga depicting prepubescent girls for the enjoyment of pedophiles; that a furry was someone, generally an autistic male, who identified as an animal, sexually and otherwise, and that this sort of thing came in a range of sordid variations. I learned about DeviantArt, where teenagers were concocting all manner of bizarre sexual trends involving depictions of themselves as *Sonic the Hedgehog* characters. All in all, I discovered that the internet had provided for the endless multiplication of subcultures, and indeed of culture, and of content. It was worth knowing about, at least in broad terms. There were dynamics in play that could prove important later, and they were mostly invisible to the media, and thus to the world at large. And some of those dynamics spoke to me—in a faint whisper, not yet fully understood—of power. I began editing pages in my free time, and hanging out in the internet relay chat channel that ED's contributors used to coordinate their work.

For as with the Craigslist experiment, some of these contributors were not content to document amusing things for their own entertainment; some felt compelled to cause drama as well. Among the most active in this regard was a fellow who went by the name Weev, a hacker of some sort. His most obvious attribute was a malevolent core, which is the kind of thing that can override comedic talent, but which in his case often drove it forward; he lacked subtlety, and even a conscience, and this made certain patterns of humor unavailable to him while also opening up horizons that were closed to the rest of us. He appeared perfectly at home with dishonesty and this, too, worked in his favor. Among his most memorable capers was his operation against a strange middle-aged fellow who was in the habit of getting into inane political debates on some forum or another; Weev created a page for him, using the fellow's full name and ascribing to him the unlikely assertion, "I want to kill six million Jews." When the fellow started threatening to sue, Weev called him, claiming to be ED's lawyer. The recording that resulted—in which Weev repeatedly refers to himself as a "qualified attorney at LOL" without the other fellow seeming to notice—was thereafter added to the fellow's page. This formula would be repeated over and over again as other victims of originally minor articles arrived at ED's internet relay chat server to beg or threaten or cajole, only to find that the ensuing conversation had been published immediately thereafter.

I didn't have much interest in that sort of thing, but I was very much taken with the idea of using Google results to do damage to actual villains. And so I briefly worked with Weev on a campaign he termed Operation Ruin, which would target regional and local political figures who, being not so prominent as to have Wikipedia pages or any coverage among national publications that Google ranked higher than ours, could be written about in such a way that our page would come up in the first few results for their name, forever.

There was a Dallas city councilman named Mitchell Rasansky, who, some months prior, had made local headlines by coming to a meeting wearing plastic vampire fangs and giving a bizarre speech denouncing a local Boy Scout who, for his Eagle badge project, had built bat hutches in a city park. "I have enough people to take care of in my district. I don't need a colony of bats," Rasansky had been reported saying, after denouncing the Scout as "Count Dracula." "We want people in our parks," he explained, "not flying mice." So I wrote a few paragraphs summarizing the incident and mocking Rasansky. Weev, as was his wont, photoshopped Rasansky's face onto some vintage gay pornography and placed it atop the ED page, which, ten years later, remains among the first results for the councilman's name.

After this proof of concept, I lost interest, for there was something else I'd discovered in all of this that seemed to hold even greater promise. Littered across Encyclopedia Dramatica's esoteric maze of high-concept novelty were references to something called /b/, a vague designation that tended to come up in the most confusing contexts and from which many of the most amusing memes seemed to derive. It was, apparently, an "image board," akin to message boards but emphasizing the posting of pictures; and it was only one of many such boards located at a site called 4chan .org. For reasons unclear to me, /b/ stood for "random."

I have noted above how the concept of Anonymous grew out of the simple mechanism whereby a post on 4chan would default to the username "Anonymous" unless the poster entered a screen name, which almost no one did. As a result, a typical message thread on /b/ in particular looked at first glance to consist of a single person having a conversation with himself. It was a rather disturbing conversation, in many cases, given how /b/ had come to exist as the internet's de facto id. The characteristic user, as far as can be discerned from the sorts of anecdotes that were posted, was a high school boy, bright but by no means a genius, and probably not terribly popular. His habits were unwholesome, his hobbies unproductive. His sexual desires were somewhat irregular. He was prone to depression and internet addiction, and both of these fed on each other. To be sure, most users likely didn't match this persona, but to the extent that there was a /b/ type, this was it. It was the sort of person who would have generally been better off in a prior age, I think, before the era of the internet and of extended adolescence.

By the time I began to frequent the message board, much of the cultural framework that would long define /b/ was in place. Indeed, some of its key aspects had already been trimmed back lest they draw heat; 4chan's founder, a kid who went by the name Moot, had felt the need to ban the "raids" that had built /b/'s reputation and which ranged in nature from generally harmless group forays into various online communities with the intention of causing amusing havoc to more consequential crowd-sourced mobs against individuals who'd somehow gotten their attention.

What these raids involved, and how they were interpreted by outsiders, may be gleaned from the first notable public account of Anonymous. In July 2007, the Los Angeles Fox News affiliate ran a story on a nefarious group of "computer hackers"—promoted elsewhere in the segment to "hackers on steroids"—who had been "treating the web like a real-life video game: sacking websites, invading MySpace accounts, disrupting innocent people's lives," these apparently being the kinds of things that one does in video games. "Destroy. Die. Attack," ran the menacing red letters that began the segment, in which the three imperatives are oddly described as "threats" in accordance with the same brand of conceptual free association for which the report has since become legendary.

"Their name comes from their secret website," the narrator continues, in reference to 4chan, which had long before developed into one of the most popular and best-known sites on the web. "It requires anyone posting on the site to remain anonymous," he adds, in reference to a requirement that never existed, since some users did indeed use names. "MySpace users are among their favorite targets," he continues, with sudden accuracy. And then the viewer is introduced to an actual human being whose profile was taken over after a list of MySpace passwords was placed on /b/ a few months prior; "gay sex pictures" were posted on his page, we learn, allegedly prompting his girlfriend to break up with him. "She thought that I was cheating on her with guys," the fellow tells Fox.

A self-proclaimed hacker, rendered the regular sort of anonymous for the purpose of the interview, explains that the agenda of Anonymous hinges on sowing chaos and discord in pursuit of *lulz*, a term our narrator explains to be "a corruption of LOL, which stands for laugh out loud," before going on to note that "Anonymous gets big lulz from pulling random pranks—for example, messing with online children's games like Habbo Hotel," an example that Fox somehow neglects to illustrate with footage of exploding vehicles. "Truly epic lulz," he goes on, "come from raids and invasions . . . like their nationwide campaign to spoil the new Harry Potter book ending." It should be noted that the sinister background music that has played since the beginning of the segment continues through this particular revelation.

We now meet the ex-hacker himself. Though once a participant in Anonymous, and thus a domestic terrorist, he claims to have since changed his ways, likewise attempting to convert his former associates to a kinder, gentler set of activities. Unsurprisingly, the fellow had little luck in changing anything at all and promptly became the subject of a harsh campaign of mockery and intimidation that manifested in the threatening answering machine message played earlier (a more complete version of this recording is now played, revealing that the caller had not only threatened our subject's life but also called him an "emo bitch"). We learn that his frightened mother responded to the posting of their address and phone number by installing an alarm system; a brief clip seems to imply that she also got into the habit of closing the curtains. "They even bought a dog," the narrator tells us, overlaying an action shot of the pet in question barking. It's also claimed that Mom began "tracking down Anonymous members" herself, fearing that her calls to the FBI might not be taken seriously, and perhaps also worrying that unless she herself took them down first, some crack team of Anonymous techno-assassins might someday manage to get past the dog.

As the segment ends, it is noted that many of Anonymous's victims of chance are hopeful that their antagonists will simply get bored and move on. "But insiders say, 'Don't count on that,'" the narrator summarizes, prompting a final statement from the unknown hacker. "Garble garble mumble never forget," the latter says, or attempts to, through the voice-garbling software that's been deployed lest Anonymous discover the identity of the fellow whose identity they posted on the web. Presumably he is referencing the group's longtime quasi-motto, "We do not forgive. We do not forget."

This first major instance of media attention set the basic pattern for countless others to come. Although that delightfully surreal degree of inaccuracy would never be reached again, it would be a rare news segment that managed to get every little thing correct. But this was understandable; Anonymous was too vague an entity to lend itself to the certainty of description that the average journalist inexplicably believes himself capable of providing, whatever the subject. For instance, "We do not forgive. We do not forget," was not really Anonymous's motto, even though it was a popular and nearly ubiquitous phrase among its participants; Anonymous could have no motto, because there was no one in a position to give it one. Likewise, a popular text laying out the "Rules of the Internet," which focuses on /b/, despite the title, begins as follows:

1. Do not talk about /b/
2. Do not talk about /b/

The reader will perhaps recognize this exhortation as a loving tribute to the film *Fight Club*. Later on, these exhortations—all the more seemingly forceful by virtue of being listed first, just like the First Amendment and the First Commandment—were taken by many as actual rules that must actually be followed. As is so often the case with budding religions, there are always those who seek to codify well past the point of certainty; also akin to religions, the rules were reinterpreted as desired by the literalists themselves, some of whom decided that /b/ also meant Anonymous, and that one must thus never speak about Anonymous (except on 4chan and associated internet relay chat networks and anywhere else that these rabbinical sorts deemed to be constituting hallowed digital grounds).

But Anonymous had expanded beyond /b/, and beyond 4chan. Other "chan" sites proliferated, each with a different emphasis and character. And after Moot banned raids, those with a taste for such things increasingly congregated at 7chan; that site's /i/nsurgency board became the chief organizing venue for the mass visits to the youth-targeted virtual hangout Habbo Hotel, for instance, where Anons donned avatars of Black men with Afros and three-piece suits and blocked the entrances to the community's pool, claiming that it was closed due to contamination by AIDS. And beyond such well-entrenched traditions as these, other methods, more sophisticated and more novel, were being incubated. In the process, people were learning skills that would someday be honed against considerably larger targets, and for more legitimate reasons. It was within the context of Second Life that I developed some of the organizational skills that would serve me well in the conflicts to come.

As Anonymous proliferated, it became even more difficult to control—for there were always those who sought to guide its path. Beyond the literalists, there were the trolls—those who subscribed to the doctrine that Anonymous was the "Internet Hate Machine," devoid of ideals and seriousness, and who enforced this program via campaigns of harassment against those who strove to change its character. They succeeded for a while, but others would come along bearing a different program, one that offered victory on a grander scale than the trolls dared to imagine, while still allowing for the satisfaction that comes with participating in the mob. This new class—later termed moralfags—could thus still appeal to those Anons who raided for raiding's sake, simply by changing the targets from the innocent to the guilty. More critically, they could also attract hordes of new participants from beyond the fold: people intent on doing actual good and often possessed of capabilities that are generally unavailable to the sort of person who really identifies, above all, as a troll. As the new blood poured in, it would dilute Anonymous until the trolls came to constitute a minority within their own digital clubhouse. In the absence of any structure, Anonymous could become anything at all.

I eventually tired of the raiding and lost interest in 4chan and its appendages. At the end of 2007 I'd moved from Austin to Brooklyn so as to be in a position to supplement my freelance writing work with whatever on-site jobs I could swing in New York. I'd already published one well-received book, a humorous polemic on the intelligent design movement that had won accolades from Alan Dershowitz and Matt Taibbi and gotten a few glowing reviews here and there. I'd written for *Vanity Fair*, *New York Press*, *The Huffington Post*, *The Guardian*, *Skeptic*, the *Skeptical Inquirer*, *McSweeney's*, *The Onion*'s *AV Club*, and a couple dozen more obscure policy journals and trade publications while also having served as the lead blogger on a failed political analysis start-up launched by the CNET founders, Political Base. After that folded, I landed another regular blogging position with True/Slant, a visually high-concept news and commentary start-up, where I specialized in mocking the work of other pundits who had the disadvantage of not being me.

As good as this may have all looked on paper, things were actually deteriorating pretty rapidly. Since early adolescence, I'd been what the twelve-step people would term a drug addict, in the sense that although I'd never been physically addicted to any substance other than nicotine, I was clearly compelled to do whichever of them happened to come along at any given moment, and also to seek them out if those moments didn't come fast enough.

Being nothing if not a child of the eighties, my first experience with powerful mind-altering drugs came around third grade, when I was prescribed Ritalin to address what I vaguely recall as having been some especially spirited behavior in school. This continued until, sitting in the bathtub one morning, I confessed to my mother that I was suicidal. I was immediately taken off the drug and remained an unadulterated child into early adolescence. But my continued childhood depression would eventually reach such a worrying point that my mother again sent me to a series of therapists. By mid-adolescence, I was on Zoloft, which allowed me to function like a regular person and even renewed my interest in other human beings, something that had waned in the interim. Now exceedingly charming, I fell in with the popular and attractive girls at school, and because beautiful girls can go anywhere and get anything, I now had easy access to drugs (and girls, which is why I was nearly expelled from high school at the end of my sophomore year after getting caught in bed with two of them while on a trip to New York to receive an award for our school newspaper, for which I'd written a comically subversive column).

Within two years of moving to Brooklyn, I'd become a drug addict in the actual sense of being addicted to heroin. Naturally this led to some difficulties, professionally and otherwise. I was invited to Rutgers to give a talk in my capacity as the author of the anti–intelligent design book, and spent the night before smoking crack because I couldn't get hold of any heroin. The talk actually went pretty well, I'm told, and it wouldn't really have mattered if it hadn't because this was a class full of college students at Rutgers. But another time I was asked to come into the office of *The New York Observer* after querying the editors about doing some attack pieces on pundits, which by this time was my specialty. I was quite visibly high when I arrived for the meeting, and though I was asked to do a piece attacking Michael Wolff—perhaps at the instigation of the *Observer*'s owner, Jared Kushner, who seems to have had the obnoxious essayist in his sights—they seem to have thought better of working with me and I never heard back from them. Wolff, of course, ended up getting Kushner first, some ten years later, with the publication of *Fire and Fury*.

After losing my apartment and spending four months on friends' couches, I called it quits and headed back to Dallas. I got a prescription for Suboxone, a powerful synthetic opiate that prevents the user from getting high off other, more destructive opiates while still allowing for a taste of the satisfaction that comes from getting high.

That solved the heroin thing, sort of, but I had larger

problems. Although I was still writing for outlets here and there, I wasn't bringing in much money, and had to turn to my father for work. This was always an option of last resort; upon nearly getting kicked out of high school at the age of seventeen, I'd taught myself basic Swahili and accompanied him to Tanzania for a venture that failed so spectacularly that the State Department eventually had to be called in to pressure a government attorney to return our passports so that we could escape back to the United States. Not long afterward I got kicked out of my mom's house and spent the summer with my dad in unhappy exile, living at his sister's home in East Texas and assisting with some sordid home-financing venture. The pattern would continue throughout my early adulthood, during which I spent probably a year in total living on my dad's apartment floors or in spare bedrooms in the homes of unlikely business partners, days spent moving office furniture for some bizarre enterprise disguised as a Pentecostal church or editing investor letters in support of some real estate deal that would invariably fail, nights spent writing and querying and submitting, my motivation rekindled by pure terror. Each time I would write my way out of the situation; it was only upon regaining independence and a modicum of dignity that I would again let down my guard in the face of my own deleterious habits.

This time was different, though, for not even the prospect of further successes as a writer could really motivate me now. Each time I wrote for a somewhat more prominent publication, there was a little buzz of satisfaction that quickly wore off. Meanwhile, a book that I'd written under contract for a small publisher that subsequently went under, and that I considered to be the culmination of my talents, had yet to be accepted anywhere else. The articles

I sold here and there didn't bring in enough for me to live like an actual adult, and I was disinclined to go back to doing the marketing copywriting and magazine filler that had often kept me afloat in the past. And then there was the increasingly obvious fact that journalism didn't really matter.

One of the first real pieces of journalism I ever wrote, during one of my living-on-Dad's-living-room-floor-because-he-didn't-own-a-couch phases back in 2003, was an article for a public policy journal on new Texas prison regulations. At the time, a female jail inmate, in on some insignificant charge, was raped by a prison guard while another covered for him from the control room. Unlike most prison rapes, this one happened to get picked up in the press. In response, the Texas Board of Corrections passed a new regulation—one making it harder for journalists to talk to inmates. After I finished the piece and got my check, it occurred to me that I hadn't really helped anyone other than myself; I had merely informed people who were already opposed to the way a particular system works of a particular aspect of it that might have been worse than they'd previously thought. If I could work my way up to more prominent outlets, I imagined, eventually I'd gain the influence necessary to right wrongs, rather than just documenting them to no visible end.

Seven years later, with a couple of the major-tier outlets under my belt and a new gig writing for *The Guardian*, it was hard to see that anything I'd done had mattered at all. Worse, it wasn't clear that journalism itself, as currently practiced, was doing much good even in those instances when the journalism was being done well. Certainly specific revelations of scandals, generally with some compelling and dramatic element included, could sometimes dislodge criminal politicians or force back the advent of some especially noxious legislation. But it was dawning on me that it just wasn't enough to make a compelling case. In a vastly complex society in which the population was heavily entertained and at least a third of its voters were actual fascists, the threshold for prompting the citizens to attend to their duties, or to compel legislators to do so via concern over reelection, was simply too high. This is to say that the basic mechanism that a republic ultimately depends upon to prevent its apparatus from being turned against its own citizenry and populations abroad was essentially broken.

This conclusion had come to obsess me in my mid-twenties, when I'd begun writing primarily about politics for a string of decently paying but short-lived online news outlets. Monitoring the day-to-day interplay between state and press during the George W. Bush years, it became more and more clear that the haphazard manner in which the news media operates had provided a massive advantage to those who understood its structural failures and were willing to make use of them, from Karl Rove on down. That these same dynamics had been recognized by others, and increasingly noted by some of the better bloggers and media critics, didn't seem to make much difference. Absent some unprecedented and well-coordinated campaign to set things right, it was difficult to see how any reversal of our politics could be pulled off. It was in 2005, I recall, that I had my first and only panic attack, having become convinced that there was nothing really holding our civilization together, and no reason to expect that a society driven by such forces as these could defend itself from whatever threats an increasingly technological globe would essentially guarantee over the next century.

But all these same anxieties—about the failures of our civics, of our media, and of my own dreams of glory—had at times propelled me to uncharacteristic bursts of hard work and discipline during my last year in New York. And though I had been forced to retreat to Dallas—and thus into the baroque milieu of upper-class criminality that had surrounded me since childhood, without ever being quite glamorous enough to be appealing—I brought with me one unique asset that could potentially address all of these problems at once. This was Project PM, which I'd created in 2009 as a proposed next-level blogging platform and which by 2012 would be publicly denounced by the Department of Justice as a criminal organization with the ultimate purpose of overthrowing the United States government.

Like I said, it was a truly unique asset.

In 2008 the struggling little publisher that had commissioned my first book now asked me to do a second, which was to be a humorous polemic against Thomas L. Friedman, Charles Krauthammer, and other Establishment commentators. After reading a decade's worth of their columns in the archives of *The New York Times* and *The Washington Post*, I had another one of those revelations that, while rather simple and not even particularly original, eventually takes on the solidity of a geometrical proof in my own mind; these periodic obsessions take a sort of control over my life thereafter, very much in the manner that a religious reformer is seized by his own mystical vision and has no choice but to follow it to its conclusion, which in the end is always conflict.

In the course of my work, I'd had occasion to follow closely the various political blogs that had come about during the Bush administration, and had been struck by the extent to which Establishment press output was now subject to highly competent peer review by some of the better bloggers—and also by how few mechanisms for such readily accessible criticism had existed prior to this. Any intellectually honest person who really wanted to know the best arguments for and against something could now find them both in seconds, simply by knowing which blogs were most likely to provide them. Any news item or commentary that a paper posted online could be dissected and, if necessary, debunked, with hyperlinks to primary sources taking the place of the mere assertions that dot television and newsprint, rarely to be checked on.

It wasn't that every blogger was more reliable than every mainstream journalist, of course; but it was undeniable that some of these bloggers had become better sources of information than many of their professional counterparts. This I'd concluded years prior. What I was learning now was that the men the Establishment had itself put forward as its own best representatives—awarding them Pulitzer Prizes and prestigious spaces in the world's most influential outlets—were actually less than worthless by any credible accounting.

Friedman, for instance, had in 2000 praised Vladimir Putin as a great liberal reformer for whom we all should be "rootin'"; went on to proclaim that Colin Powell would dominate the Bush administration; laughed off the idea that civilian casualties in Afghanistan would prove problematic for the U.S. occupation; and by the end of 2001 was celebrating the U.S. victory in that country, noting in passing that the Taliban were now "gone." Shortly afterward he won his second Pulitzer Prize for commentary. Krauthammer predicted in 1998 that the U.S. intervention in Kosovo would result in a Vietnamese-style "quagmire"; mocked those who predicted the quagmires that actually did occur in Afghanistan and Iraq; and then took an unusual stance among conservatives when he proposed that "the surge" would fail—and then, nine months later, after it became commonly held that it had been a success, suddenly proclaimed it to be a success. Through it all, he continued to shore up his status as the right's most respected pundit. At no point during this period did either of these men make any especially successful predictions that might balance out the record and bring them back up to the status of a flipped coin.

Nor does there seem to be anything else particularly redeeming in their work, and in fact both can be shown to exhibit the most astonishing hypocrisy with regard to their pet issues. Krauthammer insisted throughout the nineties that the Arabs were culturally incapable of democracy and then spent the Bush years attacking those who expressed the same opinion or even more nuanced reservations about whether this particular attempt at installing democracy would actually work as well as advertised, all without ever acknowledging his own bizarre shift. Friedman had not only given Putin the thumbs-up but also mocked the idea that there was any good reason for the United States to gather intel on Russia; in 2008, when Russia invaded Georgia, he denounced those who had failed to anticipate the threat. During this same period he also seemed to decide, inexplicably, that he was an old China hand, assuring his readers that the Middle Kingdom would never seek to censor its people's internet access; shortly afterward that government rolled out the Great Firewall, the most comprehensive internet censorship protocol to be established by any major country before or since. It's worth pointing out that Barack Obama was photographed with a copy of one of Friedman's books early in his presidency.

Every well-informed person is intellectually (if perhaps only passively) aware that those who climb to the top of a given industry are not necessarily the ones who ought to be there. And of course I had lately worked in the specific capacity of a political media critic, so was already unusually attuned to the remarkable incompetence one finds in the upper echelons of the field. But the sheer extent of the problem really was nonetheless astonishing. The U.S. commentariat constitutes the nervous system of the most powerful entity to have ever existed on earth, such that even minor failures by that class can translate into major disasters. Here we had substantial failures occurring over and over again without ever seeming to diminish the influence of those who had repeatedly been proven wrong concerning what they themselves had proclaimed to be the most crucial questions of our time; if anything, their prestige only increased even as they led the empire further astray.

Presently, I became fascinated with a related problem: that there did not seem to be anything to be done about this. One could present as airtight a case as one liked and get it published in a prominent venue, as I'd done lately by selling hit pieces on Friedman and Krauthammer to *Vanity Fair* for use on its website. But not only was there no guarantee that any good would come out of this; it was also virtually guaranteed that nothing would come out of it, as outlets like *The New York Times* could viably ignore that sort of criticism under most any circumstances. As I came to see it, there was a certain high threshold of public attention that would need to be met before the editors of *The New York Times*, for instance, would find it necessary to address even the most profound and unanswerable case against Thomas Friedman; it was the point at which that case had been brought to sufficient attention among other publications and the reading public that to ignore it further would incur a greater loss in prestige than could be expected were *The New York Times* itself to acknowledge the issue, such as via a statement by its ombudsman or some such thing (for I am not such a wild-eyed dreamer as to think that Friedman's column would ever be actually discontinued by the chiefs of the publication merely on the demonstrable basis that it is of zero value and has in fact done actual harm).

The only manner by which such a high threshold of buzz could ever be reached, I decided, would be through deliberate coordination. I would have to convince some large number of bloggers to participate in a sort of Thomas Friedman Day, whereby everyone would more or less simultaneously post some example of the columnist's failings and link to each other's output on the subject. This would set off a sort of chain reaction of attention even among non-participating bloggers, prompting comment from at least one or two of those who are followed closely in turn by producers and editors and the like—and who thus sometimes set part of the day's news agenda—plus perhaps the in-house bloggers of the mainstream outlets.

I set about recruiting bloggers, during which time the original idea began to evolve. As long as I was putting together an ad hoc network of bloggers who were reasonable enough to see the Friedman problem and adventurous enough to go along with my eccentric ideas, I reasoned, why not also harness them into some sort of more permanent entity whereby any crucial yet underexposed story could perhaps gain traction via this same deliberate process of "force multiplication"? And as long as I was populating a blogger network to compete with the lurid clickbait that carries a natural advantage in a society such as ours, why not try to supplement its array of superior contributors with an improved platform structure, too? Drawing upon what I'd seen as both a media critic and a political blogger, I came up with a few small improvements on existing platforms that could collectively be incorporated into a sort of cross-platform meta-network. Next I began recruiting, both directly via emails to specific bloggers I considered above par, and indirectly via the various outlets for which I was writing, where I used my columns to beat the drum for collaborative media reform and to provide the broad outlines of my project (sometimes to the confusion and horror of my editors).

Between my constant harping on the failures of the established media and my increasingly ardent evangelism on behalf of the untapped potential of the internet, I had managed to accumulate an audience of the sort from which such dedicated individuals could in fact be recruited—knowledgeable people possessed of what used to be termed "civic virtue" but with a growing sense that the institutions that made up our civics were fundamentally flawed beyond all normal means of repair. I was still only a very minor figure operating in a media ecosystem saturated with personalities and pundits, and I commanded only a relatively small readership. But my audience was different; it didn't want to be just an audience anymore.

So while I was recruiting bloggers for a network I'd already planned, I was also getting inquiries from regular citizens who wanted to help out as well. I accepted all the interesting ones, on the grounds that it's better to have a makeshift cyber army than to not have one, and that at any rate I'd have no problem finding something for them to do, what with the world being broken and largely devoid of my own input and all. The possibilities tended to suggest themselves through the particular skill sets of the recruits, of whom I had about seventy-five by the end of 2010; in addition to the handful of media people, many were academics, some were working scientists, others came from finance or information technology or both, while the remainder were scattered among so many odd professions as to defy summary. My second-in-command was, of all things, a retired legal counsel for the IRS. There were, in addition, a couple of more prominent figures available to me. Barry Eisler, a former CIA Directorate of Operations covert officer and a bestselling thriller novelist, reached out to offer his assistance after reading a piece I'd written for *Vanity Fair*'s website in defense of the journalist Michael Hastings, in which I'd made mention of his involvement in Project PM. Hastings himself had come to my attention while the two of us were both writing for the online outlet True/Slant before it was bought out by *Forbes*; he and I turned out to share certain views of the media, and the two of us would go on to collaborate on my various grandiose plans by which to fix all of this, mostly via phone discussions. (A few months after we met, he slipped off to Afghanistan, and the article that resulted led to General McChrystal's resignation due to Hastings having accurately reported what the fellow was actually saying—a seemingly dastardly trick for which Hastings was promptly attacked by much of the "serious" press.)

Project PM continued to evolve throughout 2010. Using Google Docs, email, and internet relay chat servers to communicate, we set about designing the inter-platform blog network as originally planned while also fleshing out a similar project about which I was now far more excited—a sort of civic participation platform by which large numbers of people could be quickly and efficiently organized into co-operative activist entities that would be well defined yet still capable of evolving quickly, and in a way that would entail the consent of everyone involved. These entities I called "pursuances" while the schematic itself would be known as the "pursuance system." The plan was that Project PM would eventually operate along these lines while also making the software available to others, who could launch their own pursuances; over time, a loose global network of citizen pursuances would come about, incubating and then disseminating new information-age techniques in the fields of activism and philanthropy, and so tackling problems while also giving rise to a sort of ecosystem of non-institutional cooperation.

In the meantime we'd thought up two pilot programs, one of which involved matching scientists with working journalists to facilitate improved science journalism, the other being a clever plan thought up by a patent lawyer who would select abandoned hundred-year-old technology and distribute step-by-step blueprints in African villages where these devices could be easily built and operated; to cover printing costs, we'd sell advertisements to African firms;

distribution could be done in large part by existing networks of NGOs, such as Bikes for Africa, one of the nonprofits we'd approached about adapting our system—for this was intended not just to allow self-organization by individuals but also to incorporate existing institutions, which would be able to make far better use of its supporters by way of this platform.

It was also built to expand perpetually, without running into the problems that I'd observed among other online enterprises. For the first few years of Reddit's existence, that outlet—wherein users submit posts from other sites and comment on them—attracted a body of participants who were early adopters almost by definition, comprised largely of people who tended to be better informed and somewhat more intellectually curious than the average person (and thus far more than the average internet commenter, naturally). Possessed of a variety of careers and educational backgrounds, Reddit's user base could usually be depended upon to point out errors, add necessary context, and otherwise provide useful commentary on whatever news items were posted on a given day—and the more useful of these tended to be voted "up" by others, such that they would gravitate toward the top of the page, where they would be the most accessible. Thus Reddit was, for quite a while, the single best source of information available to the public.

In some respects it still is, but even by 2009, there had been a noticeable deterioration in participant quality as Reddit became more popular, attracting waves of new users. Obviously not everyone who came to Reddit after any particular point was less capable than those who frequented the site in its early days, and certainly many were better. But to the extent that there are substantive differences between early adopters and "later adopters," a population that is flooded with the latter will naturally change in character to some degree or another, and in this case the changes tended to be negative.

The question of how one could set in motion something that could perpetually grow on its own without seeing an average decline in participant quality over time, then, would have to be addressed if our "civic platform" were to self-organize into something both large and viable. I concluded that although one could never ensure against this entirely, one could certainly guard against it, and meanwhile reduce the damage that could come from less capable users down the line. You would simply start with a population of high-quality participants, each of whom could bring on several other participants, and so on. This wouldn't prevent deterioration over time as some associates of associates of original users turned out to be less than adept, but such a grouping would nonetheless be superior to the results yielded by allowing anyone in, while being able to grow faster than would be possible if some static group were doing all the recruiting.

More important was that the very nature of this system would reduce the problems entailed by those low-quality participants who did manage to get in. Anyone could create their own civic entity, and grow it however they liked; but to join someone else's, one would have to apply for the position in question. As these entities grow from their early core users outward—generally through a process whereby each new user has the right to bring on others connecting directly to them, and so on—new participants are usually located on the growing margins of the entity, where they interact only with the person who brought them in until such time as someone higher up chooses to link to them as well, or offers them other positions elsewhere in the network. Submissions of data or whatever else must be approved by each next person up the line, thereby providing a sort of automatic filter. Some exceptions would have to be incorporated so as to prevent situations, typical of institutions, in which users on the margins end up being better-informed than those above them—for instance, by allowing anyone to send a message to anyone else within the entity, once, with that ability to be renewed if the recipient thinks the idea or finding to be worthwhile—but all in all, the dynamics we proposed could allow our entities to theoretically grow faster and larger than a normal organization without becoming stagnant or forcing founders to micromanage a massive array of individuals.

Things were proceeding rather encouragingly on that front, and under different circumstances I'd probably have gone on to run a network of fairly mainstream, respectable activist outfits, perhaps giving the occasional TED talk about what a great guy I am and how neat and fantastic my ideas are—instead of going to war with the government and then being thrown in prison. But two factors ensured that things would take the course they did.

For one thing, I am not a philanthropist by temperament; rather I'm closer to what was known in the eighteenth and nineteenth centuries, not always with admiration, as an adventurer. Certainly I have a very visceral hatred of what I perceive to be injustice, but I also have a deep longing for public honor. Like Romans of the senatorial class under the Republic, I regard fame as an entirely reasonable, even commendable objective. And though I like to make myself helpful, and was indeed excited about the Africa project in particular, I had no interest in being famous for helping people. Rather I wanted to be famous for overthrowing things—for attacking established institutions and beating them through cunning and force of argument. It just so happened that there did indeed exist all around me institutions that were silly or corrupt or even outright evil in some cases, and so my natural inclinations often turned out to be of some use to the public, but that was largely coincidence.

The other factor in play was the budding conflict between the world's nation-states, led by the United States, and the world's emerging anti-authoritarian net-based entities, chief among them WikiLeaks. From the fact that I've just had to coin the clunky term *emerging anti-authoritarian net-based entities*, one can probably gather that this was to be an uneven contest. And from the fact that I was around this time plotting to saturate the world with a web of self-replicating cooperative entities that I secretly hoped would solidify into a global network of effective opposition against states and anything else with more power than myself, one can likewise imagine that I had some eccentric and frankly megalomaniacal ideas about the role I myself was to play in the coming conflict (incidentally, I formulated this plan while living on a friend's couch in Brooklyn and smoking her cigarettes because I'd spent all my money on heroin; such is the boundless regard I had for my own capabilities that I could nonetheless confidently chalk up the broad outlines of far-future propaganda wars). When Julian Assange reported on Twitter that he and other WikiLeaks volunteers were being tailed by U.S. officials and that another had been detained, I saw it as one of the early shots in what would become a decades-long struggle that would come to define this century. By this point I was convinced that WikiLeaks, which was still largely unknown but already being targeted by the United States and other states for its tendency to publicize inconvenient documents, would serve as the linchpin of a new, alternative political order, and I wanted a seat at the table. I was committed to the coming struggle, then, both by philosophy and by ambition.

There were other developments pointing toward global conflict as well. Although I'd stopped participating in raids and other 4chan silliness after I'd left Austin for New York, I'd made a point of keeping up with Anonymous. That was easy now that Anonymous was regularly making headlines.

In early 2008 someone posted to YouTube a clip of Tom Cruise giving a bizarre talk on the myriad virtues of Scientology, apparently having been made for distribution among church members. He spoke in manic tones about how only a Scientologist can really help car accident victims, jumping from subject to subject in a monologue interspersed with uncontrollable laughter and obscure acronyms. He denounced "SPs," Scientology-speak for the "suppressive persons" who stood in the way of the church's ultimate triumph. To a true believer, the clip was no doubt inspiring. To the average member of the public, it was an amusing glimpse into the actual nature of this hypercommercial techno cult.

Using the Digital Millennium Copyright Act as a pretext, Church of Scientology lawyers soon had the clip taken down from YouTube. Another copy was put up; it was taken down, too. This went on for some time as word spread and more people managed to acquire copies that they could edit in small ways in hopes of evading whatever detection algorithm the church was using to find them. Finally *Gawker* put the whole thing up on their front page and proclaimed that they wouldn't take it down until such time as armed men actually swarmed their office with a court order.

The Church of Scientology and the internet already had something of a history. Back in the mid-nineties, when Usenet message boards were still the rage, the organization's lawyers had pursued legal action against one particular forum, alt.religion.scientology. This came after someone had posted documents that the church's lawyers claimed to be "trade secrets." Among other things, those documents spelled out the pseudosecret doctrine taught to members only after they'd reached a certain level within the church. And although this doctrine had been leaked before, it wasn't readily available—at least, not yet.

A funny thing happens when an attempt is made to forbid access to online information. Rather than preventing exposure, such an act tends to guarantee it. This phenomenon is now commonly referred to as the Streisand Effect. In 2003, Barbra Streisand got upset over pictures of her beachfront residence having been posted on some obscure corner of the internet as part of a web-based project documenting coastal erosion. So she got her lawyers involved. By the time the ensuing case was dismissed a few months later, hundreds of thousands of people had viewed this entirely innocuous picture after having learned of the dispute from media reports and online gossip. Prior to all that, the picture had been accessed exactly four times.

The church didn't have much more luck than Barbra

Streisand's attorneys did in suppressing information. Despite the legal wrangling, the church's secret doctrines were freely distributed from a number of venues after 1995. What's more, Scientology had made itself a lot of enemies and done a significant degree of damage to its public image, particularly among the internet savvy. Of course, they didn't get a whole effect named after them, like poor Barbra Streisand did. On the other hand, there was nothing inherently embarrassing about Streisand's house, whereas the secret doctrines of Scientology were vastly problematic; among the most interesting was a foundation myth involving billions of alien souls being imprisoned in volcanoes on Earth, and later latching on to the human psyche, from which they could be removed only through methods designed by a moderately successful sci-fi author and ceremonial magic enthusiast named L. Ron Hubbard, who founded the organization. Presumably such a revelation is more likely to be accepted in the context of well-regulated initiatory rights after the celebrant has spent years paying for church courses; having it available on the internet to anyone who cared to look these things up—prospective members, for instance—was a significant liability.

All in all, the church faced the same fundamental problem that confronted every powerful institution that had passed into this new and different age in which it was now harder to keep secrets and virtually impossible to suppress them once released. But unlike most powerful institutions, the church had no hard power with which to defend itself, and little soft power outside a relatively small number of adherents. It was vulnerable in a way that states were not. And there are those who can smell blood over broadband.

In the wake of the Tom Cruise affair, another video appeared on YouTube. The visuals consisted entirely of a sped-up scene of clouds moving through the sky, a modernist glass building in the foreground. It was accompanied by a text-to-speech reading of something that was half manifesto and half threat:

> Hello, leaders of Scientology. We are Anonymous.
>
> Over the years, we have been watching you. Your campaigns of misinformation, your suppression of dissent, your litigious nature—all of these things have caught our eye. With the leakage of your latest propaganda video into mainstream circulation, the extent of your malign influence over those who have come to trust you as leaders has been made clear to us. Anonymous has therefore decided that your organization should be destroyed. For the good of your followers, for the good of mankind, and for our own enjoyment, we shall proceed to expel you from the internet and systematically dismantle the Church of Scientology in its present form. We recognize you as serious opponents, and do not expect our campaign to be completed in a short time frame. However, you will not prevail forever against the angry masses of the body politic. Your choice of methods, your hypocrisy, the general artlessness of your organization have sounded its death knell . . .
>
> Knowledge is free.
>
> We are Anonymous.

We are legion.
We do not forgive.
We do not forget.
Expect us.

Within twenty-four hours of being posted, the video had received a hundred thousand views and become the subject of widespread speculation; *Gawker* and other outlets ran it prominently on their sites.

Some doubted that anything would come of it. But anyone with a firm command of Western history might have recognized that there was a precedent for mysterious messages appearing from the ether, declaring the advent of anonymous guardians who would strike against the enemies of reason and usher in a new, more enlightened era. In that instance, the messages proved correct, and the enlightened era arrived as promised, delivered in large part by men who operated behind closed doors, recognizing each other through symbols.

Over a period of several years in the early seventeenth century, there appeared in Western Europe a handful of manifestos proclaiming the existence of a body of luminaries, bearers of secret knowledge that gave them powers beyond that of the common man. The Rosicrucians, as they were known, were now declaring themselves to the world, though they would remain in hiding both in obedience to their mystic doctrines and as a means of better carrying out their ultimate mission, which itself was to be understood as religious and social reform to be followed by a superior political order. The manifestos, along with a later document setting forth an allegorical "chemical wedding" between a queen and a king, made use of Hermetic and alchemical terminology that would have been familiar to much of the educated class of that era. Some set out in search of this secret society that appealed so keenly to their intellectual curiosity, and to their most fervent hopes for the future; a few even applied to join by publishing letters directed at its scattered ranks, who must certainly have been ever on the watch for those worthy of joining. The Rosicrucian affair was poorly understood by modern scholars and at any rate was viewed largely as an unimportant curiosity until the 1960s, when Dame Frances Yates published *The Rosicrucian Enlightenment*. Here, she convincingly demonstrated that the manifestos were perceived, and likely intended, as a call for renewed confrontation against the Catholic Church and particularly the Hapsburg powers. The Rosicrucian-ascribed "chemical wedding" allegory was rooted in the recent marriage between the Protestant figures Elizabeth Stuart, daughter of James I, and Frederick V, Elector of the Palatinate. This was presently to be seen as a crucial development in the struggle of Protestantism and indeed the forward-thinking element of European life at that time, given the expectations that James would throw the strength of England behind whatever new wars were to arise between the two faiths on the Continent. For his part, Frederick V did indeed pursue the mystical role that was set before him, agreeing to be crowned King of Bohemia after its rebellion against the Hapsburgs. Hereafter he led his new realm into war against the forces of the old. The result was the Thirty Years' War, which laid waste to Germany.

This was a time in which educated men associated magical doctrines with reason and progress, and indeed with a restoration of the superior world that educated men knew to have existed many centuries before. In this context, mystical teachings that had again proliferated in Western Europe after rediscovery and translation by Italian and Greek scholars were seen as inherently forward leaning, not conservative, whereas to be a Hermetic thinker was to be a reformer and intellectual, even a futurist. Bohemia was one major center of Protestant mysticism and religious activism, and had been for several centuries; Heidelberg, from which Frederick had ruled, was another such center. And it had been Elizabeth I's court astrologer, John Dee, who coined the term "British Empire"—a concept that, merely by being spoken into being, and thus presented as a real possibility, became more powerful than any incantation.

Of the authors of the Rosicrucian documents we know nothing other than that the third "chemical wedding" manuscript was eventually claimed by a ministry student who publicly wrote it off as a sort of game, or prank—and who may or may not have disavowed a genuine youthful intent to excite revolutionary sentiment out of concern for how this would be taken by other, more conservative Lutherans. But as there was almost certainly no actual Rosicrucian society fitting the description put forward in the first two documents, the exact origin of these proclamations is rather secondary. What matters is the effect that these ideas had on the imaginations of men. The Rosicrucians didn't exist. But the desire existed—for religious reform, for political experimentation, and, crucially, for a mastery over nature that began as magic and ended in science.

Believing that others had begun on this path, men were inspired to join them. Failing to find any group like the one described, these men went on to create it. Elias Ashmole, an antiquarian and magician, had once written a letter to the Rosicrucians seeking admission; as it was later found among his own papers, it's unclear if this was the draft of a letter sent out for publication or was instead a sort of symbolic exercise. Either way, his life, and those of others, had taken the path, and set the world on it as well. Ashmole and people of similar character would go on to found the Royal Society, which would give the world science, and transform it beyond recognition. They would likewise form the core of the Freemasons, who though they never had any unified structure or even an agreed-upon secular function, would later provide a convenient forum for anti-monarchical and sometimes anti-clerical sentiment, gestating revolutionary movements in France and the Americas that would alter the character of human association. Tellingly, they would instead serve as a force for political and social conservatism in the United Kingdom, which reminds us that rendering an organization semi-secret is no defense against it coming asunder like anything else. At any rate, the wildest Rosicrucian myths could not approach the reality that was to follow. But the reality flowed from the myth.

Anonymous had an advantage over the Rosicrucians in that it really did exist. Nonetheless, given the culture's relatively small number of participants versus the hordes that would be needed to do the job as described, its proclamations against Scientology were no more immediately enforceable than the seventeenth-century pamphlets proclaiming a new and freer Europe built on an energetic mixture of experimental reason and Protestant mysticism. But the Rosicrucian pamphlets had given focus to energies that had lain latent within forward-thinking Europeans, acting on their imaginations in such a way that compelled them to act in turn on the world around them. The "Message to Scientology" video could do likewise, and could moreover bring the constituency of seekers into an organization that was ready to receive them right then, at that very moment. This would only happen if, as in the seventeenth century, the latent desire was there. Such desires need not have anything to do with Scientology in and of itself, or even with justice. There are yearnings in the human heart that build empires and bring them down. And where no army exists, one may be raised simply by pretending it does, and by making people see it.

On the morning of February 10, 2008, people began arriving at a Church of Scientology branch in Sydney, Australia. Many wore identical masks of pale, stylized faces adorned with archaic mustaches—Guy Fawkes masks, as they were known, having originated in a traditional English festival commemorating the capture of the Catholic terrorist of the same name. Some held signs bringing attention to the church's various atrocities; others handed out pamphlets to passersby wherein were listed embarrassing aspects of its history; still others shouted out random 4chan memes. Within two hours, well over two hundred people had assembled. The local press couldn't help but take notice and report on the pretext for the event.

The very same thing was happening in Perth, Melbourne, Adelaide, and Tokyo. As the sun rose that day over the world's major cities, crowds formed in front of dozens of church locations across the world, wearing the same masks, shouting the same bizarre slogans, pointing to the same embarrassing information regarding what the church really was and what it really did. Altogether, the first round of protests had brought out some ten thousand people in some 143 cities. It couldn't help but spawn countless media reports that were of course obligated to say a few words about why so many people were hanging out in front of buildings wearing masks and shouting memes and distributing leaflets, and what those leaflets said, and why these people cared enough to say it, and what this all might mean. Additional protests were held a few weeks later and then off and on for the next several years.

The campaign itself was a partial success. For decades prior, Scientology had managed to pull off an unusual balancing act, growing immensely and achieving religious brand recognition while also managing to keep its more egregious characteristics largely out of sight. Certainly many who had heard of it were vaguely aware that it was some sort of kooky self-help thing that all the Hollywood types resorted to when they needed to get off drugs or convince themselves that they weren't actually gay. But for an organization that had engaged in as baroque and somber an array of abominable acts as were here directed toward its paying members and those who spoke out against it, the church had nonetheless managed to keep its darkest aspects largely out of public view. It had accomplished this via the same strategy that it had used in seeking to rid the internet both of its secret theology and of the Cruise monologue—by covert intimidation and unprecedented misuse of the legal system.

In 1991, *Time* ran a cover story titled "The Thriving Cult of Greed and Power," an investigative piece that drew from testimony of former church members. The author was pursued by Scientology employees and lawyers who seem to have been looking into his own background; other lawyers prepared a suit against *Time*, which the church lost, but not before getting their message across. A few years earlier, a journalist for the *St. Petersburg Times* reported having been similarly hassled after depicting Scientology in a negative light. Then the same thing happened to a journalist from the *Boston Herald*. For years afterward, Scientology received relatively little negative coverage, even as it continued to expand.

Safety in numbers applies to journalism just as it does to anything else. The Tom Cruise video had provided a two-week window during which every journalist could be assured that they wouldn't be the only ones saying something mean about Scientology. More important, it provided them with a hook to do so (hooks are very important in media, even if they mean nothing in terms of what may actually be of life-and-death significance to the populace). Anonymous's campaign, entailing protests, distributed denial-of-service (DDoS) attacks that rendered websites inaccessible, hacks of data, and the like ensured that this window of opportunity would be extended and that there would always be a ready pool of interviewees ready to provide punchy quotes or point reporters to damning bits of information.

Anonymous was a machine that focused attention—a sort of spotlight that could be turned toward whatever needed to be exposed, and attacked.

But who was turning the spotlight?

3

The Robespierre Complex

Gregg Housh was born outside Dallas to a father who robbed banks and stole cars for a living along with a small group of friends who in turn served as Gregg's childhood role models. After his dad fled to escape an impending arrest and the responsibilities of fatherhood, Gregg grew up in relative poverty, which he would overcome through natural cunning. There was a video arcade in the area called Tilt, with a certain machine that awarded tokens on a more or less random basis; somehow Gregg noticed that one of the many flashing lights on its exterior blinked in an odd way at certain times, and that if one hit the button at such a point, the game would pay out in tokens that he could turn around and sell to other customers at a bargain rate. When a security guard caught on, Gregg cut him in, thereby securing protection. He made enough to buy a computer, which he learned to program well enough that he was doing it for local companies by the time he was sixteen. More important, he'd already learned a great deal about how the world really works.

Like others who made computers a career back in the nineties, Gregg came to frequent internet relay chat servers, a primitive but robust medium of communication conducted within chat rooms with names like "#c++" and "#StarTrek-STG." Alongside the conventional population of system administrators asking each other for pointers and auctioning off vintage action figures, IRC channels played host to a more colorful element of criminal hackers, including some who were less interested in making money than in outwitting the corporations that owned the infrastructure they themselves were building. Naturally Gregg fell in among them.

He was introduced to the warez scene—the underground network of those interested in disseminating pirated software—by a kid younger than himself. Presently Gregg, who had a penchant for the organizational side of things, had managed to vastly expand the operations of one warez outfit he was involved in, finding new sources for unreleased software in exchange for access to their own catalog and negotiating in-kind trades for better hardware by which to further expand their reach. His crowning achievement was getting indirect access to a Sprint lab that was experimenting with the cutting-edge technology of broadband; by making a deal with a staffer, he was able to secretly employ the firm's own hardware to distribute the stolen intellectual property of Sprint's fellow tech giants. Now their warez syndicate had more bandwidth than most governments—all the better to get a beta build of Windows 95 out to the public a year before the product's release date. Theoretically, every program ever devised could be made available to everyone in the world for free. Someone was going to have to go to prison.

Eventually the FBI swept through the warez community, picking up many of the key players, including Gregg, whose apartment in his adopted city of Boston was among those raided. There followed months of interviews, lie detector tests, and offers that entailed him cooperating with the bureau against, variously, his fellow warez kids, child porn producers, and credit card thieves. He spent several years in limbo, waiting to see if any of those offers would come to fruition, watching as most of them ended up falling through for unfathomable reasons, trying to figure out what sort of life he should plan for afterward. Finally he was charged and given a reduced sentence in return for whatever he did agree to cooperate on, which itself remains a subject of controversy. During his stint in federal prison, he learned an up-and-coming programming language that he knew would soon be in demand. He already had a job lined up when he got out.

Because Gregg doesn't smoke, drink, do drugs, or play organized sports or video games, and could no longer engage in the explicit criminal activity that had formerly made up his chief recreation, he needed something that could scratch a similar itch without guaranteeing a return to prison. Luckily, he found 4chan.

The raids on Habbo Hotel and similar "/b/tard" outings were certainly amusing, but didn't quite reach the level of employing Sprint's own infrastructure to give away Microsoft's flagship product. But soon came the war on Hal Turner, and with it, expanded horizons; when the Tom Cruise incident went down some months afterward, there were many who could be convinced that the church, though vastly more powerful than anything Anon had gone up against before, was nonetheless now within its reach. By this time, the center of gravity had moved from 4chan itself to a handful of IRC servers, including one called partyvan.org, where Housh was a regular. He and a few others created a channel in which to brainstorm in private, and they came up with the idea of posting a declaration of war against Scientology on YouTube, in the hopes of attracting a couple of hundred new participants to the IRC and putting them to work. Instead, thousands arrived.

Still operating from their invite-only channel—called "#marblecake" after the dessert a girl involved was eating at the time—the half dozen conspirators were now faced with the problem of organizing an unceasing flood of people with little knowledge of Anonymous culture, and doing so within a milieu that eschews open leadership. But they had the aid of one of the fellows who ran the server, who, bemused over the sudden appearance of so many outsiders, was just as interested as they were in getting things under control. With the server admin's cooperation, it was decided that channels would be created for every major city, and that anyone joining the server would be prompted to choose the one nearest them; this ended the chaos of having a thousand or so people in one channel, where anything one typed would scroll off the screen in a microsecond, but it still left the problem of what would come next—for without central direction, nothing would.

So the #marblecake crew established a shadow government. They watched each regional channel, looking for natural leaders, and then approached each one via private message explaining that they had a plan that could only succeed if some degree of unity could be established—and that it could never be made explicit that such unity derived from a secret leadership, even though that's exactly what was happening. By disseminating "suggestions" in such a way that they seemed to be the result of local consensus, #marblecake's agents managed to provide the illusion of decentralized control, necessary to stave off the inevitable long and unproductive arguments that inevitably result when a certain sort of minor participant is unwilling to accept his or her actual status; this would be a particular problem with Anons themselves, some number of whom would always prefer the fiction that they were equals in an evenly distributed movement.

In addition to pushing for protests as the most viable method of using its thousands of recruits, this de facto command-and-control structure was sufficient to inject needed coordination into what would be a tricky enterprise. Scientology staff have a tendency to identify and harass its opponents—sort of like Anonymous, actually, except that the church also has the ability to file nuisance lawsuits even in the course of committing its own arguable crimes (one fellow I'd known from my Encyclopedia Dramatica days, an English transplant to L.A. who went by the moniker Old-DirtyBtard and who would later join Project PM, was identified and then sued by the church for his role in the upcoming campaign; later he killed himself). And so those attending protests would have to conceal themselves as best as possible, which meant they'd need masks, preferably all of the same design. The success of the recent film *V for Vendetta*, the protagonist of which wears a Guy Fawkes mask, had ensured that plastic versions could be ordered from the Warner Bros. website; as a bonus, both the film and the original graphic novel were steeped in anti-authoritarian themes, shifting the mask's association from that of crankish seventeenth-century Catholic terrorism to aggressive civil disobedience.

Even beyond the basic coordination that makes a central directorate a useful thing to have, #marblecake could also attract and then disseminate expertise in a way that more amorphous enterprises couldn't. A veteran of Greenpeace made his way to the server and managed to get a message to Housh that he had advice for whoever was running things; invited to the secret room, he provided a lecture on all the little ins and outs of overseeing protests, which, he explained, was both science and art, and not something one accomplishes simply by telling people to show up at a certain place at a certain time with a certain grievance. That info and other tidbits were conveyed to prospective participants via a video titled "Call to Arms," as well as through #marblecake's growing network of chat room satraps.

Just as the Greenpeace leader could find them, journalists could, too, simply by sending messages to the YouTube account that was then the most visible manifestation of an otherwise amorphous non-organization that was still little understood. And so the #marblecake crew, and Housh in particular, were able to control the messaging even beyond what capabilities they already had. This would accelerate some months into the protest campaign, when Housh himself was identified by church security after allegedly running onto church property during an event in Boston. Having determined Housh's extensive role in the strange and troublesome information war that was now being waged on their organization, church lawyers took Housh to court in a case that received significant local attention, turning him from Anonymous to Boston celebrity, and later something of a national figure. And although the settlement legally barred

Housh from going anywhere near Scientology for a set period while also making him more cautious about his own future role in Anonymous, it also established him as the point man for every journalist intent on covering the movement; he was essentially the one person you could go to for quotes and on-the-record background. Since editors tend to emphasize the obtaining of quotes from connected subjects over anything else, Housh's unofficial new role as "press facilitator" allowed Anonymous to get the expanded coverage that it had previously missed out on due to structural press failures. Happily, Housh was also naturally good with reporters and an effective advocate for whatever Anonymous was doing at any particular time. This would have been less crucial a job had Anonymous not been about to embark on a global crusade against the most powerful institutions in the world, engaging in a strategy that would entail attacking things widely seen as the most fundamental symbols of legitimacy while also making the case that the attacks themselves were legitimate.

The difficulty of effectively presenting that argument within the confines of American popular news media is amusingly illustrated by an appearance Housh made on CNN toward the end of 2010. Anonymous had just launched distributed denial of service attacks on the websites of Mastercard, Visa, and PayPal, bringing each one down for a few seconds each. Although the PayPal attack arguably caused actual difficulties for the firm, the credit card websites had no connection to their actual operations; they'd been symbolically struck down so as to bring attention to the sudden and coordinated move by each of these firms to stop processing donations to WikiLeaks in the wake of the release of U.S. diplomatic cables. This de facto embargo, naturally, had been prompted by the U.S. government.

"The hacker group Anonymous obviously likes to stay undercover," announces the horrible British harpy who was serving as CNN host. "But our next guest says that he's been associated with them for years. He says he speaks for the organization and shares their views. Gregg Housh is the administrator of a website called Why We Protest. And he joins us now live, from Boston. Prepare to show your face, Gregg!"

She issued this challenge in the general direction of the in-studio video feed on which Housh stood unmasked as usual, having done television interviews under his real name and appearance for over a year now.

"You say you speak for Anonymous. We can't verify that, so talk me through it."

"I have . . . never said that I speak for Anonymous," Housh replies. "That is something pretty bad to say in the eyes of Anonymous. Simply by being here in front of you, I'm not Anonymous. Here's my name, here's my face." He had explained this to the producer—and, before that, to the dozens of other journalists who had insisted on referring to him as the "official mouthpiece," "spokesman," or even "leader" of Anonymous.

"Okay, forgive me for that, but I thought when you spoke to my producer earlier on that you'd said that you felt that you could speak for Anonymous."

"I can speak for what's going on. I'm sitting there in all the chat channels, I'm on all the websites, I've been involved in past Anonymous actions such as the attacks on the Church of Scientology. But I personally am not taking part in any of the illegal activities. I just am trusted by a lot of these people and I'm around all their inner circles."

"Tell us in your own words, then, what these guys are trying to achieve."

"You know, everyone on there—being that there's so many people from so many different countries—have their own ideas. But it all revolves around the idea that information is free. And one of the big goals here is . . . We live in a free society where the press has certain freedoms, journalists have certain freedoms. And from this side of the fence, it looks like WikiLeaks really is working as a journalistic organization. They're working with *The Guardian* and all these other already existing journalistic organizations to do what they're doing. So we believe they deserve those same protections. And we find it very interesting that all these organizations are canceling their accounts or denying charges, like Visa, Mastercard, PayPal. And listing off very clearly—"

"How, though, do the ends effectively justify the means?" she asks Housh, and likely no one else before or after Housh. "The means being disrupting me and millions of our viewers from using facilities like Mastercard, Visa—and Amazon, which, let's be honest, and face it, they weren't able to bring down today. Just before Christmas! How do the ends justify the means, do you think?"

"This is a very tough balance to keep here. And I'm smiling because I've been asked this question a few times today . . . We don't want to interrupt the public's livelihood . . ."

". . . but you are."

". . . because in the end we want them on our side. Some people have been affected, but in all honesty, even when Visa's website was down completely, you don't go to Visa's website to use your credit card, and their website has nothing to do with their payment processing, which was working perfectly fine."

That Anonymous's operation had not actually disrupted the economic welfare of the millions of viewers she had said it had fazed the woman not one bit; nor does she seem concerned about having just grossly misinformed those precious viewers about an issue that was important enough to take airtime away from Tiger Woods's marital difficulties. Suddenly, the issue is not that Anonymous had inconvenienced everyone, but that they had failed to do so.

"There weren't enough hackers today to bring down the Amazon site," she notes. "My sense is we're talking about a couple of thousand, fifteen hundred people around the world—and we're giving them the oxygen of publicity tonight, and there could be more by the time this story is over. I hope we're not complicit in what they're doing. But fifteen hundred," she continued, citing the number someone had made up, "doesn't sound like a lot of people to me. And they certainly weren't able to hit the Amazon site. So what should we expect next?"

As it turns out, she should have expected that Housh would end up signing a book deal for Amazon's new publishing arm less than a year later, which makes for a good lesson in and of itself, unless it doesn't.

"Well, the Amazon site didn't go down," Housh conceded. "You're absolutely correct. But the numbers are a little short—as I left for the studio, there were over three thousand people sitting in the chat channels doing this. So it's still growing. And the 'complicit' line you used there—that's a bit tough, because one of the reasons the DDoS are so effective is not necessarily that sites go down, but that every time these DDoS happen, people like me and people like you end up talking about it."

Here we have, in its purest form, the "meaning" of Anonymous. Anonymous being an organic phenomenon, rather than something chartered or even designed, this was necessarily an emergent sort of meaning, one that would have to be gradually discovered even by its key practitioners.

Two years prior, when I was setting up Project PM while living on the charity of friends, I was focused on trying to fix the media. This was idiotic, not because it was quixotic but rather because the real answer had been right in front of me. It had existed in the very name of the project, known only to me, and to those to whom I couldn't resist bragging about the allusion. "PM" stood for Panther Moderns, themselves a fictional future subcultural grouping depicted in William Gibson's *Neuromancer.* I had put off reading the book in the decade since I first tried it, having believed it to be mostly about hackers, couriers, clichéd cyberpunk trappings in which I had no interest. Then, in the midst of one of my several efforts to get off heroin, a girlfriend who worked in AI offered me her copy. It is a particularity of the opiate-withdrawal process that, in one's desperation, one becomes highly receptive to stray enthusiasms; and *Neuromancer* turned out to be ultimately concerned with information, imagery, and the unanticipated intertwining of concepts. And so when I came across a passage in which a fictional sociologist is interviewed about this bizarre incarnation of youthful savagery, it struck me as superbly profound—and, in some way, mine, by right of my sheer will to make it reality. It ran thusly:

> There is always a point at which the terrorist ceases to manipulate the media gestalt. A point at which the violence may well escalate, but beyond which the

> terrorist has become symptomatic of the media gestalt itself. Terrorism as we ordinarily understand it is innately media-related. The Panther Moderns differ from other terrorists precisely in their degree of self-consciousness, in their awareness of the extent to which media divorce the act of terrorism from the original sociopolitical intent.

The media need not be "fixed." It could simply be directed, via a sort of alchemy of spectacle.

The CNN interview was actually unusual in one respect: the great majority of Anonymous coverage after the Scientology crusade was decidedly non-hostile, and much of it was outright positive. But it was also typical in the sense of including extraordinary inaccuracies. Even the better write-ups tended to miss something important about what this movement was and what it represented. That would explain why Housh was so keenly interested when, some months prior to the CNN appearance, he'd come across an article on *The Huffington Post* that revealed an unusual degree of understanding of Anonymous.

The occasion for this piece was an ongoing attack by Anonymous on the government of Australia, which had been proposing new legislation giving the state further control over the internet on the pretext of fighting child pornography. Hundreds of government servers had been attacked, along with fax machines and other communications infrastructure, followed by a physical protest campaign and other headline-prompting measures, thereby laying the usual groundwork for the propaganda to follow. The legislation was tabled for "review" and promptly forgotten.

The most striking part of the article itself was not the atypically nuanced description of how such emergent campaigns actually functioned but rather the grandiose prediction it went on to make about what this all meant—a prediction couched in extraordinary, almost comical arrogance, as well as open contempt for any other journalist who might try to understand such an issue as this, which the author alone was equipped to assess:

> The specifics of this particular case have already been described with varying levels of accuracy by some of the more astute media outlets ranging from Wired to the BBC. Some of the details expressed regarding Anonymous will be wrong, as usual, but the details matter little as nothing is likely to come of this incident, whereas the implications for the future defy overstatement. Having taken a long interest in the subculture from which Anonymous is derived and the new communicative structures that make it possible, I am now certain that this phenomenon is among the most important and under-reported social developments to have occurred in decades, and that the development in question promises to threaten the institution of the nation-state and perhaps even someday replace it as the world's most fundamental and relevant method of human organization.

Housh shared the piece with some of his associates on the IRCs, who likewise found it interesting. Then he emailed the author, which, of course, was me.

"We are very happy with the article you wrote," began the message.

Housh and I spoke on and off throughout 2010, comparing notes on the nascent discipline of online rabble-rousing. He eventually became a fixture at the Project PM IRC, helping out here and there as my team continued work.

The conflict I'd been awaiting had materialized, and was in fact accelerating; in addition to Anonymous's campaign against Australia, WikiLeaks released the cache of U.S. diplomatic cables, prompting calls for the assassination of founder Julian Assange by a range of U.S. political and media figures. The United States' back-end economic blockade vis-à-vis PayPal, Mastercard, et al. led in turn to the Anonymous strike on those companies, which was unlikely to be overlooked by law enforcement. After the release of chat transcripts by the hacker-turned-informant Adrian Lamo, the army intelligence analyst Chelsea Manning had been identified as leaking the cables, along with assorted documents on the Iraq and Afghanistan wars and a video of U.S. forces gunning down unarmed civilians and journalists in Baghdad. Manning was arrested and eventually placed in detention at the U.S. Marine base at Quantico under conditions that were reported to be both harsh and arbitrary, leading to a growing protest campaign on her behalf.

The diplomatic cables themselves, despite some dismissive commentary from pundits who seem to have been only vaguely familiar with their contents, painted an instructive picture not just of the nuances of U.S. foreign policy but also of the criminal conduct of a range of regimes and corporations across the world. Royal Dutch Shell was seen to have bragged about its infiltration of the Nigerian government for the purpose of ensuring that a major nation would be sufficiently geared toward its own economic interests; Yemen had assured the United States that it would cover up the latter's involvement in bombings of alleged terrorist targets; the vice president of Afghanistan had been found carrying $52 million in cash on a trip abroad; DynCorp employees engaged in child sex trafficking and used young boys as entertainment at company events. Naturally, few of these revelations led to any real consequences for those involved—itself the most important lesson of all. There was one very notable exception, though.

The people of Tunisia had long been aware of the corruption of President Ben Ali and his regime, which by 2010 had been in power for over twenty years. But a series of reports stemming from the cables and covered by several of the newspapers that were working in conjunction with WikiLeaks painted an even starker picture, providing solid information by which to supplement the anecdotes and rumors upon which Tunisian nationals had previously relied in assessing their government. Tunisia being an internet-saturated country relative to other African and Middle Eastern nations, the regime felt compelled to respond by blocking WikiLeaks and other websites, which naturally brought further attention to the reports. Whereas these issues had existed in the hazy background of national life, they were now front and center, and perfectly clear. The necessary spark came a few weeks later, when a fruit vendor set himself on fire in protest after having his goods confiscated by the notoriously corrupt Tunis police. The conditions were right for the fire to spread.

Like nearly everyone else outside Tunisia, I had no idea that a revolt was ongoing when Gregg Housh emailed me about it at the end of December 2010; there had been no Western press reports on the subject other than one brief piece in *The Guardian* that received no real attention. Housh explained that some of the Anons working out of a particular IRC server were themselves Tunisian nationals, and that an operation had begun to assist with the uprising. Since this was the exact sort of thing I'd predicted some months prior and clearly had an interest in altogether, he thought I might be inclined to log on to the server in question—known as AnonOps—and monitor operations or perhaps even get directly involved. He was correct.

I arrived at the server just as things were taking off, with operations being conducted out of a channel called #OpTunisia. The main website of the Tunisian prime minister had been taken over by one of the hackers present and replaced with a message headed "An Open Letter to the Government of Tunisia." Among other things, the message proclaimed that cyberattacks on the government's online infrastructure would continue until free speech had been implemented. Other government sites were now being taken down via DDoS attacks organized out of AnonOps.

These sorts of attacks were not simply symbolic. For years prior, Tunisians at home and abroad had been using the internet to criticize the regime and otherwise promote an environment of sustained opposition. Meanwhile the government had modernized its security forces, developing an especially active cyber component capable of identifying opposition leaders via the internet using sophisticated means—some provided by French and other foreign technology firms, as we'd learn later. Among those in-country Tunisian revolutionaries who had put themselves at risk in this cat-and-mouse game was Slim Amamou, who worked out of the AnonOps IRC server and went by the handle of slim404. Shortly after I joined AnonOps, Amamou disappeared; despite his precautions, he'd been arrested.

Disruptive attacks on Tunisian government digital infrastructure, then, provided crucial support to those on the ground. Anonymous coders also disseminated a software script that could defend against police phishing tactics, an increasingly common technique by which the social media accounts of activists who were otherwise difficult to track could be infiltrated and their communications seized. Providing Tunisians with a relatively secure venue for organizing, as the AnonOps server still was at this point, also helped.

It is the nature of Anonymous that anyone with ideas and a bit of work ethic can jump right in. Thus it was that within an hour of arriving at AnonOps, I had already begun working on press and propaganda strategy. A couple of people had written a press release about the importance of the Tunisian revolution and Anonymous's support campaign. Gregg had an extensive list of press contacts that this could be sent to, as did I, but getting the sort of international focus on Tunisia that could both provide a morale boost to the protesters and build pressure against the regime was going to be tricky, for reasons I understood better than I would have liked.

That a nationwide revolt was accelerating within Tunisia did not strike many in the media as worth reporting.

With a few exceptions, most probably heard "Arab unrest" and zoned it out on the premise that there was always some degree of "unrest" in the Arab world. In fact, nothing like this had happened in Tunisia for twenty-three years—the last time the government was overthrown, that being the event that put Ben Ali in place to begin with. Regardless of whether one expected anything positive to come of these new developments, certainly they were newsworthy.

But media workers of the sort Gregg and I were contacting get untold numbers of press releases thrown at them every day. Sometimes a journalist will indeed consider some particular thing to be worthy of attention, but what one actually writes, if anything, will be determined by an array of factors going beyond mere public good. The most important of these involves a complex formula of perceptions on the journalist's part as well as on that of his editors. Some of those perceptions concern what readers of a given publication are expected to care about, whether an event or trend can be treated in some novel way, and whether the finished product is likely to gain attention elsewhere. This last factor is especially important within the hypercompetitive world of "new media," as online outlets were once classified back when they were still new. All of this has to be taken into account if one is to navigate the resulting ecosystem.

Luckily, the sheer novelty of what Anonymous was doing provided an element that could pass muster with the amoral calculus of the American press corps. And I had the connections to ensure that they'd pay attention long enough to determine this for themselves.

Michael Hastings, the journalist who had prompted the resignation of General McChrystal with his *Rolling Stone* piece months earlier and who had since become an editor at that publication, was the perfect vector by which to move the story forward. Aside from his time in Afghanistan, Hastings had covered Iraq for several outlets including *Newsweek* and was otherwise familiar enough with the region and its nuances to understand that a revolt of this sort in Tunisia was indeed noteworthy in and of itself, even beyond the involvement of a shadowy international hacker ring. He also understood what Anonymous was and why it could potentially be a major factor in things to come. So I called in a favor, saved up from the pro-Hastings counterattacks I'd performed via *Vanity Fair* and an appearance on Russia Today. On the evening of January 2, then, Hastings wrote the following on his Twitter feed: "very interesting: Anonymous, the hacktivist group, launched attacks against the Tunisian government today. #optunisia." He posted more over the next day or two in order to better ensure that the story caught on, and continued to assist. It's indicative of the media blackout preceding Anonymous's involvement that much of the press coverage immediately following Hastings's announcement emphasized our digital campaign against the regime while barely commenting on the uprising itself, which was still so unknown that major outlets could look into a matter involving Tunisia without gleaning that this was all being done in support of a massive, ongoing revolt (the messages Anonymous left on seized websites had not explicitly mentioned that revolt, as its authors, in their innocence, had assumed the Western press was aware of it or at least capable of finding out without help from hackers; in those days I would have assumed the same thing). The day after Hastings's tweet, *Gawker* ran a front-page piece titled "Anonymous Attacks Tunisian Government over Wikileaks Censorship." Although nothing was mentioned about the actual revolution, the article did describe the situation with the WikiLeaks cables, included a screenshot of the seized-and-redone website, and quoted Anonymous's press release in full. At the bottom, the author had given a "hat tip" to Michael Hastings and linked to his original tweet, thereby satisfying me that I'd done my part.

But within a few days mentions of an actual revolt by the mass of Tunisians had appeared in such places as BBC coverage of the Anonymous campaign, and so the majority of journalists who get their news from other journalists would now begin reporting on the central events in that country. Tellingly, though, AnonOps would remain the best source of info on Tunisian developments for another week or two; I was contacted at one point by a *Newsweek* journalist who was about to cross into the country and had asked Michael Hastings about getting in touch with opposition leaders in the capital. Two weeks prior, I'd known nothing about Tunisia—which is to say, about as much as the journalists who would now be covering it.

With the international outrage having been set in motion, and with Anonymous and organizations like Telecomix moving on to provide secure internet access to Tunisians on a larger scale, I moved on to one of the few other ways I could help. As the revolution was centered largely on the streets, and given that Tunisians had no experience with such things, I set out to create a guide to street fighting and demonstrations that could be distributed both online and in printed copies via residents of the capital who were working out of AnonOps. I didn't know any more about such topics than did the average Tunisian, but I now had plenty of experience in running emergent online collaboration and had already gained some credit via my media operations, which I'd naturally taken steps to ensure that everyone on the server was aware of. Plus I was an editor of sorts, or the closest thing available. So I had some volunteers scour the internet for whatever relevant tips might already be available, got in touch with a couple of "black bloc" types that you always see fucking with cops at antiglobalist protests, brought in someone who'd been involved in the cell phone–driven Ukrainian revolution a few years prior, and set up a group pad—a collaborative online document that people can edit in real time if they have the link. Soon enough we had the first version of what would become the Anonymous Guide to Protecting the North African Revolutions, a series of pamphlets with handy tips on dealing with tear gas, setting up Wi-Fi points with cell phones, documenting atrocities and ensuring coverage, circling police lines, assembling debris to cover retreats, setting up medical, spotting, and documentation teams with clear lines of command, and fortifying one's neighborhood, all translated into French and Tunisian Arabic dialect and distributed in print via coffee shops and other community nodes across the region.

Incidentally, the original name of the pamphlets referred to the "Tunisian Revolution"; I had to rename it in the middle of January 2011 because it had become clear to those of us involved, if not to the world at large, that the revolt could viably translate across the region. And we had Egyptians and Algerians on AnonOps now, coordinating on revolutions of their own and, occasionally, attacking each other over long-ago historical treachery and, I swear to God, soccer.

As street demonstrations came to be supplemented by

a series of national strikes, including by lawyers and other professionals, and as international attention had the desired result, the regime collapsed. Ben Ali fled the country, leaving it in the hands of a provisional government that would come to include Slim Amamou, recently released from jail and soon to be serving as a cabinet minister. A clip appeared on YouTube of a large group of Tunisian nationals assembling in Germany, holding Guy Fawkes masks, giving thanks to Anonymous, and proclaiming themselves, accurately enough, as "Legion."

With Egyptians assembling in Tahrir Square and small groups of dissidents now agitating in Morocco, where the government wisely gave in to some of their demands, it was time to start trying to seize control of the narrative. U.S. conservatives, sensing that it was ideologically convenient to do so, began claiming that the revolutions in Tunisia and elsewhere were essentially Islamist—something I knew to be entirely false, based on my communications with those involved. At the same time, the idea of Anonymous was gaining a certain hold over the consciousness of many net-savvy, pro-democracy Arabs who were most capable of organizing opposition; it was clear that even the prospect of Anonymous assistance could provide significant hope of the sort necessary to foment confrontation with regimes that themselves depended largely on hopelessness and on inertia that is dispelled only by novelty.

At the same time, we couldn't overplay our hand; as useful as it would be to ensure that Anonymous's role was spelled out, any claims that could be perceived as taking too much credit for the revolutions would be problematic. But the image of a formidable and serious network of noble saboteurs was powerful enough that it would have to be established even at the risk of it not quite coming off; Chanology, as the operation was called, had proven that regardless of where one's capabilities stood at a given time, one could vastly amplify them in the near future by presenting the imagery that would attract the army that everyone wanted to believe had always existed in the first place. That we essentially had such an army and had just assisted in the toppling of a government would help.

After confirming my role in OpTunisia, Al Jazeera published the resulting manifesto, "Anonymous and the Global Correction," which they ran under the name "Anonymous" and which presented my attempt to package our efforts in a broader framework that would effectively signal that the movement had a real program for international change:

> The tendency to relate past events to what is possible in the present becomes more difficult as the scope of the geopolitical environment changes. It is a useful thing, then, to ask every once in a while if the environment has recently undergone any particular severe changes, thereby expanding our options for the future.
>
> Terminology, let alone our means of exchanging information, has changed to such a degree that many essential discussions in today's "communications age" would be entirely incomprehensible to many two decades ago.
>
> As the social, political and technological environment has developed, some have already begun to explore new options, seizing new chances for digital activism—and more will soon join in. It is time for the rest of the world to understand why.

. . . and so on and so forth. The piece was received as hoped; Bruce Sterling, futurist and *Wired* commentator, ran a post titled "Anonymous Theorist Bragging to Al Jazeera," noting that he'd "heard revolutionaries talking, and this guy sure talks like a revolutionary. I don't think he's knocking off in the middle of his DDOS attacks to check out Star Wars parodies for the lulz."

By this time, I'd assisted in writing press releases, assembled a regular array of journalists and editors who would report on them while spreading the word of my involvement, gained credibility with many of the most hardworking participants at AnonOps as well as some of those who had control over the server itself, and otherwise established myself as a sort of Marat figure, both within and without Anonymous. I still had my own personal cybermilitia in the form of Project PM, albeit composed mostly of squares. And I'd figured out that I could shoot up tiny pieces of my Suboxone opiate film every couple of hours such that the opiate agonist contained therein wouldn't build up in my system, allowing me to stay somewhat high and on point for eighteen hours at a time. I was prepared for the great crisis that I'd always worried might never come.

4

Tripping Over Invisible Weapons

Tap, tap, tap.

It was another wonderful day. But then every day had been wonderful in the month since I'd thrown in my lot with Anonymous.

Certainly some complications had arisen here and there. Many of the original members of Project PM were unhappy with my sudden involvement in a mysterious international revolutionary organization, a maneuver with no obvious connection to the science journalism and experimental developmental aid programs we'd been focusing on for the past year. And the forty simultaneous armed raids the FBI had conducted a week prior on suspected participants in Anonymous's retaliatory DDoS attack on PayPal, with further arrests in the U.K., seemed to have given certain of my old associates the jitters.

But complications could be managed. I'd just announced a measure whereby the majority of Project PM members who were disinclined to follow me into an uncertain future of bleeding-edge global insurrection could continue working on our various crowdsourced philanthropy and media-reform projects under delegated leadership; I'd appointed one of our more prominent and straitlaced members, an NGO type with the Mozilla Foundation who also happened to be quite justifiably furious with me, to run all that under an entirely separate outfit. All official ties thus severed, the more militant among us could proceed to assist Anonymous in the revolutionary support measures that needed attention right then.

Even the FBI raids could be handled. By putting out messages over various Anonymous channels and tracking down acquaintances, I'd been able to get word to a few of those who'd been targeted that we'd begun rounding up lawyers willing to provide pro bono legal assistance to anyone who wanted it. This was tricky, in large part because the targets had all had their household electronics seized, including phones and modems, and also because we had no complete list of those affected; but I'd placed announcements here and there with some key words they were likely to come across when they managed to get back online. The lawyers themselves had been pulled together thanks to the veteran Yankee rabble-rouser John Penley. Like most seasoned radicals, Penley knew everyone and a half plus Patti Smith, and had a working relationship with a whole stable of left-wing defense attorneys. The upshot was that several of our people were already hooked up with members of the National Lawyers Guild plus some mavericks like the attorney Stanley Cohen, a staple of the cable news circuit who was best known for defending the accused Hamas member Mousa Mohammed Abu Marzook and was now set to represent Mercedes Haefer, one of Anonymous's chat room moderators. Mercedes was a teenage girl from Las Vegas whose entire family had been herded into their living room and held at gunpoint while federal agents ransacked their home on the chance that she may have been one of thousands of people who loaded a corporate website too many times.

Tap, tap, tap.

It was reasonably satisfying to watch Penley invoke the New York activist lawyers, who had thereafter begun to multiply and call forth their pro bono brethren from California and Oregon and whatnot until my Gmail in-box had fattened with demands for wrongs to right. Things took an irritating turn when it came to light that Cohen and the National Lawyers Guild folks hated each other. Presumably this was why the NLG asked me for exclusive across-the-board representation of all the raid subjects—something I was in no position to give, as I had no official role within Anonymous, which didn't even officially have members, much less legal liaisons, and also because there was no obvious reason why several dozen people should be required to accept such an arrangement. Luckily I was approached by another lawyer out of California, Jay Leiderman, who had no dog in these particular fights and was interested enough in the issues involved to help anyone I sent to him in perpetuity, to an extent that he would soon become known to the press as "the Anonymous lawyer." With the legal defense structures now self-sustaining, I'd entertained myself further by getting a couple of the raid victims in touch with reporters to talk about the FBI's innovative new children-at-gunpoint initiative.

But all of that had been in the very recent past, which by the measure of my new life might as well have been three summers ago in terms of residual emotional impact. A month of round-the-clock involvement in the Tunisian revolution had completely reoriented my expectations as to what an average day should entail, and what it might yield. Our colleague Slim Amamou, after all, was still a minister in the new government; this naturally inspired the question of what else might be possible. So now I demanded from life a glorious momentum that I knew would likely end in a crash, to be sure, but not before taking me quite a ways forward. Crashes can be survived. All that mattered now was the fulfillment of my new emotional requirements, which were really very simple: repeated and measurable victories over the unjust, an increasing degree of influence among the just, and public honors accompanied by the prospect of more and greater honors to follow.

The honors were already materializing. Just the other day I'd been mentioned in a *New York Times* cover story, itself dealing mostly with the expansion of our revolutionary assistance program from Tunisia into Egypt, where protests were growing in Tahrir Square; I'd been quoted on the matter of the recent FBI raids as "Barrett Brown, who is helping to organize a legal defense for those who might be prosecuted." I liked how no explanation had been given as to who I was or where I'd come from; I was simply Barrett Brown, whose emotional requirements did not extend to titles. The world would just have to accept this phenomenon wherein Barrett Brown appears from out of the ether to provide lawyers to the deserving or consultation to the neophyte or expert advice on street insurrections to the oppressed. I can also write press releases.

Tap, tap, tap.

The fact that I was obviously very close to succumbing to a manic episode of the sort that had occasionally thrown my life into terrifying disarray in my earlier years did not bother me at all.

Tap, tap, tap.

The satisfaction over the *New York Times* mention had of course already worn off. It was a fine thing, then, that a team of Anonymous hackers had just completed their own raid on the corporate servers of FBI-linked intelligence-contracting firm HBGary and its subsidiary, HBGary Federal. The hack was in retaliation for an incident a day prior in which HBGary Federal's CEO, the navy intelligence veteran Aaron Barr, claimed in an interview with the *Financial Times* that he had Anonymous by the balls—that he'd infiltrated its chat networks and used some proprietary technique involving the comparison of log-in times to identify its key participants, including members of its "leadership." The article also noted that he was scheduled to meet with the FBI about his findings.

Although everyone concerned knew that we were subject to surveillance by various governments, this new development caught us by surprise. But one of the great things about amorphous internet collectives run by Information Age delinquents is the speed and decisiveness with which they can react to previously unknown enemies. A day after the *Financial Times* article went up, the websites of both HBGary and HBGary Federal were under the direct control of a team of Anon hackers, their uninspired marketing copy now replaced with Anonymous propaganda to the effect that Anonymous does not forgive and Anonymous does not forget—along with a hyperlink leading to seventy thousand emails the team had taken from servers shared by the two firms, comprising years of communications with other, similar "intelligence contracting" companies as well as the government agencies to which these firms provided various mysterious services.

Tap, tap, tap.

Just now I'd gotten off the phone with Penny Leavy, HBGary's president, whom I'd directed to the AnonOps chat server that she might plead her case before the quasi-revolutionary cyberbandits who had seized control of her company and who, as I explained to her, could sometimes be reasoned with. Now I was expecting another call, from Barr himself. This was the man I intended to destroy.

Tap, tap, tap.

You have to flick the syringe to get any air pockets down to the bottom of the opiate solution, away from the needle, so they won't get into your vein when you shoot. I mean, you don't, really; as William Burroughs once related, if air bubbles could kill there wouldn't be a junkie left alive. But I enjoy flicking it just as I enjoy every aspect of shooting up. I like ripping just the tiniest little piece of Suboxone from an eight-milligram strip. I like dropping it into the spoon. I like dipping my finger into the cup of ice water I keep on my desk for both drinking and narcotic preparation purposes and then letting a single drop fall into the spoon. I like watching the Suboxone dissolve over the next minute or so and then drawing it into the syringe. There follows some period of tap, tap, tapping until the moment feels right. The moment didn't feel right.

My phone rang. My girlfriend, prone on my bed and browsing the internet, handed it to me without looking up. The area code was unknown to me; presumably it emanated from one of those bullshit states that aren't Texas or even New York—Virginia, say, where all these toy fascist Pentagon groupies tend to congregate. I set my laptop to Record, put the phone on Speaker, and answered the call.

It was Aaron Barr. This would be our first direct engagement, though not our first indirect one. That would be the press release the hacker-humorist Topiary and I had composed before the hack, titled "Anonymous Admits Defeat." Its purpose, to the extent that it had any, was to keep the HBGary execs as confused about our intent as we still were about theirs; I'd posted it on my account at the left-wing blog platform Daily Kos, had it posted on the obscure websites where Anon distributed such things, and emailed it to the array of press outlets that had been covering our goings-on of late. We'd peppered the statement with gratuitous and obscure inside jokes and references to an old computer game I'd started playing again recently: "As Mr. Barr has discovered in spite of our best efforts, Anonymous was founded by Q last Thursday at the guilded Bilderberg Hotel after a tense meeting with one Morrowind mod collection, which itself includes the essential Morrowind Comes Alive 5.2 as well as several retexturing packs, all of which seem to lower one's FPS . . ." Topiary, whose tastes ran more toward *Zelda* and, for whatever reason, *Sonic the Hedgehog*, made sure to throw in something about Barr having successfully collected a large number of "gold rings." The nonsense had continued for several paragraphs.

Later perusals of the firm's emails would confirm that our obnoxious handiwork had indeed left our enemies divided in confusion. "They still don't get it," Barr had written afterward to a vocally worried HBGary exec, Karen Burke, in one of several bizarre exchanges between the firm's principals, to which we were now hilariously privy. "They think all I know is their irc names!!!!! I know their real fing names." Actually, he didn't; as we'd demonstrate after getting our hands on his notes, Barr's supposed technique for matching internet handles with real identities based on comparisons of log-in times on different social network platforms was not as viable as he'd found it convenient to claim.

"I'll look at the blogpost," Burke had replied, "but I am concerned about escalating the 'brawl.' They seemed freaked out on the Daily Kos post."

"No they are not freaked out. They don't get it . . . Greg will tell you," he replied, citing Greg Hoglund, the CEO of HBGary proper, who was still erroneously convinced that Barr had things under control. "They think I have nothing but a heirarchy [*sic*] based on IRC aliases! as 1337 as these guys are suppsed [*sic*] to be they don't get it. I have pwned them! :)"

Barr and I greeted each other and made brief introductions. His strategy was to convince me that he'd meant no harm, in hopes that I'd get the hackers to take down the link that he and the other execs were rightfully terrified about being made public. That link, as noted above, led to a file containing some seventy thousand emails that Topiary and a handful of others had stolen from the two firms, representing several years of communications with other "intelligence contracting" outfits as well as government clients. I'd just taken down one of those links from the aforementioned Daily Kos post as a favor to Penny Leavy, who'd told me—falsely, as we soon learned—that HBGary itself had been unaware of Barr's plans to assist the FBI. My strategy was to draw Barr out, lull him into a false sense of confidence, and then catch him in some demonstrable lie that, being recorded, I could subsequently use to discredit him. It was clear that this man chased glory just as hard as I did, albeit apparently unrestrained by any personal or ideological code of conduct. I would have to deny him the ability to gain any further media traction in the hours to come; the limitations of the press are such that once a narrative is established, it's difficult to de-establish.

Now, as Barr completed his claims of pure intentions, I explained to him that even the sample research he'd provided to the *Financial Times* about the supposed leadership structure of Anonymous was nonsense—the idea of an AnonOps administrator called Q being the founder of Anonymous was especially ridiculous, given that the half-accidental origins of Anonymous were not even secret—and that we were concerned that his data would lead to more raids, quite likely on innocent parties whom his analysis had mistakenly identified as key members of an entity that was now being heavily targeted by law enforcement in a dozen countries. He conceded that his research was not completely accurate, but denied any ill intent.

"I never planned to sell the data to the FBI," he said, as I lit a Marlboro Red and petted my girlfriend's kitten, which had managed to find a space on my desk amid a forest of mostly empty Dr Pepper cans that each doubled as an ashtray. "The FBI called *me*."

This wasn't exactly true. As we'd discover from the emails soon enough, Barr had been trying for an audience not only with the FBI but also with the Pentagon, and had in fact also parlayed his alleged intelligence coup into a meeting with the intelligence- and military-contracting giant Booz Allen Hamilton; intriguingly enough, one of the firm's vice presidents had flown him out to its offices just a few days ago to discuss the NSA-linked firm's own unspecified project involving WikiLeaks and Anonymous. Although I didn't have all this information yet, I knew enough from the circumstances of the *Financial Times* piece to deduce that Barr would be lying fairly regularly throughout our conversation. Anyway, it wasn't clear how the FBI would have known about his supposed success in tracking down Anons before the *Financial Times* article came out unless he'd been the one to contact them to begin with.

But this wasn't the time to point that out. The best tack to take with someone who can be expected to lie is to make a show of believing him, thus encouraging him to lie further, to make him comfortable enough that he'll produce more and more inaccurate statements until such time as he stumbles so badly that you're both aware of it, you and he—you and he and everyone else who'll eventually get to hear the recording that you're secretly making. Because you yourself never had to train to be devious, as Barr did, because you yourself are a veteran junkie for whom deception is not a job skill but the very stuff of everyday life.

Tap, tap, tap.

And indeed, as Barr—this military amateur, this corporate intelligence dilettante—grew more confident, he tried to sell me on the notion that not only did he mean us no harm but he'd actually done us a favor. He'd *helped* Anonymous, he was saying now, comparing his intent to that of a hired penetration tester who hacks into a firm's network and thereby helps its management identify previously unknown security flaws. "Even if I get a portion of Anon folks," he was telling me, "I mean, look what they can do. It just proves the point—that if I can even get a partial on Anon, social media is a problem. And that's what I'm talking about. It's not about prosecuting Anon. It's about—am I using the publicity that

Anonymous is getting? Absolutely. Just like anybody does, just like Anon does and everyone else does—you use the publicity that's out there in order to get your message heard."

"Right, no, I understand that." I did indeed.

"I'm running . . . I'm running a business. I'm not trying to, you know, attack Anon—I'm not releasing and have not released publicly any names."

"Let me ask you a question real quick," I cut in suddenly, putting my cigarette on top of a Dr Pepper can and picking back up my syringe and otherwise getting ready to close in for the kill. He was overreaching now, with this claim that he was trying to be helpful. "Sorry to interrupt you. Let me ask you a question. Did you ever supply Anonymous with the research you had gathered, like before you started talking to the press about it, for instance?"

A pause. "No."

"Okay. So you didn't—were you planning on doing that at any point?"

"Who would I provide it to? Who would I provide it to?" he demanded, in the manner of someone who very much would have liked to help, if only such a thing were possible.

"Uh, the people in the IRC that you think are leaders . . . That might have been a good start."

Now came the longer pause, the stumble-made-manifest, when both knew one had fucked up, and my real work was done. I hit a vein and pulled back on the plunger, prompting a twisty column of blood to shoot forth into the syringe—this verifies that the needle has indeed found a vein—and pushed the plunger back in. And then I stepped into the pause that Barr had left unoccupied and I told him how things really were, in the real world. I explained that our hackers had been right to hit his servers as they had, to defend Anonymous from an international police onslaught—Anonymous and the random people he'd quite incorrectly identified as being Anons. For his notes had just been posted online along with some annotations that a couple of AnonOps had added explaining where and how he'd been wrong, and some of the people listed therein were already angrily coming forward. And I explained that I was particularly unhappy with having seen in his notes a copy-pasted chat message from myself about an upcoming meeting at my Project PM server concerning the building of secure networks for use by Egyptian activists, as of course Barr was working with a government that had an unfortunate tendency to provide intelligence to the very dictatorships we were helping those activists to oppose. All of this was meant for public consumption, naturally, and not for Barr, as the amoral are immune to moral appeals and must thus be destroyed.

Presently I tired of myself and ended the lecture. Barr resumed his explanations, presumably for form's sake, and I took the opportunity to light another cigarette and move my girlfriend's cat (named Minou, which is French for "Pussy") off my desk before he or she or whatever it was knocked over any more Dr Pepper cans. Then I glanced at the Anonymous chat room to which I'd sent HBGary's president, Penny Leavy, who was still hoping to get us to stop reading her firm's emails:

> PENNY: You want me to fire Aaron and donate to bradley mannings fund?
>
> SABU: yes penny

HEYGUISE: aaron should maybe donate some thing too
EVILWORKS: kidneys

Things seemed to be well in hand. Probably it would be a good idea to send over Barr, whose voice was still droning through my speakerphone; he seemed to have run out of unsustainable declarations of friendship and was now issuing vague legal threats that I was too high to find interesting. Anyway, my own attention was drifting—I was in the mood to play some *Fallout: New Vegas* on my other laptop—so it was time to wind down the conversation, upload the recording, and brief the Anons on what I'd learned so they could take their turns interrogating our trampled foe.

"Well," I said, "you'll have plenty to talk about at your conference next week." From the bed, my girlfriend giggled, still looking at her phone.

I tore off another piece of Suboxone and dropped it in the spoon.

I'd been informed of the hack prior to its completion so that I'd have time to prepare the grounds for the conflict that would inevitably follow. When the seventy thousand emails had been extracted and made accessible, a gaggle of journalists I'd briefed beforehand were already poised to start combing through the contents. Conspicuously absent from this informational scavenger hunt was *The New York Times*; a contact there who'd already written about our work in North Africa told me that this new development didn't quite "sound like a *New York Times* story." The extraordinary revelations to come, then—which over the next month would be covered by countless news organizations around the world and thereafter summarized in a dozen books and documentary films—would be discovered almost exclusively by journalists from smaller outlets, and in some cases by individuals with no journalism background whatsoever. When *The New York Times* did run a piece on all this some days later, it merely served to recap events that had been reported over and over again in the intervening weeks.

Within twenty-four hours of the hack, the first articles began to appear. It turned out that Barr and his working partners at several other contracting firms had been approached by the influential lobbying firm Hunton & Williams on behalf of two clients: Bank of America and the U.S. Chamber of Commerce. Both institutions were looking to arrange covert campaigns of cutting-edge dirty tricks against their respective enemies—the Chamber hoped to discredit several left-wing activist organizations, including Stop the Chamber and Codepink, that had been bringing renewed attention to the organization's ongoing involvement in the writing of legislation. Meanwhile, executives at Bank of America had apparently grown concerned over Julian Assange's announcement that he'd obtained information proving wrongdoing on the part of a major U.S. bank, which they presumably believed to be them. Barr—along with employees of the increasingly prominent data analysis giant Palantir, another contractor called Berico Technologies, and a highly secretive company known as Endgame, had been asked to put together a presentation detailing how these troublesome dissidents could be put out of commission.

Team Themis, as the outfit called itself, came up with a variety of despicable and in some cases illegal solutions, which they detailed in a series of emails and PowerPoint slides. WikiLeaks, it was written, could be brought down in part via "cyber attacks" against the organization's servers in Sweden and France, with the object of obtaining "data on document submitters"—which is to say, whistleblowers. The plans also called for fake documents to be anonymously provided to WikiLeaks that they might thereafter be called out as fabrications, thus discrediting future releases, as well as operations by which to intimidate WikiLeaks' key supporters. One document singled out the then *Salon* contributor Glenn Greenwald as someone who should be "pushed" and thereby forced to choose "professional preservation over cause" as a result of unspecified harassment.

The U.S. Chamber of Commerce, meanwhile, wanted information on its domestic political opponents. Barr made a point to demonstrate both his tactical prowess and his absence of inconvenient scruples via means we shall let *The New York Times* describe, as they did a few days after it had been discovered by others: "Mr. Barr recounted biographical tidbits about the family of a onetime employee of a union-backed group that had challenged the chamber's opposition to Obama administration initiatives like health care legislation. 'They go to a Jewish church in DC,' Mr. Barr apparently wrote. 'They have 2 kids, son and daughter.'"

As if this were not exciting enough, Barr had even created an official slide, marked with the logo of HBGary Federal, in which he notes his ability to "gather personal information and information about immediate family" coupled with "SNS searches for family members." Other slides prepared by Themis laid out specific vectors of attack against U.S. Chamber Watch and Change to Win, organizations that the Chamber had identified as key targets. Two of these proposals merit quotation in full:

- Create a false document, perhaps highlighting periodical financial information, and monitor to see if US Chamber Watch acquires it. Afterward, present explicit evidence proving that such transactions never occurred. Also, create a fake insider persona and generate communications with CtW. Afterward, release the actual documents at a specified time and explain the activity as a CtW contrived operation.
- If needed, create two fake insider personas, using one as leverage to discredit the other while confirming the legitimacy of the second. Such work is complicated, but a well-thought out approach will give way to a variety of strategies that can sufficiently aid the formation of vetting questions US Chamber Watch will likely ask.

Most remarkably, the emails revealed that all of this had been set in motion by the Department of Justice, whom Bank of America had approached to ask for help in going after WikiLeaks.

Examining the initial findings, it was the "insider personas" concept that stood out to me in particular. Infiltrators had existed about as long as there had been entities to infiltrate, and the practice had remained in heavy play throughout the modern age. But it had always entailed significant costs, including the training and deployment of individual operatives who worked, for the most part, in physical space, and who thus had to control for appearance, account for their own comings and goings, and engage convincingly in real time with individuals who might differ significantly from the operative in their worldview, background knowledge, and a dozen other things—and who not only have certain distinct behavioral expectations that the operative must consistently fulfill but also in some cases will be specifically looking for any deviations that may mark him as an infiltrator. The resulting cat-and-mouse game is played with varying degrees of sophistication by both sides, right down to the low-stakes level of the plainclothes cop who mingles unconvincingly with protesters in such a context that it doesn't really matter if they suspect him or not. But in any event, a serious infiltration operation by state or private interests has always required some expenditure of time and resources, a range of special skills on the part of the operative and his support team, and a wide assortment of potential risks to both the operative and those who deployed him.

That this age-old practice had been adopted for the internet was hardly surprising; the more fundamental phenomenon of sock-puppeting was, by 2011, already well established, and the comparable use of infiltration by law enforcement against criminal online networks had been documented for years. It was understandable, then, that few observers among the press focused much on the "persona" angle of Team Themis's proposals, riddled as they were with so much else of legitimate concern. I myself neglected to think through the implications of this concept of the "persona" in the first few weeks. This is less understandable, as I was better equipped than almost anyone else to take a guess at what the logical next step of such a practice would consist of, and the threat it would represent to the very basis of self-government. As it happened, I didn't have to guess; soon we would know for certain.

It is a sort of truism that the Information Age diminishes barriers. But what exactly this means is less obvious, and vastly complex, because it means so many other things, all at once, across the span of human experience. Individual observers representing particular backgrounds and industries may reasonably expect to envision some potentially viable new function or stray unintended consequence of mass connectivity, at least within the framework of a handful of subjects with which the individual is conversant; this is how innovation occurs in the first place. But as Robert Heinlein was fond of pointing out, it was easy to predict the advent of the automobile but nearly impossible to predict the profound social changes that followed in its wake—such as the reinvention of relations between the sexes as courtship broke free from the confines of the parlor, of chaperonage, of family itself.

When an industry is not only secretive and little known to outsiders but also compartmentalized to such an extent that even insiders cannot expect to know much about what it does in totality, the difficult and crucial task of envisioning consequences becomes nearly impossible. When it deals with something as fundamental as information, and disinformation in particular, it also becomes incomparably relevant to all other affairs, which are conducted in accordance with that same information. The intelligence-contracting industry is as opaque as it is consequential. It is a breeding ground for dangerous capabilities that are all the more dangerous for being so little understood.

I was equipped to understand the dangers because I'd designed some of those dangerous practices myself. One of the things that Encyclopedia Dramatica had covered was the practice of pedo baiting, which entails playing the role of an underage child online with the intent of attracting a pedophile. This is usually done with the intention of reporting the subject to the police (and, in the case of NBC, competing with other, less vapid news programs for ratings). How widely this is done and by whom is naturally unknown, though in 2016 NPR ran an interview with a young woman who reported doing this on an ongoing basis; I documented other instances of the phenomenon myself in years prior, in my capacity as an armchair internet scholar for ED. Later, when I started thinking more seriously about what the internet really meant, and how much of this remained to be explored, it occurred to me that such a thing as pedo baiting could be exponentially weaponized in the following manner:

1. Catch a pedo in a chat room as usual. Give him your phone number and tell him to call you.
2. The number is actually to a law enforcement agency with appropriate jurisdiction.
3. Point out to the pedo that you have a chat transcript showing that he called the agency at a particular time in pursuit of an underage girl; that the agency naturally has his phone number and records of him calling at that very moment, and that unless he wants them to be provided with the missing piece of the puzzle in the case of the guy

who just called us and hung up, he will have to comply with occasional orders. The first such order is for the subject to perform this very same stunt and catch two additional pedos within forty-eight hours.

4. As your self-propelling blackmail-fueled pedo-slave army expands automatically, provide further orders as desired, to be distributed down the pipeline.
5. For best results, assigned tasks should not be so onerous as to meet the threshold whereby some sizable portion of your digital slaves will find it worthwhile to revolt or call your bluff.

Set aside your practical objections, which I can assure you I've already considered and solved, and your moral ones, which are obviously irrelevant to a thought experiment and likely vague nonsense at that, and you begin to understand what it means to live in a world in which so many barriers have disappeared so suddenly. A few decades ago, such a project as this would be, if not impossible, rather unlikely to be pursued in the first place, because the incidental barriers to pulling it off would be far too high. Today it could conceivably be carried out by a lone teenager. And as is now documented via such things as the NPR profile, lone teenagers have indeed pulled off the first several steps, to the point of successfully blackmailing adult men. Some seem to have made a living off it.

And then there was Anonymous. The barriers to global organizing en masse had fallen to such an extent that a highly coordinated campaign against Scientology had been carried out in a few days by people with little relevant expertise.

Instrumental assistance to a democratic revolution, previously the purview of figures like Lafayette, had been successfully rendered to Tunisia. In the Nixon era, a network of Catholic peace activists and other antiwar elements spent several months in preparation for their burglary of an FBI field office, where they stole the files that would reveal the agency's criminal COINTELPRO operation. Anonymous had carried out an equivalent operation within twenty-four hours of it having been conceived. They did it as a lark.

Aaron Barr was the first person we'd come across from the other side who seemed to be exploring the new landscape with similar vigor, even impulsiveness. Surveilling the AnonOps IRC server was not difficult in itself, since all one needed was an address to log on and get into the public channels, and this was well enough known by this point that we even had a "Press" channel for reporters. People came in and out of the main channel all day long, and some never really "left," instead remaining idle such that it was common for some hundred users to be present, with only a dozen or so actually talking at any given time. And so when Barr created the username CogAnon and appeared a few weeks prior, he didn't even have to interact with his subjects, as an undercover would be required to do when infiltrating a radical meeting hall. He could pick and choose who to talk to, in private messages to individuals if he preferred. Barr could sit in every channel on the server—with the exception of HQ, where moderators and particularly well-liked contributors hung out and to which one had to be invited—and document everything. He could leave his desk, go to sleep, work on something else, come back, and push a few buttons to save every conversation that had occurred in the interim, each message helpfully annotated with a time stamp. It was easy, and not even original; law enforcement agents had been doing essentially the same thing for at least a few months, as we knew from aspects of the recent PayPal raids and the indictments that had followed, which made clear that conversations had been similarly monitored.

It looked as if things would come down to the same cat-and-mouse dynamic that had been in play for centuries, and with the same general results. The Information Age had conferred certain advantages on both sides of the game, but as far as could be determined from these latest events, these would cancel each other out.

Then, a few weeks into the Themis scandal, it became clear to me that this wasn't actually the case at all.

It is telling that the technology known as "persona management" was discovered by one of the independent researchers who'd been rummaging through the remaining HBGary emails after the press, being the press, had moved on to other things. A post by a blogger at Daily Kos quoted several emails showing that HBGary Federal had responded to a U.S. Air Force request for proposals to produce software capable of allowing a single human operator to oversee some large number of fake online people, complete with fleshed-out backgrounds and capable of interacting with real internet users without raising suspicion. Given what both the state and its favored contracting firms had just been caught planning, even with relatively straightforward technologies, and taking into account the history of the U.S. intelligence community as a whole as well as the increasing frequency with which foreign actors were managing to steal such technologies, this was an especially striking development. Someone such as myself, who had designed self-replicating blackmail mechanisms as a hobby, couldn't help but be horrified at the implications of others creating more viable information weapons . . . It was for this reason that I now repurposed Project PM to oversee a crowdsourced investigation into the intelligence-contracting industry as a whole.

From the clues available from the emails, a Project PM researcher managed to find a patent—filed by IBM and listing several inventors with ties to the U.S. military—describing persona management in further detail. The software portion that allowed operators to better handle the business of mass deception appeared to be rather far along, particularly given that this patent was a few years old. Meanwhile, the firm that actually won the USAF contract HBGary had bid on—a company called Ntrepid—was an absolute mystery in and of itself; a *Guardian* reporter who pursued the issue early was unable to find out where it had come from and who owned it. Later, my researchers came upon tax filings proving that it was a wholly owned subsidiary of Cubic, itself a massive weapons and infrastructure consortium that would come up again and again in the years to follow. But other than a few pieces in *The Guardian* and *The Atlantic* that mostly repeated what we'd already put out ourselves, persona management received little serious attention. But it would appear again, years later, in a context so obviously dangerous that even *The New York Times* couldn't ignore it.

Within a month of the Anonymous raid, Barr had resigned from his position as CEO of HBGary Federal (which soon ceased to exist), Palantir's CEO had apologized, and there were calls in Congress for a formal investigation.

All of this was deeply satisfying to many on our side, who saw it as a great victory for Anonymous. They were right, but it was also indicative of how bad things really were and how little chance activists had against the powerful and lawless. Palantir, cofounded by the billionaire Peter Thiel, had disentangled itself from the scandal largely unscathed, claiming that Themis had merely been an aberration pursued by two overzealous employees acting without authorization. In fact, several email threads that largely flew under the radar of the press demonstrated the involvement of a half dozen participants, including the firm's lead counsel, Matt Long, whom I later managed to get on the phone and record Barr-style. But only the most thoroughly implicated employee, Matthew Steckman, was put on leave pending an investigation—and then promoted after the press had lost interest; as of 2016 he was head of business development and living in D.C. Barr himself got a new job at another contracting firm almost immediately.

Meanwhile, the bid to proceed with a Congressional investigation, led by Democratic Rep. Hank Johnson of Georgia, was running into a suspicious degree of opposition. Johnson started off by writing a letter to several federal agencies requesting information as to whether the firms involved might have broken the law with the participation of the federal government itself, and further asking for specifics on related federal contracts. Immediately, Rep. Lamar Smith—a Texas Republican who chaired the Judiciary Committee—released a statement declaring that, although he appreciated Johnson's interest, "It is the role of the Justice Department to determine whether a criminal investigation is warranted." This was certainly convenient for the DOJ, which had of course played a significant role in that which was to be investigated. It was also convenient for Smith, whose major donors included AT&T and other tech firms with a history of engaging in potentially illegal conduct with these same government agencies. As it turned out, the DOJ declined to investigate itself and its powerful intelligence-linked corporate partners.

If anything, the immediate aftermath of Team Themis would signal to others within the fast-expanding intelligence-contracting sector that, in the very unlikely case that one's illicit plot was revealed, there would be no real consequences for anyone involved. Themis hadn't been so much a cautionary tale as a green light.

No one had more to fear than us in this respect, given that we had just tweaked the noses of some dozen clearly amoral organizations that either had links to the state or were the state. And we'd already been targets even before the HBGary hack. Toward the end of February 2011 I found an exchange between Barr and one of the vice presidents of Booz Allen Hamilton in which Barr provides updates on his opposition research against Anonymous: "I have made significant progress on the group and have 80–90% of their leadership mapped out. Meeting with Govies next week." A separate email clarifies the focus further: "just a status [update]. I started to look more carefully for wikileaks ties within anonymous . . . there are many. BTW, anonymous is looking for its next effort to get involved in and is looking to resurrect operation payback in support of wikileaks."

This was written a few days after Barr was actually flown out to meet with the Booz VP at their office, apparently to discuss some ongoing "project" that Booz was overseeing. Perhaps in connection to this, Endgame Systems had prepared a thorough and surprisingly accurate report on Anonymous, compiled for some unknown party, which included an assessment of the likelihood of Anonymous escalating its attacks on Western governments should Julian Assange be assassinated. In this context, it was somewhat alarming that Barr had referred to me—in one of the other exchanges seized from his personal accounts—as a key leader of Anonymous.

It was also clear that the people we were dealing with were almost comically unscrupulous. In the days leading up to the hack, as Aaron Barr prepared his media blitz at our expense, his de facto boss Greg Hoglund of HBGary proper instructed one underling thusly: "I think these guys are going to get arrested, it would be interesting to leave the soft impression that Aaron is the one that got them, and that without Aaron the Feds would have never been able to get out of their own way. So, position Aaron as a hero to the public. At this point they are going to get arrested anyway." This was the industry that the federal government had made in its own image, and granted dominion over all other things.

We kept looking through the remaining emails, with Project PM being entirely repurposed to oversee the crowdsourced investigation that I was now intent on seeing through to the end, whatever that might consist of. We documented our findings on a wiki we'd set up for the purpose, Echelon2.org, which would come to serve as the world's most comprehensive repository of information about the increasingly powerful intelligence-contracting industry that had mushroomed into existence over the past ten years.

Other hacks by Anonymous and similar outfits yielded additional data; much else could be gleaned from public records, such as patent applications, if one knew just a bit about the industry and its individual participants, as we now did.

Two themes were making themselves plain. One was that the apparatus by which the powerful could interfere with the flow of information via net-based black ops was proliferating widely even as it got more advanced due to the budding free market in services and technologies. The other was that traditional press structures were largely incapable of either discovering such things or adequately pursuing them, whereas crowdsourced journalism, properly curated, sometimes could.

But we needed those press structures nonetheless; aside from the amplification power that *The New York Times* or NBC could bring to the table so as to at least create opportunities for national focus on opaque problems, there also still existed professional journalists who could accurately assess leads, follow them up, and force the degree of sustained attention that we often struggled to achieve via our websites, Twitter accounts, and attention-grabbing hacks. In a couple of instances, then, my lust for glory lost out to my increasing hatred for the contractors and my desire to see their work disrupted, even if that meant handing scoops to others. In the weeks after the hack I provided one of my most competent contacts, Michael Riley at *Bloomberg Businessweek*, with emails to and from execs at Endgame Systems in which were discussed, among other things, their dealings with the intelligence community, as well as their desire not to be listed on Team Themis documents and to otherwise exist as merely "silent partners" per the wishes of their "clients," who appeared to value discretion more than

Barr did. A few months later *Businessweek* came out with its story revealing that Endgame, which had NSA ties and had been founded by the hacker-turned-Pentagon-employee Chris Rouland, had acquired the ability to seize control of infrastructure across entire regions—including airports in Western Europe—and was renting out these capabilities to unknown non–U.S. government customers for a few million dollars a month.

There was one story I was intent on doing myself. Romas/COIN was among the many operational monikers that one would come across in perusing the HBGary emails, usually in mysterious and unhelpful contexts; this one stood out as particularly intriguing because it was mentioned as having something to do with Apple. The *Forbes* tech blogger Sean Lawson had openly wondered about this in February, but lost interest after an anonymous commenter chimed in to the effect that there was nothing of interest here, since COIN stood for counterinsurgency (the acronym had just been rolled out with astute marketing flair by the Pentagon, which had largely replaced a jumble of old urban warfare techniques and presented it as a game-changing new strategy in the war they'd been losing). And since anything having to do with counterinsurgency is necessarily benevolent, as Vietnam showed us, and also taking into account that there was certainly nothing suspicious about the idea of Apple being involved in tactical warfare, the press naturally declined to pursue the story.

In fact, COIN can also stand for counterintelligence, as in the FBI's illegal COINTELPRO apparatus that had been used against antiwar and civil rights activists until its discovery in the early seventies. And that's exactly what it stood for in this case, as explicitly noted in one of the email attachments I came across as I investigated the program over the course of a month. To do so required a more systematic examination of the emails, as few of the messages between the firms involved actually included the program's code name; rather than simply searching for the term *Romas/COIN*, one would have to gradually familiarize oneself with the names of executives, small partner firms, technologies, and procedures so as to accumulate more and more key words for searches while also piecing together the nature of the project itself, which in accordance with industry protocol is never explicitly laid out. But a general picture emerged along with some telling details here and there as I went through a year's worth of email exchanges between Barr and executives at several far more prominent firms, like TASC, Inc.—and entirely obscure ones, like Archimedes Global—with which HBGary Federal had teamed up to compete for the relevant government contract when it next came up for bidding.

Whatever it was, Romas/COIN was at that time being run for the government by Northrop Grumman, where Barr had worked on it during his stint there (he'd even named it: as Barr proudly explained to his TASC counterparts, "Romas" was a variety of Middle Eastern tarantula). It was an operation of strangely tremendous breadth—producing a superior product sufficient to edge out his old employers would apparently entail the integration of several dozen little-known capabilities involving mass surveillance of social networking trends, natural language processing, and content production, while also drawing upon seemingly mundane products and services from a dozen small firms, including cell phone game companies. There were also face-to-face meetings not only with Apple but also with Google's "national security division." Perhaps most crucial was coming up with a badass name; one TASC employee asked if they could call their program iteration *Saif*, the Arabic word for the sword that executioners use to decapitate criminals; this, he noted, would be "cool."

I called up the TASC executive John Lovegrove to ask him for comment, explaining that I was doing a story on the project for a major publication. He informed me that he "can't talk about that" and that even his refusals to answer were "off the record." I informed him that this wasn't how the whole off-the-record thing worked, and then posted the recording on YouTube, which shortly thereafter removed it on the grounds that it constituted "harassment." So I made a new video in which I read the transcript out loud, doing Lovegrove's lines in a variety of comically undignified voices.

The finished article—an article that, after all, dealt with a massive all-in-one data mining/surveillance/propaganda apparatus that united the world's most powerful information technology companies with the world's most powerful government in large part under the auspices of a man now best known for seeking to destroy opponents of powerful institutions for money—was supposed to serve as the first of three pieces I'd agreed to write for Al Jazeera on the subject of intelligence-contracting operations directed at the Arab world, and was set to appear in English and Arabic on its website. Then, for reasons unclear to me, another editor was brought in—Christopher Arsenault, an American who'd previously been with the CBS News radio division—and asserted that the piece "lacks pull."

> To over-simplify, I am left thinking: Who cares about all these e-mails and junk after I read it. You need to

> humanise the issue a little bit. And explain clearly to someone who isn't familiar with the issue why they should care about this. As it stands, the piece reads too much like a technical document.
>
> I am hoping you can talk to some privacy advocates (start with the ACLU and go from there) about why this is scarey, and then have them comment on particular aspects of the case. Ideally, I would like you to talk to someone who is a victim of data mining. Please do at least 4 solid interviews.

I explained to him that people who have been data mined don't know that they've been data mined because it merely entails the absorption of existing information on the internet and is done on the level of entire populations in order to establish patterns and thus doesn't target individual victims; that there was no actual journalistic value to talking to privacy advocates about why this was "scarey," or to anything else he was proposing; and that I had no choice but to take the story elsewhere. Immediately the original Arab editor came back into the picture and said it could go up as is in just a few days. He returned again, apologetically asking for more opinion to be inserted, which is the only request I always entertain, and afterward suggested a few minor changes, including a more comprehensive introduction to both the article and the three-part series. Then I never heard from Al Jazeera again, and they stopped responding to my emails. Later I would talk to other journalists who'd worked for the outlet, who explained that these sorts of bizarre occurrences were growing more common and seemed to have much to do with internal politics among the Qatari royals who owned the network, some of whom were supportive of certain clandestine U.S. operations so long as they were targeted at the kingdom's regional enemies. Really I was less bothered by the ham-fisted censorship than I was by having had to interact with an American network radio producer.

I took the story to *The Guardian*, dashed off a quick announcement piece in which I summarized my findings, and linked back to the full report on Echelon2. Aside from the left-wing website Raw Story, no U.S. outlet of any note even mentioned the program. Russia Today, always happy to embarrass the United States, had on Lieutenant Colonel Anthony Shaffer to confirm the significance of the revelations, and *Der Spiegel* ran a piece on the extraordinary absence of American coverage. Crikey, a small Australian outlet, also ran my full report. That was it. In cases such as this, some will inevitably posit an active conspiracy to repress information, whereas in reality it usually has much more to do with the fact that editorial decisions are often made by people like that CBS producer.

After this vastly obnoxious episode, I was even more inclined to put out information by proxy, which is why, when I was provided with a file stolen from Raytheon demonstrating the firm's upcoming software intended to detect leakers via changing patterns of behavior, I passed it on to Ryan Gallagher, another journalist who'd interviewed me a few times on security matters and whom I thus knew to be capable of doing the story.

Anyway, I was now too busy for conventional journalism. My career as a revolutionary was taking off.

5

The Age of Ambiguity

Though the ocean looks uniform from the shore, and thus easily understood, well-informed people accept that complexity and variation exist under the surface, only to be known through study and experience; they would not claim to be oceanologists simply by virtue of having gone to the beach.

But many of these same people will nonetheless proclaim broad principles of media and politics with a confidence they would not dare to apply to oceanology or engineering. Thus we hear that "the media" is, variously, the economic tool of its corporate owners, or the propaganda apparatus of its left-wing reporters, or the instrument of one or another intelligence apparatus. We hear similar assertions about governments, and segments of governments.

In the effort to understand, we may go too far in personalizing institutions, and even entire industries; we may forget that none of these things really exist. It is only individual human beings who have agendas—and these agendas are themselves complex expressions of political and personal drives, some unconscious. So long as institutions must be comprised of individuals, then, institutions will have fractures, gradients; they will be many things, and in combinations that will change over time.

We speak and think in models. And so we say that "*The New York Times*" wants to accomplish this, or that "the CIA" is after that. So long as we recognize this as shorthand, necessary for describing broad, shared tendencies and the institutional structures that were originally created to drive these individuals along some specific path, we can indeed speak in such terms and profit thereby. If we forget this, we risk losing the plot.

We cannot afford to lose this particular plot. The survival of a free and moral society requires that some large portion of the citizenry be in a position to assess the nature of powerful institutions.

This is all easily enough understood, and even those most guilty of personifying forces in ways that miss important complexities are obviously aware that *The New York Times* is not a person, and that the CIA itself doesn't really want anything. The problem with obvious things is that they are easily disregarded.

Had I believed that the intelligence community was a particular creature with a particular agenda, I would have been more confident in brushing up against it, for a singular agenda may be assessed and worked around. Had I thought that the press could be understood in terms of covert state control, or corporate greed, or ideological mission, I could have proceeded under its gaze in accordance with some expectation of its behavior.

But I'd been in a position to know that although all these beliefs about the press were actually true to varying extents that differed from outlet to outlet, the real problem lay elsewhere. Certainly news coverage is subject to conscious direction, including economic pressure dictated by advertisers; one clear example is the incident in which Monsanto successfully killed an upcoming TV news report on the potentially carcinogenic properties of milk containing its hormones. And news coverage is indeed subject to the ideology of those who assign, produce, and present the stories; this can be as blatant and top-driven as what happens at Fox News, or as subtle and near-unconscious as the choices regarding terminology and emphasis that any news reporter makes every day.

More dramatically, the United States has a long documented history of intelligence community interference with Western press outlets, ranging from such things as the *Time* founder Henry Luce's active cooperation with the CIA to that agency's long-running partial infiltration of outlets and wire services under Operation Mockingbird. There is good reason to believe that such operations are far diminished from their Cold War peak, and that any that remain are relatively inconsequential. But indirect methods involving tech-based disinformation—and, more prosaically, the cultivation of that mediocre sort of reporter who, in the absence of any particular talent, is forced to build a career on scoops—do still seem to be in play, sometimes in a manner that can tilt crucial national decisions in one direction or another.

The best example of how all of this works in practice is the Judith Miller affair, when Miller—a *New York Times* journalist who shared certain ideological affinities with neocons and supported their Middle East ambitions—accepted false information from Dick Cheney's chief of staff, Scooter Libby, to the effect that Saddam Hussein had received uranium from Nigeria; this was quickly followed by true yet classified information intended to discredit a U.S. diplomat who'd publicly refuted the false story. Most egregiously, from an ethical standpoint, she characterized Libby to her readers as a "former Congressional staffer" so as to launder the source. Others at the *Times* had objected to the uranium story on its merits, but the editor in charge is said to have dismissed the warnings. This was not because the editor was a hawk, or a CIA plant, or concerned about losing Nigerian advertisers. It was more likely because Miller was an award-winning journalist whose ongoing "scoops" reflected prestige on the editor himself.

As all of this later became the subject of a criminal investigation on the one hand and an apologetic series of public inquiries by *The New York Times* itself, the Miller affair produced an unusually robust case study of how the interactions between editors, journalists, sources, and government officials can shape stories, and thus national consciousness—and the roles that careerism and personal ambition play in real life, if not in the poorly ordered imaginations of armchair press critics. Here we have ideology and conspiracy, to be sure, but we also have something far more deleterious, and all the more troubling because it so commonplace: we have the haphazardness of the whole thing. We have the end result of a press system that was never designed by earnest technocrat-kings to achieve some high-minded civic end, but that instead grew piecemeal to serve the desires and self-delusions of both its customers and its practitioners. It is an industry comprised largely of poorly compensated, job-insecure functionaries who must produce a degree of content on every complex subject that happens along in the public view, and who must do so with limited time, subject to the whims of editors, and within an economic framework that presents media professionals with a choice: either reward the salacious interests and childlike attention spans of a large part of the public, or risk everything in an appeal to that virtuous minority who care about the truth above all and are emotionally and intellectually equipped to understand it.

This was the ocean I would now have to cross, pursued by sharks. (The sharks are the cops and the spies and whatnot.)

After the sort of journalists who actually discover and flesh out stories had decided that Anonymous qualified as such, it was time for the major outlets to call sloppy seconds. I was contacted by the dean of hokey Beltway journalism, Michael Isikoff, then working for *NBC Nightly News*, who wanted to do a story on whatever it was that we were doing. He told me, though I could have guessed, that NBC's producers were most interested in having Isikoff and a camera crew visit "one of these hackers" and "watch him hacking," an arrangement that no serious hacker would ever agree to even in the face of Isikoff's cute assertions that he could ensure anonymity, and which would have at any rate been entirely devoid of any value to the public beyond entertainment. After I'd finally convinced him on the first point (naturally I didn't bother pursuing the second), it was agreed that he would come interview me at my apartment instead.

Here I was playing a dangerous game. Over the past two months, I'd continued to strengthen my position within Anonymous, having won varying degrees of acceptance from those veterans of the movement who loomed large over the AnonOps IRC while also expanding my media relations work. But I'd been careful not to do any of this in a way that could draw reasonable criticism. Unreasonable criticism was unavoidable in this environment, the population of which is best expressed as consisting of the Noble and Clever, the Noble Yet Dumb, the Ignoble Yet Clever, and the Ignoble and Dumb. The Noble tribes could certainly take issue, on both pragmatic and theoretical grounds, with the degree of control I was accruing over communications and other things, but there was precedent for this that could partially defuse the theoretical criticisms, and so long as they accepted that what I was doing was ultimately useful, I would be largely insulated on that front. The Ignoble and Dumb could, in sufficient numbers, generate anti-Barrett chatter along various lines, factual and otherwise, itself only dangerous to the extent that it could be taken seriously by the journalists who were now dropping by AnonOps on a daily basis.

The Ignoble Yet Clever were most dangerous of all. Anyone who held any influence in Anonymous was subject to a baseline degree of resentment from those motivated chiefly by a desire to believe themselves equal to anyone else in the movement, regardless of what they'd actually done; someone who spoke publicly about Anonymous was a particular target. One of those who'd been arrested in the U.K. in conjunction with the January FBI raids turned out to have been set up by some other Anon who'd used his screen name in a chat during the Visa/PayPal et al. attacks, writing a series of incriminating messages under that name on the major IRC channels that everyone knew to be monitored by law enforcement. The fellow had made himself a target by providing a quote to the BBC using his Anonymous moniker. Incidentally, his charges were dropped when the circumstances became clear; contrary to American practice, British prosecutors tend not to pursue the demonstrably innocent.

A few others had spoken to the press in such a way that left the impression that they were portraying themselves as leaders, and were hassled in a less dramatic manner. Gregg Housh had survived in this capacity by denying both the role of spokesman and any current personal involvement in anything whatsoever, taking pains to present himself as a mere observer. Still he took unwarranted criticism, generally from those with little stake in the outcome of the activities he was supporting (which he usually did only at the request of those involved), and who were thus immune to the argument that this was a necessary method of getting the word out about increasingly high-stakes operations that were themselves ultimately intended to change perceptions. Since I was not only actively involved in operations under my own name but also still technically a journalist with a professional obligation to note that I was connected to some of the events I was being quoted on (and writing about myself, as I often still did for *The Guardian* and other outlets), that wasn't an option for me. Even had it been, my own agenda required that I be associated with the things I was risking myself to help accomplish; had George Washington not been accorded due prestige for his role in the French and Indian War, his later career as a revolutionary might never have taken off.

Nonetheless, I'd managed to get this far without attracting so much negative attention as to make my job impossible, and had meanwhile built up a base of support among those who knew the specifics of what I actually did and who cared about outcomes. Many of the interviews I gave to journalists were on background, intended to ensure that the resulting articles would incorporate our point of view, and I'd made a point of regularly referring reporters to others in Anonymous who I knew could speak cogently about the movement. Most important, I consistently disavowed the title of "spokesman."

But as with Housh before me—who'd once had to argue with a CNN anchor about whether he was the spokesman for Anonymous, only to find that his own opinion in this matter was granted no more weight than that of a television producer with whom he'd had a brief phone conversation—the title is hard to avoid. If Housh couldn't escape the designation even as he regularly disavowed any current connection to Anonymous whatsoever, someone like myself who was demonstrably involved in ongoing operations and was furthermore in the habit of talking like a McKinley-era labor organizer was doomed to this double-edged title, particularly given that even some Anons themselves had begun to think of me as such; in the post-HBGary IRC chat with the execs Penny Leavy and Greg Hoglund, while I was on the phone with Aaron Barr, a visiting reporter was told by one particularly active Anon to talk to me on the grounds that I was the movement's "public face," an assertion that went uncontested by anyone present. Here, anyway, was the convenient side of the phenomenon; to the same extent that it put me at risk, both the accurate assessment that I was someone the press could get cute quotes and factual information from, and the inaccurate view that I held some formal spokesperson role that I had perhaps granted myself would serve to route journalists in my direction, giving me that much more control of the message even as I lost control over my own public identity. Had people deemed me the Duke of Lancaster, I would likewise have denied it, but anyone who insisted on raising levies for my war with Spain would not see them refused. And should I sack Barcelona, and the other brigands become upset that I have been proclaimed a duke by others still because my actions happen to appear duke-like, I will sympathize with that resentment, and try to assuage it when possible, but let us remember that we are ultimately here to kill Spaniards.

At any rate, references to me as "Barrett Brown, spokesman for Anonymous" had already begun appearing in some articles. This was the natural result of some of the systematic press failures that I'd already grown obsessed with, and that I now had a rare opportunity to study closely even as it damaged my ability to function.

The first of these is a tendency toward fill-in-the-blanks journalism whereby sloppy reporters present their misunderstandings as fact (thus a reporter sees me referred to in *The New York Times* as speaking about Anonymous, and decides that I must be the spokesman). The second is the desire by editors, and thus by reporters who must please editors, to present their sources as especially knowledgeable and as close to the situation in question as they possibly can (thus a reporter with a major outlet whom I've just explicitly told not to refer to me as a spokesman responds via email with the declaration that "it's our policy"). The third is the inevitable practice, by harried media professionals with limited time, of getting the bulk of their information from existing articles (thus after a few mentions of me as spokesman, the references quickly proliferate, along with other, more unique errors that can thereafter be traced as they spread).

The problem for me is that all these little nuances are unknown to the general public, and so the average person who saw me referenced as a "spokesperson for Anonymous" would assume that this was the title I'd given out myself, because otherwise why would a reporter write such a thing? The average Anon would think likewise—and there were vast numbers of such Anons who would never see my own explanation, having no connection to the venues out of which I was working. Worst of all, the average *journalist* didn't understand these things much better. Soon enough, then, my press-appointed title would mutate into "the self-appointed spokesperson for Anonymous," a perverse development that gave me the air of an absolute charlatan while doing untold damage to my ability to recruit, to persuade, and—later, when my life was on the line—to attract critical support.

With these things already in play, doing NBC was a gamble. But to turn it down would be to miss a major opportunity to force attention to the companies and government agencies that had weathered the HBGary firestorm; to present the case for Anonymous and "enhanced civil disobedience," as I'd taken to calling it; and to establish myself as a public jurist on the order of Gore Vidal, whose own compulsion to proliferate himself across the face of our civilization I understood perfectly well. Declining never seriously occurred to me.

The interview itself was rather soul-crushing, though this wasn't entirely NBC's fault. My girlfriend had convinced me to get off Suboxone, so I'd refrained from renewing my prescription. The plan was for me to kick immediately after the visit from Isikoff, but then his arrival ended up being delayed four days. By the time he did arrive I'd already run out and begun the withdrawal process, which is less intense than that of heroin but lasts about four times longer. I had liquor and weed and ibuprofen to help me through it, but there are few things in life more hellish than having to explain the exact nature of your role in an anarchist cyberinsurgency to Michael Isikoff while in the opening phases of dope sickness.

And the exact nature of my role was indeed on the agenda (see the second of three systematic press failures from a few paragraphs back). Pressed to describe the nature of my role, I told Isikoff that, if we had positions, I would be something akin to a "senior strategist at a think tank." I also took pains to explain that this was not actually my title, and that although I was clearly involved in some of these operations and additionally did press work on behalf of particular groupings of participants at their request, there was nothing "official" about any of it. The editor of the Dallas city monthly *D Magazine* was on hand for the interview, which he was going to be describing in the course of a long profile he was writing on my recent adventures; as he would later quote me from this conversation, which he'd audio recorded, "Anonymous is a process more than it is a thing.

I can't speak on behalf of Anonymous, because there's no one who can authorize me to do that."

Though the resulting newscast wasn't completely idiotic, and summarized the crucial instance of Anonymous's support for the Tunisian revolution, it did manage to go into the dramatic details of the HBGary hack without bothering to mention that we'd uncovered a conspiracy to subvert democracy involving several major corporations and the DOJ. Nor did they see fit to mention that I myself was a longtime journalist and author; instead Isikoff described me in the voice-over simply as a "cocky twenty-nine-year-old college dropout." Brian Williams himself had just introduced me, somewhat more flamboyantly, as "an underground commander in a new kind of war." Worst of all, for me, was Isikoff's inevitable and vastly inaccurate voice-over declaration that "he calls himself 'senior strategist.'" In the end, it had been more important to NBC to present their source as someone high up the chain than to relate the actual nature of the subject to the public.

The segment was another wound in my side, though not fatal; on the plus side, it would lead to further scrutiny by better journalists with more serious outlets, and thus further opportunities to win the propaganda war. And for all the inefficiencies and silliness of the press at large, we were indeed winning; coverage of Anonymous was almost universally positive, if not always accurate.

One particular reaction to the NBC segment was especially telling. Someone on 4chan posted a screen capture of me sitting in my chair during the interview, dressed as usual in a blazer, cowboy boots, and blue-and-white-striped oxford button-down. The accompanying text was something along the lines of, "This hipster douchebag is pretending to be the leader of Anonymous," adding that—as he himself had discovered via a Google search—I was actually a journalist with some large number of outlets, something that NBC hadn't pointed out. He concluded, inevitably, that this was the visible manifestation of some plot by the CIA or whoever to gain control of Anonymous by working with the press to present its own undercover asset as the acknowledged leader. What's striking about this (other than that a twentysomething male can go to the trouble of wearing a blazer every day of his life and still be denounced as a hipster) is that this major news outlet's bizarre omission regarding an obviously relevant factor in its story that could have been addressed in a mere two seconds was so inexplicable that someone who noticed it might well struggle to account for such a thing without concluding that it must have been intentional. It is not just those within the Establishment press who ascribe to it far more deliberation and competence than it deserves; those who mistrust it from the outside tend to do the very same thing.

Beyond that, it was a sign—one of many—of the ambiguous position one could hold in public life, even in an age when information is an order of magnitude more accessible than ever before. Rather than narrowing down various perceptions and possibilities toward that one, singular reality supported by the preponderance of available information, the great proliferation of outlets and the sheer amount of material out there actually seemed to lend themselves to the fragmentation of story lines. Of course anyone possessed of competence, time, and an actual will to understand could still approach the truth in most instances, but such things are at a premium. Thus it was that I would read, variously, that I was someone working with Anonymous; a journalist working with Anonymous; a journalist "embedded" with Anonymous, on which I was simply reporting; a journalist who had latched on to the Anonymous banner to promote myself without having actually done anything; a natural leader "respected across the board by all of Anonymous's members"; or any number of other mutually exclusive descriptions. In early 2012 I was asked to appear on a taped Bloomberg panel and listed as a "security expert"; in truth, I knew less than the average newspaper technology correspondent about the basic elements of computer networks and had to have people like Gregg Housh help me any time my own laptop went down. Project PM was almost inevitably described as having been founded in the wake of the HBGary hack, rather than two years prior for an entirely different purpose. A later book on Anonymous by a writer for *Forbes* listed me as have been born and bred in Houston, a city I grew to despise after having spent only four hours among its benighted and tacky natives.

And this same degree of fractured memory on the part of our press was also aiding some of our enemies. Certainly Aaron Barr would always be known to search engines as the fellow who resigned from his own company after Team Themis. But anyone who played more than one role could easily be known entirely for one aspect of it. Peter Thiel, founder of Palantir, would be the subject of dozens of profile pieces, along with his increasingly powerful firm; very few of them mention the time that Palantir conspired to subvert democracy, pretended not to have been involved, waited out the press, and then promoted the man they'd managed to designate the sole scapegoat in spite of a dozen emails proving otherwise. Even the critical profiles tended to omit this.

It wasn't enough to establish the facts. The facts would have to be continually reestablished, even fought over.

I was a mess throughout much of this time. In April I flew up to New York City with my girlfriend to deliver a speech at City Hall as part of a Rally for Information Freedom in honor of Chelsea Manning that I'd helped to organize without managing to wriggle out of it afterward. While there, I was also supposed to meet with the lawyer Stanley Cohen regarding the ongoing legal defense efforts of various arrested Anons, as well as with early Project PM consultants like the journalist Michael Hastings and the media-savvy mathematician Jonathan Farley. I got ahold of some heroin less than two hours after touching down at LaGuardia and had already picked up a habit by the day of the rally. After the speech, which I gave while moderately dope sick, we retired to a nearby bar, where Gregg Housh and I were attended by the press and a sprinkling of information activist groupies. Catalina Saldana, an old girlfriend of sorts with whom I used to get high, came by and offered me some speed in earshot of my then girlfriend, Nikki, who promptly instigated a heated argument in front of reporters.

I maneuvered the party back to Brooklyn and left everyone standing outside a walk-up apartment building for ten minutes while I bought heroin from my old Puerto Rican gangster buddies, having claimed I was merely going to buy us all some weed (in my defense, I did also buy weed). Back at the friend's apartment where I was staying, Catalina and I sneaked off to get high and make out like in the old days. Later Hastings and I conferred in my friend's kitchen on how best to confound our feckless enemies in the orthodox press. It was the last time I'd see either of them alive; during my imprisonment, Catalina would jump off a building on the anniversary of the death by overdose of a mutual friend with whom I'd also been briefly involved. Hastings would be dead within two years, killed in a single-car accident.

Before heading back to Dallas, I met with Cohen. He told me that the government would likely prosecute me under the Racketeer Influenced and Corrupt Organizations statutes. I snorted some heroin in his bathroom and then visited another old girlfriend.

In those days of frantic activity, multiple instances of Skype, Gmail, IRC, and more obscure platforms lay open on my laptop at all times. My universe centered on my desk, itself covered in overflowing ashtrays and used syringes and coffee cups in which floated the corpses of insects—but my universe extended out across the world, and into its hidden places.

Anonymous grew ever more significant and thus ever more worth fighting over. We fought over tactics, philosophy, prestige, credit. Hackers like Sabu, Topiary, Tflow, and Kayla gained followers and detractors within Anonymous and outside of it. Our occult power struggles leaked out into the media, which we all wielded against one another in subtle and not-so-subtle ways; several of us had become celebrity adventurers, and it was now necessary for us to secure our individual legacies, especially from each other.

Still, we mostly remained focused on the enemy. I spent

Sunday mornings on the phone, rousting executives out of bed to demand answers about projects they'd thought were secret. I did this to one Booz Allen vice president on several occasions. Afternoons were spent collaborating with Topiary and others via Skype as we tried to piece together patents and vague emails into something that the press might run with; in the evenings I got drunk and stoned and addressed Anonymous over the movement's in-house internet radio programs, trying to incite the digital mob into greater and greater feats of insurrection.

The chaos accelerated. Anonymous attacks on the CIA, on Congress, on Booz Allen, on the Syrian regime, on British intelligence and law enforcement agencies became routine. Sometimes emails and other data would be stolen as well; Project PM's volunteers would devour it all. Chelsea Manning was being subjected to mental torture at Quantico; we made vague threats and specific demands, followed by some light probes of the base's computer networks; the Pentagon announced it was investigating; I went on Russia Today to tamp things down, the requisite attention to Manning's situation having been successfully generated. HBGary's CEO, Greg Hoglund, called me one evening, clearly drunk, to say he knew I was behind the ongoing press campaign against him; I recorded the conversation and played it for the visiting documentary filmmaker Brian Knappenberger, glowing with pride over my latest cyberpunk trophy. Sony sued a young man for uploading a guide explaining how a PlayStation could be altered to run custom software; Anonymous hacked Sony again and again for weeks, costing the firm hundreds of millions of dollars and prompting another congressional inquiry—this time into Sony itself, for its failure to encrypt the customer data that someone stole in the process. There were arrests and rumors of arrests, and rumors of snitches, of CIA infiltration; there was talk that I myself was a CIA agent charged with taking control of Anonymous; more realistically, there were rumors that I was a megalomaniacal drug addict who would one day take things too far.

Michael Hastings went back to Afghanistan and exposed a two-star general's ongoing use of psyops against visiting senators to encourage further commitment to the war. There are times and places in which this would have caused a major scandal, but twenty-first-century America isn't one of them.

DDoS attacks of a severity available only to institutions with considerable resources were directed at our Echelon2 .org website, bringing it down for weeks until we moved the site to another host with the means to protect it; thereafter it disappeared from the Google index altogether, only coming back after the *Wired* reporter Quinn Norton made public note of its absence. No explanation was ever provided.

Topiary and a few of the more prominent hackers began working mostly under a separate outfit, LulzSec, under the banner of which they carried out an amusing reign of terror causing an estimated billion dollars of damage to various firms, and dominating the news cycle through the summer of 2011. A security firm called Imperva publicly declared me to be the spokesman for LulzSec; when I objected, pointing out that I'd never been to its IRC server and had even criticized the group in interviews, they updated their post to note that I denied being the spokesman for LulzSec.

A small-time marijuana dealer was kidnapped in Veracruz by the Zetas drug cartel and held for ransom, a routine occurrence in those days other than that the dealer happened to be connected to the Mexican contingent of Anonymous, which operated out of another IRC server; they threatened to release the names of seventy-five Zetas-affiliated police officers and cabdrivers they'd supposedly stolen from a government server earlier that year if the fellow wasn't let go, which he promptly was. I came out in favor of the controversial operation and assisted those involved with the press, which itself promptly decided that I myself was in charge; major outlets ran analyses concerning whether I might perhaps be beheaded in uptown Dallas by Zetas enforcers, to whom they ascribed almost supernatural capabilities. At first I laughed off the idea; as time went on, I wondered if perhaps the danger was real and I was merely unable to see it through a haze of opiates and mania. OpCartel, as it was known, eventually fizzled out; I made a few halfhearted efforts to obtain information on U.S. cartel activity, and worked on the skeleton of a plan to get Mexican journalists working with their American counterparts to report such things as could get them killed in-country and rebroadcast it all to the Mexican public from here, but I found that I lacked the wherewithal to get anything accomplished. A journalist with one of the Mexican TV networks flew up to interview me; after getting visibly drunk, I left him at the bar for twenty minutes while I met with a neighbor who could sell me a couple of hits of Suboxone, which I'd gotten back on but kept running out of for some reason. Upon my return I crushed up the pill and snorted it at the table before concluding my earlier point about how I would consider going to Mexico to lecture the head of the Sinaloa cartel on human decency, a proposition the journalist listened to with more politeness than was warranted.

Several dozen members of the Polish legislature donned Guy Fawkes masks on the floor of the chamber as Anonymous led an unprecedented global protest-insurgency against the Stop Online Piracy Act, the proposed U.S. legislation that would have given the U.S. government open-ended power over the internet. I looked into the possibility of moving to Tunisia and securing political refugee status for myself and other activists with the assistance of Slim Amamou, who'd become minister of youth and sport, but then he resigned in protest over one thing or another. Documentary filmmakers arrived with increasing regularity, and I started appearing on Russia Today every month or so via Skype in order to explain why a government or corporation had been hacked and why this was a justified and in fact insufficient response to some act of perfidy by our enemies, who were the enemies of mankind.

A prominent conservative blogger and California state prosecutor with whom I'd spoken on occasion, Patrick Frey, asked if I could get Anonymous to do something about a blogpost by another conservative blogger, Jeff Goldstein, who'd written a piece with a headline to the effect that Frey was an antisemite—a disingenuous assertion that Goldstein had made to prove a "point" about some idiotic dispute the two had engaged in. As the headline appeared on the first page of his Google results, Frey was concerned enough to have reached out to a group of hackers through me.

FREY: As long as any way is legal, I'm all for it

ME: well what if it's legal . . . but

FREY: Do I need to hear the rest?

ME: nope

FREY: There you go. It's legal, you say? Great!

I went up to New York to meet with publishers alongside Gregg Housh, who was hoping to sell a book on Anonymous and his own life in general and wanted me to cowrite it. While there, I attended the first couple of days of Occupy Wall Street. I didn't notice Aaron Barr, who'd rebounded from the HBGary thing and showed up on the first day of Occupy with his hair dyed blue as a sort of disguise. Upon being recognized by a reporter, Barr claimed he was just there out of curiosity, though he struggled to explain the dye job. In fact, he and another, similarly colorful "security firm" exec named Tom Ryan were there to sign up for mailing lists and forward them to the FBI. Unfortunately, they accidentally cc'd them to a reporter they'd been corresponding with, and the whole thing ended up in *Gawker.* Meanwhile, Ryan challenged me via Twitter to meet him and Barr at a Midtown tavern; high on coke, I headed over with a voice recorder in my pocket and spent an odd half hour listening to Ryan tell me that the address we'd put up for his company Provide Security on Echelon2.org was actually the address of some mafia front, and that I was thus in danger. I'd say this was the most ham-fisted veiled threat I ever received in those days, but I'm sure there're others I've forgotten. At some point I lost my little baggie of coke and left shortly thereafter.

Journalists flew in from Germany and the U.K., and I harangued them about the military-industrial-cyber-intelligence-prison-surveillance complex while wiping blood off my arm. My girlfriend and I had apocalyptic fights over my drug use; I replaced her with a series of compliant Anonymous groupies. Topiary disappeared from the internet, then reappeared amid a flurry of rumors, then was arrested, as were several other prominent Anons; the foremost of the remaining hackers, Sabu, continued to operate as the leader of Antisec, which waged ongoing war on governments and security firms, increasingly with the assistance of another hacker who went by a variety of different monikers but whom I knew primarily as "O." When Housh signed a contract for the manuscript about his life with Anonymous with me as cowriter, to be delivered eight months later and published in a year, the *Daily Mail* instead reported that I'd just signed a book deal about my life with Anonymous, which was either out already or coming out at some point in the future and which at any rate I was currently promoting.

Further arrests and raids went down across Europe. One of my most active Project PM collaborators, a young Scandinavian who had spent time in the Skype channel with Topiary and myself, was raided by local police and charged with "harassment" under circumstances that were later found to be irregular and indeed illegal, though not before they'd gotten his data. Michael Hayden, director of the NSA, gave a speech in which he asserted that Anonymous would soon be capable of seizing control of U.S. power plants. A conference call between the FBI, Interpol, and several European police agencies—during which they discussed strategies in the upcoming court cases of arrested LulzSec affiliates and ongoing operations against the wider movement—was accessed by an Anon, recorded, and posted online to the palpable glee of reporters. An article in *The Huffington Post* announced that Aaron Barr had lost his new job; his boss was quoted explaining that Barr had spent much of his time pursuing Anonymous instead of working. This wasn't terribly surprising to those of us who had continually dealt with mysterious attacks and disinformation campaigns since February; years later, we would learn how much of this had in fact been state-sponsored.

The year 2011 ended as it began, with a sophisticated hack on a state-affiliated corporation that ostensibly dealt in straightforward security and analysis while secretly engaging in black ops campaigns against activists who'd proven troublesome to powerful clients. Just as with HBGary, I was informed of the hack on Stratfor before it was concluded so that I'd be ready to handle the aftermath. Along with five million emails, O, Sabu, and a few others had also taken customer credit card numbers, which O released to the public after using a few to make donations to the Red Cross. Several of us opposed that move for a variety of reasons that I put forth in a statement, immediately redistributed by WikiLeaks, asking that the press focus on the revelations to come—especially given what we'd uncovered from the last raid. I was also concerned that the initial plan, which was to dump all the emails into the public space without review, might cause additional problems, so I asked and received permission from Sabu and O to call Stratfor's execs and offer to redact anything that could potentially endanger their overseas informants. I made the proposal to one mid-level executive who said he'd relay it to the firm's president, but by the time I noticed that the fellow in question, Fred Burton, had called back, the hackers had already decided to provide everything to WikiLeaks, which could then release it all in a more systematic way. The first round of revelations demonstrated, among other things, that the FBI had been sharing its files on PETA with Coca-Cola through Stratfor. This "risk assessment" firm had also spied on activists in Bhopal for the benefit of Dow Chemical, lest their campaign to secure further reparations for those maimed or orphaned in the Union Carbide disaster prove too successful. The bulk of the contents would later be published by WikiLeaks.

On March 5, 2012, I received a communication from an unknown person telling me that the FBI was about to raid me. It was more specific than other messages I sometimes received along these lines, so I considered taking my laptop to a friend's for the night. Then my mom asked if I wanted to come and stay over at her house, something I did regularly; I decided this would be a good idea. The FBI rang the doorbell at her home the next morning at six thirty, explained that they'd just raided my apartment, and asked if I had any laptops I wanted to hand over. I declined. They left.

I started to hide my laptop but my mom took over, placing it in a kitchen cabinet on top of some pans. Meanwhile I started getting calls from *The New York Times* and CNN and the like asking me for comment on that morning's Fox News exclusive: several LulzSec hackers had been raided and/or arrested that morning, including O, who turned out to be an anarchist activist named Jeremy Hammond. Sabu—a certain Hector Monsegur from the projects of Manhattan—was revealed to have been turned by the FBI in June 2011, and had since been secretly working with them. Tellingly, the FBI hadn't mentioned to Fox that I'd been raided as well; it wasn't the sort of thing to which they wanted to bring attention.

Meanwhile, CNN had arranged to interview me about the incident over Skype, so I went to take a shower before I went on. Then an FBI agent came into the bathroom and told me to come out and get dressed. He led me downstairs to where my mom was sitting at a table under guard. Some two dozen agents searched the house for hours, taking everything electronic. Then they gave me a copy of the search warrant and left. My mom cried.

Brazenly enough, the warrant listed Endgame Systems, HBGary, Project PM, and Echelon2 as subjects for search. The Dallas district attorney told my lawyer I'd likely be facing some unspecified fraud charges and that my mom was facing a count of obstruction of justice due to the laptop's having been placed in an inconvenient location before any warrant had actually been served. I kept this latter threat under wraps at her request while working to bring as much attention as possible to what was happening, having recognized from Fox News' omission about my raid that the FBI's strategy was to avoid bringing any focus onto my own "investigation"—and that the only defense for my mother and me would be public outrage. I sent a copy of the search warrant to Michael Hastings, who ran it at *BuzzFeed*, his new employer. Then I bought another laptop with some of the remaining advance money from the Housh book deal, which would eventually be canceled. Project PM's investigations resumed; there was nowhere to go but forward.

Soon enough another hack, of a contracting outfit called Backtrace Security, which had been rumored to be working for HBGary over the last year, revealed what many of us had long suspected—that much of the harassment directed at myself, my volunteers, and journalists sympathetic to Anonymous was being directed by HBGary itself, and that at least one of those overseeing the campaign was meanwhile acting as a compensated FBI informant. One fellow who'd somehow found and then posted my unlisted address online and tagged it to the attention of the Zetas turned out to be an ex-military buddy of the HBGary executive Jim Butterworth, as Butterworth himself noted in one of the newly released emails. Others involved had posted my mom's address for the same purpose. I'd taken screenshots and made public note of all these things as they'd happened, but never managed to get any press to pay attention to what probably struck many orthodox journalists as amorphous internet drama. Nor could I have gone to the cops, even had I been so inclined; the FBI was in on it. My attempts to get other journalists interested never got any traction. Gradually it became clear that this was something I'd have to handle myself.

After returning to Dallas from another trip to New York to appear on a *Bloomberg Businessweek* panel on security (the one in which I was introduced as an expert on such matters), I decided to try to get off Suboxone again in preparation for my inevitable arrest and incarceration; I was aware that I'd probably be denied bond on whatever spurious nonsense the FBI would come up with, and I wanted to spare myself a prison drug withdrawal. While I was at it, I figured I'd also stop taking Paxil, the antidepressant with which I'd recently replaced the Zoloft I'd used to treat depression since early adolescence. As it turns out, sudden discontinuation of Paxil tends to bring on a manic state. Between that and the sudden influx of emotions that up until then had been kept at bay by opiates, I was constitutionally incapable of just waiting out the forces arrayed against me and against my mother. I was now, even more than usual, at the mercy of my own questionable impulses.

In early September 2012, I went on my porch with my laptop, set up the camera, and began talking. I spoke about the last year: about Themis, about the FBI, the DOJ, Booz Allen Hamilton, Palantir, HBGary, Endgame Systems. My plan was to force the issue—to explain from beginning to end what the FBI and HBGary had done, linking to the screenshots and emails I still had on hand, and doing all of it in such a way that there was no chance of being ignored. I announced that the feds were threatening my mother. And I made a threat of my own—that I'd do the same sorts of things to the lead agent on the case, Robert Smith, that Aaron Barr had been planning to do to activists, and that HBGary had since done to me.

Barr, I reminded viewers, had proudly exhibited to prospective Themis clients his ability and willingness to dig up dirt on activists' children using social networks, something that had been reported at the time. I summarized what could now be documented about efforts against myself, my supporters, and my family. "I know what's legal, because I know what's been done to me, and if it's legal when it's done to me it's going to be legal when it's done to fucking FBI Agent Robert Smith . . . so that's why Robert Smith's life is over. And when I say his life is over I don't say I'm going to go kill him, but I am going to ruin his life and look into his fucking kids, because Aaron Barr did the same thing, and he didn't get raided for it."

I also noted that the FBI itself had justified its odd decision not to make public its raid on me as a safety measure so that the Zetas wouldn't get access to my mother's address—an accidental acknowledgment, then, that HBGary's moves to reveal that very information had endangered my family, and that the FBI's failure to act on this meant that I existed outside the protection of the law. Here I added a legalistic flourish—since the FBI acknowledged the danger from the Zetas, and as it was known that Zetas sometimes conducted their raids in the guise of police, the feds wouldn't mind "if

I shoot any suspects." But I added that I intended to shoot any FBI agents who tried to raid me again anyway, as I considered their efforts to constitute a criminal conspiracy on behalf of private interests that had proven themselves to be above the law.

Satisfied that whatever happened now, I had at least made my case and done so in a manner that was unlikely to get lost in the day's news, I sat back to relax with my current live-in Anon groupie. That evening, as I presided over a Project PM video conference, I heard a rustling at the door; thinking it was a friend, I walked over with my forty-ounce beer in one hand and opened up. Then I was on the floor with someone's knee in my back, my arm bones pressing into my ribs, which were being forced inward into my organs. I screamed in pain. Someone in fatigues asked me where the modem was, then unplugged it. The girl cowered in the corner as men in black fatigues secured the apartment, weapons in hand. One of them stepped on my ankle and ground it into the floor. I looked up at him. He smiled.

NEMESIS

6

Another Hidden Country

Of the thousands of people who are indicted by the federal government each year, prosecutors win convictions against more than 95 percent of them. It's a number that's suspiciously evocative of reelection results in phony democracies, yielded through techniques that would be familiar to those living in them.

In many cases, the process begins with a secret grand jury, which, along with a magistrate judge, hears only from the FBI about a target that the FBI has decided to pursue. The result is akin to walking into a room full of people after your ex-girlfriend has spent half an hour telling everyone what a horrible person you are—except that your ex-girlfriend is also paid to do this, and in fact her career prospects are directly related to the extent that she's able to get everyone there to hate you. Naturally, the grand jury almost always indicts.

The defendant—as the target is now designated—isn't initially privy to the things the feds have been telling the grand jury about him, which doesn't matter in and of itself since the grand jury's role is complete. What does matter is that in many cases, the magistrate judge who will be ruling on all manner of life-and-death pretrial motions is the same one who's already heard the FBI accuse you of various things under circumstances in which they can freely lie not only without consequences but even without you or your defense team knowing what's been said. You may find out later on; in the meantime, you'll have to pick up clues from what the FBI is willing to say about you while you're sitting there, a lawyer at your side, and theoretically able to challenge their testimony at your initial court appearances.

The first such appearance is usually a bond hearing, where the FBI explains why the defendant must not be released before trial, but instead immediately subjected to punishment in the form of being remanded to a jail that is almost always worse than the prisons to which the guilty are eventually sent, and where he will be incapable of maintaining his life, his finances, and his family in good stead for however long it takes before he is sentenced—a period that can range from a few months to several years. The defendant can argue for immediate release on bond—through his lawyer, who may have been brought on to the case an hour prior and is thus usually somewhat less conversant with the relevant circumstances than are the FBI agents who could have been watching him for a year. All this, at any rate, was my situation.

Even so, getting out on bond might still be within reach for many defendants if it were not for one other aspect of the federal system that tends to surprise even those who were already skeptical of such institutions. This is the tendency of FBI agents to lie under oath even when the lies in question may be refuted by the public record, and the tendency of judges to nonetheless take these lies at face value even when they don't necessarily make a lot of sense even on their own merits.

Let's have a look, then, at the transcript of the September 14, 2012, bond hearing in the case of *United States v. Barrett Brown*.

Most of the proceedings centered on Special Agent Allyn Lynd, who took the stand and went about explaining the background to all this for the dubious benefit of Magistrate Judge Stickney. After some preliminaries, Lynd held court on the subject of doxing, the process of finding and making public information about people, which I'd vowed to do to Agent Robert Smith.

> LYND: In particular as far as the doxing goes, which their release of personal information, I saw numerous Tweets about doing that. It compared the production of the personal information called the doxing, which I know from my previous experience to be release of personal information. He also discusses at length in these—using it—doing to Agent Smith what was done to Aaron Barr, who was an executive with H.B. Gary, and basically they released his information and tried to ruin him financially and get him fired and other things like that.

If you've been following this book closely, you may realize that I did not threaten to do "to Agent Smith what was done to Aaron Barr," but rather to do to Agent Smith what Aaron Barr had been trying to do to others, including investigating their children and using any information gained as leverage. The exact quote was "because Aaron Barr did the same thing, and he didn't get raided for it." But it wouldn't do to talk much about Aaron Barr lest it be too obvious that I was mostly trying to make a point. At any rate, the point was lost; Lynd had managed to reverse it. Thus continued a process that had begun behind the scenes well over a year prior, with the first secret search warrant applications submitted to Judge Stickney—the FBI would make regular use of outright falsehoods of clear relevance to the charges themselves, most of which could be easily exposed as lies via the briefest review of the public record. These would be supplemented by literally dozens of smaller, less explicitly relevant lies, dishonest rewordings, and convenient omissions, nearly all of which could have been documented as false, and often intentionally so. In both cases, I could have refuted nearly everything were I simply given access to the documents in question and provided with an opportunity to present the results to the judge sitting twenty feet away from me.

Such an opportunity would not be forthcoming.

> LYND: I listened to some various recordings he had stored on his computer, whether it be a phone, contacted H.B. Gary officials and extorted them.

Obviously, no such thing ever occurred—and this accusation would eventually be discarded as too clearly false even for a court setting, given that the recordings did indeed exist and some of them were on YouTube. As would this one:

> LYND: He says he's going to kill Agent Smith . . .

. . . which would also be difficult to maintain in light of my statement, "And when I say his life is over I don't say I'm going to go kill him," followed by a threat to "ruin his life," which would be a lot of trouble to take over someone whom I was planning on murdering anyway. Anyway, the allegation that I'd threatened to actually kill him would vanish into the same baroque void as the SWAT business, to be replaced by the slightly less absurd idea that I intended to simply injure him and then take him to court. As would this:

> LYND: I also know from looking at some of the portions of his computer that when they do doxing it's in preparation for something called Swatting, which is where they try and obtain a false 911 call to the residence of an individual in order to endanger that individual. He has one discussion in there with other individuals, particularly an individual named Neal Rauhauser, about swatting other people in the past and getting even with them and things like that.

. . . which, again, would never be brought up again by the DOJ, being not only false but the exact opposite of the actual truth. Neal Rauhauser was one of the many strange characters I'd rubbed up against in the course of online activism—a political social media specialist with bizarre habits, such as the creation of sock puppets by which to manipulate others to mysterious ends. The California prosecutor and blogger Patrick Frey—the same one who'd once asked me to have Anonymous deal with a blogpost by an enemy of his—had suspected Rauhauser of involvement in an incident in which he himself was swatted. Afterward he'd asked me about the fellow, who he knew had hung around Project PM's IRC at one time before being banned, and who had also tried to present himself as involved in Anonymous; at Frey's request, I forwarded to him every email Neal had sent me mentioning Frey. Nonetheless, Frey seemed to suspect that I, too, was involved in whatever nonsensical feud the two were engaged in, despite having been friendlier with Frey than I ever was with Rauhauser, and despite having just sent him a half dozen instances of my personal correspondence with this person. Incidentally, the first time I ever saw a reference to "swatting" was when Jennifer Emick—a former Anon who'd gotten into some conflict with Gregg Housh and other veterans of the Scientology operation and who later worked as a compensated FBI informant while also going after me on behalf of HBGary—had written a public post claiming, among other things, "Rumor is, this little creep is trying to have me 'swatted.'" Since Lynd obviously found nothing that would indicate I'd ever done any such thing or expressed any interest in doing so, despite having all my laptops, phones, email accounts, and the entirety of my IRC chats for several years, I can only imagine it was Emick or Frey who gave him the idea, which he simply ran with as best he could.

Eventually Lynd came to the tale of my raid the previous evening, after which he and another agent had driven me to the county jail to await transfer to the federal building I was sitting in now, ribs and organs still injured.

> LYND: He also made all sorts of comments, admission about how he was actually guilty of the underlying offense which had caused the March search warrant.

This is especially cute since I would never be charged in connection to any of the subjects listed on that search warrant, as we'll see, and which listed HBGary, Endgame Systems, and the Echelon2.org website on which we compiled information about the crimes those particular entities had engaged in with a little help from various state agencies.

> LYND: He talked about how he had so much that the FBI had no choice but to come and do searches.

This is actually true.

> LYND: He talked about other members of Anonymous and where they were located, their true names. He blamed a lot of it on an individual named Sabu, who he then told us was Hector; I can't remember his last name. He is in New York in the projects. He went on at great length about it.

This, presumably, was intended to demonstrate to the judge my great personal familiarity with Anonymous hackers, and thus guilt by association. I suppose it worked, as the judge didn't seem to find it suspicious that an FBI agent who had just yesterday been told the full name of a wanted hacker involved with what he claims to be a dangerous international conspiracy would not have actually written down that name. Of course, what I really told Lynd was that it seemed as if Hector "Sabu" Monsegur, whom the FBI had bragged to Fox News about having turned last June, had ultimately been working for them, not us, when he oversaw the dozens of hacks against major firms, including Stratfor, that he'd been involved with from that point on, and that it was neat that he'd likely get less time than I would and that the FBI would somehow manage to pin the blame for stuff like Stratfor on people like me who couldn't have stopped the hack even if they'd wanted to. Lynd's implied ignorance as to the role of the most famous FBI informant in the country, who had been directly connected to his longtime target, may be confusing at first; later, the purpose of this bizarre gambit will become clear.

Lynd's testimony, like all testimony, came in the form of answers to questions—in this case from the prosecutor, Candina Heath, a strange little person whom I find it difficult to describe beyond that, but who will ultimately do a pretty good job of describing herself via the motions and transcripts we'll be meandering through as the narrative proceeds. But this will happen only gradually; for now, she is shadow; she is darkness.

> HEATH: Do you know whether he has traveled anywhere in the United States or overseas?
> LYND: He has.
> HEATH: And how do you know that?
> LYND: Both in postings and he told us about having lived in Tunisia before.

In fact, I had never been anywhere near Tunisia, though I had indeed lived briefly more than five thousand miles away, in Tanzania, a decade prior. This could indeed be honest confusion; at any rate the purpose is to illustrate that I am a "flight risk," one of two attributes that prosecutors seek to ascribe to defendants in order to deny them bond. The other quality is being a "threat to society," already well established via my fictional murder threats and extrapolated deployments of SWAT teams to the homes of my enemies, but still to be established further just for good measure. Tunisia, as you'll recall, was the country that several of us worked to assist in its aspirations toward democracy while we ourselves were being spied on by Aaron Barr for profit.

Later, we hear a bit more about my crazed obsession with HBGary Federal, the company that was spying on me, and then we are told, in whispered tones, of:

> LYND: Project PM, his hidden investigation into these alleged conspiracies.

. . . which, I'm afraid, was not as well hidden as it could have been, what with my accidental references to it in *The Guardian*, *Vanity Fair*, and *Der Spiegel*, plus, I believe, our website.

Eventually, the prosecutor and Lynd move from HBGary and death threats to Stratfor, the company the FBI had known to have been hacked for three weeks before I did.

> HEATH: And the Stratfor hack or compromise that was done of their system, that was done by members of Anonymous?
>
> LYND: It was, ma'am.
>
> HEATH: That was back in December of 2011; is that correct?

LYND: I don't remember the month but late 2011, yes, ma'am.

HEATH: And within a day or two Mr. Brown had that data, or some of that data on his computer and was actually making it public; is that correct?

LYND: I believe we had a portion of that data on his computer, yes, ma'am.

HEATH: And he was making it public?

LYND: Yes, ma'am.

Now it was our turn. The public defender I'd been appointed that morning, Doug Morris, had enough information from our brief time together to know a bit about what to ask Lynd so as to bring the subject back to Sabu and the FBI's oversight of the hack I was apparently to go down for.

MORRIS: And at some point you came in to an investigation of Mr. Brown being in one of these groups; is that right?

LYND: Not exactly, sir. Again, I'm not the agent investigating Mr. Brown as far as his involvement with Anonymous; I'm the agent investigating Mr. Brown as far as his threats against Agent Smith, so if I'm misstating something that's because of my lack of understanding of Agent Smith's investigation. But as I understand that investigation Mr. Brown has self-proclaimed himself to be a spokesman, so to speak, for Anonymous, and was also targeted from various other activities he had done, chats and other things he had done that made it appear from other agents' cases that he was involved in some of these specific criminal acts, such as the Stratfor—release of the

> Stratfor data, and that was where his investigation came in. It wasn't initially the whole group but it was acts directly attributable to Mr. Brown.

As would be revealed later, when earlier grand jury and secret search warrant documentation was provided during discovery, the investigation had actually preceded Stratfor by six months, and had begun after the HBGary affair. That the search warrant had not even listed Stratfor despite having been served five months after the hack had occurred was one of many clues that had already made this obvious, even if it didn't bother the judge. But my lawyer hoped to drill down on this issue, which was being presented as proof that I had probably committed a crime and thus might as well be placed in jail right away to save time.

> MORRIS: Okay. So it sounds like some attack, cyber-attack of Stratfor has occurred?

And then Judge Stickney shut down the questioning.

> THE COURT: It's all in the affidavit and when you have time to read it I think you'll be clear about all that but this Agent is testifying to more recent things.

If you happen to recall that it was the FBI agent and the prosecutor who had brought up Stratfor and spoken at length about my supposed crimes against the firm, along with things that had happened with HBGary some nine months prior to that and a trip I took to Tanzania or Tasmania or Tallahassee when I was seventeen, and that my lawyer simply wanted a chance for the defense to address these very same issues, then you're doing better than Judge Stickney. Remember how I said that you're "theoretically" allowed to contest the allegations against you? Yep.

Undeterred, Morris went on to try to get Lynd to admit that, contrary to some of his rhetoric on the stand, I'd never actually done anything violent. But Lynd had that covered:

> LYND: Well, sir, I disagree because he's having conversations on the computer regarding the swatting activity and I would consider that to be a violent activity.

. . . further confirmation, if any is needed, that the FBI considered its allegation that I had done any such thing to be central to its argument that I should spend the next several years in jail while I fought whatever charges to come. As noted, this claim evaporated thereafter, never to be spoken of again. It had served its purpose.

Lynd and Heath may have been concerned about the optics regarding my mother, whose threatened indictment had spurred me to vow to investigate Agent Smith and his family to begin with, and thus might make me a subject of some sympathy. And so the two of them made a point of explaining how clearly guilty she herself was of obstruction of justice. Sure, they hadn't actually seen her hide the laptop. But Lynd testified that, during a five-hour search of the house, they all just happened to have eyes on Mom when they came upon the kitchen cabinet where the laptop had been placed.

> LYND: We observed the mother as we got closer to that area getting very agitated and then she basically went into a fetal position as we found the computer.

Obviously, my mom did not "basically" get on her hands and knees and then press them against her body while lying on the floor. Or at least I don't think she did; when they found the laptop, while I sat watching from a few feet away, she was in another room.

If I have done my job adequately as a memoirist, and provided some sufficient sense of my vices and my virtues alike, the reader will by this point have some conception of what I felt, handcuffed and silenced, as I watched this agent of the state bear false witness against my mother, myself, and my cause, with the ultimate intention of destroying each. Everything else in my life—from birth to violent arrest through the entirety of my imprisonment—I have since recovered from. That particular morning is the sole exception. Even reading the transcript is difficult for me.

I was denied bond.

SAN ANTONIO, 2012 (Reuters)—

> A self-professed leader of the computer hacker group Anonymous was arrested by authorities in Dallas, officials said on Thursday.
>
> "He was arrested and brought in for booking about 11 p.m. last night," said Dallas County Sheriff's spokeswoman Carmen Castro.
>
> She didn't know why Barrett Brown, 31, was

> arrested, saying there was no offense listed on the booking sheet. Brown was turned over to the FBI, she said . . .
>
> He is best known for threatening to hack into the computers of the Zetas, one of Mexico's deadly drug trafficking cartels.
>
> Brown did not immediately return a message left on his cell phone on Thursday . . .
>
> In a monologue riddled with obscenities, Brown says he plans to "ruin" Smith's life, adding that the FBI has threatened his mother with arrest and posted pictures of his home on line.

This is where things stood upon my arrest—a wire service piece that would color local and nationwide press on my case, introducing the novel, garbled claim that I'm best known for something I never actually did and disseminating the "self-professed" phrasing that essentially presented me as a crank (seven years later the outlet made a correction). This was what I would have to build from if I was to survive this, and to make something out of it.

Despite the uncertainties and anxieties that come with being imprisoned without having actually been charged with anything (for I was being held on a criminal complaint; they had thirty days to indict me), I enjoyed the rhythm of jail life from the moment I arrived to my first real cell. Part of this was due to my ongoing manic state from going off the Paxil, which largely extinguished any concerns that might have otherwise plagued me about the future or even the present; that I couldn't climb into my top bunk bed without excruciating pain in my ribs and organs was of less import than getting my hands on a decent book. It was also partly attributable to the eight-milligram strips of Suboxone I started receiving from the nurse each morning, which, for the first few days, got me especially high after a month of taking a quarter of that while further minimizing the rib-and-organ issue. Thus I was well equipped to enjoy my initial few weeks of jail, just as Solzhenitsyn did under far worse conditions while nonetheless noting that jail is where the spirit soars. Why I happen to agree with him will become clear by and by.

Because the feds now arrest far more people than can be held in the federal government's own jail units, I'd been taken to the Mansfield Law Enforcement Center, a rundown facility that functioned mostly as a county lockup and now brought in huge amounts of money for the little town of Mansfield by hosting federal prisoners without actually providing them with the basic amenities that they're technically entitled to. These were jail units that had been intended to hold people for a few days while they awaited release on bail or transfer to state prisons. Whereas federal lockups give inmates their own cells that they share with no more than a couple of people, the setup at Mansfield provided for no privacy whatsoever. The din of two dozen men and a television ended only at night, and sometimes not even then.

Rather, most of the dozen or so individual units, or "ranges," were made up of a single "dayroom" with a TV, a shower stall, and several metal benches, with three large cells running off the room, divided from it only by clichéd black steel prison bars. Each cell contained four bunk beds along with a sink-and-toilet unit. Twenty-four men, most yet to be convicted of a crime, lived together in a space smaller than an average two-bedroom home. And they left this space only rarely, to go outside and walk on a strip of concrete for one hour each weekday (or each weekday on which we actually got our recreation time), or to be led by an officer to a family visit or lawyer meeting at the front of the building, or to be thrown in solitary confinement for some transgression. Theoretically, they were also entitled, as federal prisoners, to go to a little "law library" down the hall any day they requested. In reality, Mansfield lacked the staff to take anyone to the law library most days; and unlike libraries at actual federal lockups, these lacked the computers with searchable, perpetually updated databases of case law necessary to effectively relate one's own case to the thousands of others that might have come to define how it would be viewed within the esoteric construct of U.S. federal law. The physical volumes on hand were well out of date, and became more worthless each day as districts around the country introduced new precedents and obliterated others. (A few years later, I'd be held in a similar facility where there was no law library at all, contrary to U.S. law and basic decency.)

My fellow prisoners constituted a fairly typical cross section of federal defendants throughout the southwestern United States. Perhaps a third were Mexican nationals who'd been arrested on charges of reentry—coming back into the United States after having been deported. Of these, one always encounters a good portion who were brought to the country as infants, built a life here, got married, even had children of their own, but who are nonetheless regarded as Mexican citizens and are repeatedly thrown back into a nation with which they may be largely unfamiliar; some don't even speak Spanish.

The other large categories include mid-to-high-level drug dealers whose cases are federalized by virtue of being said to constitute a "conspiracy" (that all manner of comically peripheral figures may be roped into such charges has brought this legal instrument into disrepute even with some prosecutors); people with weapons charges (generally those with prior felonies who are thus barred from being around guns and then got caught with one); various assortments of fraud that the feds have deemed to impact interstate commerce (sometimes tenuously); bank robbers (banks are federally insured); relatives of someone who was the target of an investigation and who has also been indicted to put pressure on the original target, with those charges often being dropped once the target gives in and pleads guilty (most of these are females, who at Mansfield were kept in their own unit down the hall); and those facing child porn charges involving the internet. You'll also encounter American Indians, whose reservations are federal land that magically federalizes even minor crimes in accordance with the white man's magic.

We need not describe here any particular inmate I was with those first two months at Mansfield, nor otherwise begin our inquiry into the trials and tribulations of life in an American jail, for I was about to be moved anyway. First, though, I got my indictment. On October 3, 2012, I was charged on three counts: threatening a federal officer; conspiracy to make publicly available restricted personal information of an employee of the United States; and retaliation against a federal law enforcement officer.

The good news was that each of these charges was somewhat flimsy. The "make publicly available" count required that the defendant actually try to obtain information about the subject that was "restricted" so as to make it, well, publicly available. The conduct that the indictment listed consisted of me asking my live-in groupie to find information on Robert Smith over the internet, and her doing so. Later, when the feds fleshed out this accusation in further filings, they admitted that what she had performed was a Google search. Since anything Google yields is, by definition, publicly available, one couldn't *make* such information publicly available.

Both the threat count and the retaliation counts, meanwhile, required that the defendant threaten actual violence against the fed in question, whereas of course I really hadn't. The DOJ obviously realized this, which was why they not only removed the end of the key sentence involving me doing to Robert Smith what Aaron Barr had done to activists but also threw in a variety of entirely unrelated statements from weeks and months past, mostly from my Twitter account. Such as:

> Don't know how to shoot? You've got five years to learn. Maybe less.

. . . which I stand by, incidentally. Or:

> Have a plan to kill every government you meet.

. . . which is clearly a tweak on the moronic saying "Have a plan to kill everyone you meet." Or:

> Kids! Overthrow the U.S. government lol

. . . which the indictment noted was followed by a URL, though without noting that the URL went to a Blondie video on YouTube (yes, I'd been smoking weed). Or:

> Everyone in Anonymous with balls is either with us or awaiting trial. Don't wait. Retaliate.

. . . that final tag being, I think, a fine specimen of revolutionary phrase making that I'm proud to note I coined myself, and at any rate not indicative of violence, much less violence toward Robert Smith. Then, when they did manage to throw in a tweet that at least mentioned Smith, it was this:

> If what HBGary did to me was legal, it will be just as legal when I do some of it to #AgentRobertSmith

. . . which of course had the unfortunate aspect of reiterating that what was intended was not violence, since HBGary obviously didn't cut off my legs or anything of the sort. And the following—taken from my video address and following the portion where I narrate how one of the FBI agents who raided my mom's house referred to me in my presence as "the bad guy"—suffered from the same deficit:

> From now on I *am* a bad guy, and I'm going to prove that in the coming months, using the court system, using the media, using my group Project PM . . .

. . . which, in the context of the DOJ's broader argument, would presumably indicate that I was planning on shooting Robert Smith and then criticizing him on television, writing about him on my website, and taking him to court.

Finally, the DOJ found a quote in which actual murder was advocated. That I hadn't actually said it was secondary:

> On September 10, 2012, Barrett Lancaster Brown used his Twitter.com account BarrettBrownLOL, and re-posted the message "A dead man can't leak stuff . . . Illegally shoot the son of a bitch."

I did indeed repost this message—a quote from Bob Beckel, a Fox News commentator who had said this on air about Julian Assange, apparently without having drawn the attention of the FBI. When I saw this on the indictment, I assumed that it would be the most ham-fisted and dishonest gambit the DOJ would employ in my case—which I also thought was a shame, as certainly every attempt to misrepresent me that we could easily demonstrate to be a falsehood would make it plainer that the DOJ itself knew the actual facts weren't on its side. No judge could take any such prosecution seriously.

I was young and innocent then, accustomed to the relatively straightforward milieus of private espionage and postmodern digital insurgency.

A few weeks later I was transferred to Fort Worth Federal Correctional Institution's jail unit facility. This meant losing the small collection of books I'd received in the mail, along with anything else that wasn't legal papers or couldn't be misrepresented to benighted Mansfield jail staff as being legal papers, or concealed somewhere in the collapsing folder in which I carried my legal papers and pen-and-paper role-playing game booklets that Officer Rusk thinks are part of my arrest report. The move was due to my public defender's request that I be examined by court-appointed psychologists—like so many things, unavailable at Mansfield—so as to determine whether I was "competent to stand trial." The lawyer assured me that this was merely so that we could get someone to officially document that the things I'd said about the FBI were brought on in part by my attempt to get off opiates and the ceasing of the Paxil, though I could tell that he probably thought I was delusional, too, what with all the "factions of the intelligence community are retaliating against me for my work exposing its secret programs" stuff.

Whether he believed it or not didn't matter, since I'd be replacing him as soon as possible with a private attorney. But it was necessary that the public know. And whereas I wasn't yet in a position to ensure that this would happen, I had with me, among my indictment papers, criminal complaint papers, and fantasy games, a letter I'd received some days prior from a certain Kevin Gallagher—a programmer and occasional visitor to the Project PM IRC who was in a position to know exactly what was going on, and who was willing to run the inevitable propaganda and legal campaign from the outside.

Upon arriving at Fort Worth, I reported to the doctor in intake that I still had injuries that hadn't been looked at from the SWAT raid, and that I would also be going through opiate withdrawal, since the federal prisons, as opposed to U.S. Marshal–supervised lockups like Mansfield, didn't give out Suboxone. The next day I was escorted to the prison's medical facility—minus the books I'd just acquired from the jail bookshelf and all my other property, including legal papers—and placed in a locked room. Here I would spend the next several days, being fed through the door a couple of times a day and given dwindling doses of some mild barbiturate and ibuprofen by a nurse. Although I was glad they were treating my withdrawal with something, I wondered when I was due for the operation on my ribs that I was presumably being prepped for. None of the staff, including an assistant warden who came by one time on her weekly rounds, could explain what was going on or when I'd be released from this particular room; indeed, the assistant warden told me it was impossible that I'd simply been placed in this room without explanation and left there for six days. On the seventh day, a psychologist came by, opened the little door slot, and asked me a series of questions such as what day this was, what city I was in, and whether I could name the current president. I told her I could name all of the Roman emperors from Augustus to Septimius Severus.

"Listen to me," she interrupted. "I'm not your friend. I'm not here to have a conversation with you."

"Okay," I blurted, taken aback.

"I'm here to see if you're mentally capable of being released from here back into the jail unit. That's all."

I told her who the president was.

She turned, nodded to someone out of my view, and left. I was released an hour later. Upon arriving back at the jail unit, I was informed that there was no bed space right now.

I was placed in the Special Housing Unit for a couple of days until there was room for me.

Still under the weather from Suboxone withdrawal, and having been looked at by a BOP nurse who told me I probably had "contusions" that would heal in time, I began my career as an actual Bureau of Prisons inmate in a real Bureau of Prisons facility. And although this was still a jail unit and not an actual prison yard, one could still get glimpses of what those yards were like. For one thing, Fort Worth, like many such "federal correctional institutions," had both a jail unit and a prison yard, and although inmates from the two are prohibited from having any contact, the same pool of corrections officers is used to oversee each. And the physical setup of the unit is more or less the same as the individual housing units in most prisons, federal and state alike.

This near-universal structure, which in assorted slightly different incarnations will serve as the backdrop for much of our tale to follow, should be familiar to anyone who's watched television prison documentary programs. It consists of a single huge rectangular room with steel cell doors lining the first and second floor on both sides, with stairs and a walkway servicing the top tier, or "range" (a term that can refer to either the unit as a whole or the top or bottom portions). The officer assigned to the unit for one of three shifts—breakfast to dinner, dinner to evening lockdown, evening lockdown to breakfast—has a little "station" comprising either an elevated structure on the floor or an office with a window on one of the floors. There may be other offices connected to the range used by the case managers and counselors who minister to inmates; there will usually be a workout room, which may or may not have anything in it; and the five or six limited-use computers provided to each unit for inmates will be either in another little room or set up somewhere in the huge main room, which itself is invariably known as the dayroom and is taken up largely by steel tables and stools.

Within this setting, replicated thousands of times over across the whole of a faltering empire, millions of men and women have carried out a peculiar sort of life, one drastically limited by geography but quite rich in adventure, peril, and heartbreak, as if huge portions of these things had all been compressed into that small space.

I recall my first impressions of all this, viewed through the prism of the tales I'd picked up from veteran convicts at Mansfield. I'd been told that racial segregation was universal in prisons, and that although the races mingled at jail units, one would be ostracized and perhaps attacked for, say, sharing a cigarette with a Black guy on a real "yard." But depending on the prison, further divisions could exist within this self-established apartheid; the Blacks might all be expected to fight the Hispanics in a given context, but in other contexts they will fight among themselves in accordance with gang alignment. Elsewhere, division was by "car," a term that could refer to a number of things, as we'll see, but that here designates inmates hailing from a particular region. Thus at some prisons outside the state I would be aligned with the other Texans of all races and backgrounds against, I hoped, the Oklahomans.

The truth of all this was complicated by two factors. First, the prisons—particularly the federal prisons—were changing quickly as the focus of federal authorities changed, and as the world outside changed. Second, the sort of people who end up explaining these things, or anything, to anyone, are more likely than the general population to suffer from expert-itis, whereby a person—usually male—overestimates his own knowledge of a subject and proclaims broad principles that may not be principles at all. Thus it was that, although there are certainly prisons where all this racial and regional regimentation still exists—particularly among maximum and medium security facilities—there are also plenty where it doesn't.

But many of the inmates I watched in those first few days were previous offenders facing long sentences, and would thus more likely than not do much of their time in those places where the strictures of race, gang, and region did still very much apply. And so as I watched Blacks and whites work out together, and Tangos and Paisas play cards, and Californians and Texans share nachos, it occurred to me that jail units were like the lobbies of online games, where Red and Blue, Survivor and Infected, Axis and Ally chatted amicably in the moments before the round began and the killing started.

Free to fraternize for now, I made friends, and, better, acquaintances. There was the Vietnamese guy who seemed to be in on some sort of sex-trafficking charge related to a whorehouse he ran in the area, and who invited me to stay at his casino in Ho Chi Minh City if I were ever so inclined. There was the rather odd cellmate I had early on who claimed to have taken remote-viewing courses from one of the instructors who'd been mixed up with the CIA's foray into such things, who sometimes transmitted to me messages from my long-dead grandfather, and who'd had a bit part in one of the *Nightmare on Elm Street* films wherein he's sitting at a bar and turns around to look at a character who's just walked off-screen (as this would be literally impossible for a human being to make up, one must assume it to be true). There was the weird Black kid, known popularly as "Suicide" for having requested to be on suicide watch at some point and now very much intent on proving his toughness after this soft, white-ish aberration. There was Suicide's uncle, who was in on an entirely different case involving embezzling from a financial firm he'd been employed with and who wanted nothing to do with his obnoxious nephew (I shared cells with both of them at different times so I got to learn all the nuances). There was the nineteen-year-old white kid known as "Strawberry" for his slight build and red, close-shaved hair, who had robbed a bank for two hundred dollars. There was the relatively educated bearded man in on a gun charge in connection to a regional motorcycle gang, who claimed he was innocent and who gave me all sorts of advice on the law and prison procedure that turned out to be mostly worthless, and to whom I gifted my extra copy of *Decline and Fall of the Roman Empire*. There were the other members of the same motorcycle gang who explained to me that the old man was full of shit and totally modified that assault rifle for someone who turned out to be an FBI informant.

And there was the very tall and formidable-looking white fellow named Cody, who was the leader of various Aryan gangs that—despite being divided into different factions that sometimes went to war—were here assembled into a makeshift car for the duration of their jail stay. I first had occasion to meet this fellow when he approached me in the rec yard—acting in his capacity as de facto shot-caller for all the "good white dudes," by which is meant whites not under suspicion of snitching or pedophilia—and asked me what I was in on. I explained my history as best as I could.

"But you ain't messin' with no kids or nothing?"

I denied having any sexual interest in children and referred him to the news accounts that were still floating around the unit. Since these sometimes referred to me as a hacker, I would regularly be approached by other inmates requesting that I do various vague and improbable things with computers; on one occasion a guard asked me about acquiring documents that a possible acquaintance of mine had reportedly stolen from NASA on the subject of UFOs.

The amusing thing about Cody was that he'd been given as a cellmate a guy from South Carolina who was basically Truman Capote without the unpleasantness—small, pale, fey, and gay—and didn't seem to have objected to the presence of this "punk" insomuch as Capote, as we'll go ahead and call him, had not been found beaten to death on his first day. I asked Capote about this.

"He basically sees me as so bizarre that I'm essentially an alien," Capote explained, "so none of the rules apply to me."

The Aryans, having determined that I was not only a good white dude but also a celebrity inmate and a sort of leader in my own right, courted me from time to time on behalf of their individual groupings—here represented by the Aryan Brotherhood, the Aryan Brotherhood of Texas, the Aryan Circle, and the Order. One ABT even let me review an internal gang document, circulated among members at both state and federal prisons, laying out the group's policies. Some of this was prosaic stuff, including reminders that members are not obligated to give any of their commissary to another ABT. Much was said about some recent war between the ABT and either AC or AB (I forget which one) and how it had come about due to a misunderstanding that had since been resolved.

Strikingly, the document also proclaimed that ABT is not, in and of itself, a racist organization. This was technically true insomuch as its current charter did not expressly designate it as such, and as I would find, not every single member was particularly racist, even if the great majority definitely were. Naturally there are few progressive, left-wing gangs for whites to choose from, and membership in nonwhite gangs is usually inconceivable (with some exceptions, including the white friend of mine from Fort Worth who was an active Tango, complete with appropriate tattoos, and who seems to have won this status due to long-standing neighborhood and professional ties to other members; white Crips are more rare, it seems, but not altogether unheard of). There is some subset of white inmates who, cast into a maelstrom of historical racial violence, find white supremacy compelling. Others merely find it convenient, as other white inmates seem to join exclusively for practical purposes, or out of fear; in any case they will spend some large number of formative years submerged in the milieu of institutional race war. They train together, develop ties with one another, and instruct their recruits in matters ranging from ideology to tactics.

Thus it is that the federal and state governments have been inadvertently radicalizing huge and uncertain numbers of young white men for decades now, compressing them into spaces filled largely with violent criminals, and then returning them to society, now enmeshed in some neo-Nazi network or another and individually more dangerous than when they were first arrested for selling weed, or selling meth, or working at a clinic that committed Medicare fraud, or modifying a firearm, or failing to pay child support, or nothing at all. An American prison is many things, and among them is a Nazi training camp.

One afternoon, an Aryan came to my cell and provided me with a quick overview of the Norse runes he had tattooed on his abdomen, and how, properly chanted, they could evoke the presence of various entities. Then he demonstrated the chanting, which requires that one sort of vibrate one's larynx and stomach muscles or something (I have trouble with occult anatomy).

While he was doing this, my Tango cellie came in to let us know that a problem was transpiring with one of our white comrades. We stepped out onto the second-tier walkway and were debriefed by another guy as we watched developments below. A white kid had walked out of the little library/computer room and collided with some big rookie cop who promptly decided that this constituted an assault on an officer, and was now preparing to have him placed in the SHU. As an actual staff assault is punishable by up to five years in the hole as well as a significant increase in custody level points, which in turn decide whether one gets to go to a relatively carefree minimum security "camp" or a blood-drenched maximum security war zone, this was a significant development.

But most of the other whites were just sitting around watching rather than trying to help, and thus it was left to my Norse high priest associate and me to intervene. That was best accomplished, this wise Son of Odin explained to me, by making it clear to the authorities that to follow through with the dastardly plot would bring about a Ragnarök of inmate disorder, which itself would result, aside from anything else, in the staff having to lock down the unit for some number of days, during which they end up having to hand deliver meals, mail, and medication to fifty cells. And though ranking officers and the administration officially take the side of staff even when one of them is clearly at fault, in reality guards who make extra work for everyone else without a very good reason are likely to get passed up for promotion. They're also likely to get stabbed if they try that sort of thing at certain mediums and maximums, where lifers and those who don't care if they end up as lifers set the pace for staff behavior—and any one of the hundred inmates here could end up being that particular guy who missed a last-chance visit with his wife and child before being shipped to Wyoming simply because the guard who now works his range decided to start trouble in his jail unit four years ago. The guard won't recognize the convict; the convict will recognize him.

In order to make this somber narrative plain to the jail lieutenant and the handful of low-ranking officers who'd come in to appraise the situation, the high priest and I began agitating among those whites we identified as being possessed of sufficient civic virtue or racial solidarity to join us in our peacock display of potential riot. As each new berserker joined us, our ranks swelled until we comprised a sufficiently noticeable cohort, all standing on the top tier and staring at the cops. I was, at the time, even less of a physically menacing specimen than usual. But I was known to be a crazed anarchist revolutionary who may or may not be the leader of Anonymous and who may or may not have threatened to hack the Zetas and who would absolutely have no problem endangering himself and others to prove a point and at any rate would definitely brag about the whole thing in a book years later.

The guards uncuffed the kid and assigned him to a face-saving duty of wiping down the officer station with paper towels and Windex. My raven-flanked colleague went to his cell to chant a hymn of thanks to Freyja (I assume).

Still, the guards weren't that bad here. "Correctional officers," as they're known to nobody who's actually been in a prison, can be divided among several overlapping categories that are often readily identifiable. "Here's the deal: you don't bother me, and I won't bother you," announces the ten-year BOP veteran who's probably in the middle of a divorce and may or may not have just taken a Xanax and sold thirty others to an inmate, and who promptly disappears for the next eight hours. "Everyone be ready at ten fifteen for cell inspection," says the female officer with the crazy eyes, who may also volunteer to watch the rec yard in order to demand that inmates not take off their shirts in front of a "lady."

But the average officer is equal parts stickler and timekeeper, ignoring some rules (it would be impossible to enforce them all, or even to know them by heart; there are manuals and manuals of regulations) while going to extraordinary lengths to enforce others. Here at Fort Worth, we had a middle-aged Hispanic day officer who was most notable for bringing his little Dallas Cowboys lunch box in with him each day, and for otherwise ignoring everything around him. But one day he determined that the porcelain sink behind the officer station had been used by some inmate to wash his plastic bowl or some such in direct defiance of the little sign saying OFFICER USE ONLY and spent five minutes screaming for the perpetrator to identify himself. When this didn't happen, he declared that he would now call SIS—the BOP's Special Investigative Service—to review the camera feeds. Then he got on the phone, made his request to the acting SIS lieutenant that he personally review hours of footage so as to solve the Case of the Utilized Sink, and was apparently told to go fuck himself, because he hung up the phone and dropped the issue thereafter. And I continued my policy of using the officer sink to get hot water for coffee and to pour it back out when it got cold, just as I had a half hour prior. Yeah, that's right.

The only officer on hand who bears describing on grounds of blatant misconduct was a short, muscular Black guy named Soa who would do things like stop me in the food line and tell me that the collar on my jumpsuit was sticking up and needed to be pulled down immediately. One day, the inmate orderlies whose duties include cleaning the horrible old showers found that someone had defecated in one, and one of them made the mistake of informing Soa of this. This appears to have happened before, and is easily ascribable to the fact that this jail unit is home to some unknown number of mentally deranged inmates who've been sent over for psychiatric evaluation. Nonetheless, Soa summoned everyone to the dayroom to give a demented speech to the effect that he had been unaware that he was "baby sittin'," and that he was going to make sure the feces stayed in our shower "just so you can smell it." In fact, the orderlies had already disposed of the feces, because it was feces.

This was a rather telling incident. This longtime BOP officer clearly wasn't concerned about the consequences of threatening a hundred witnesses who were the actual victims of this incident with the prospect of having human feces kept in their shower area. I was vaguely aware that inmates could write some sort of official complaint about such things, but I quickly deduced that none of the veteran inmates were going to bother. Both the officers and the inmates seemed to implicitly agree that inmates had no real recourse in the face of due process violations.

Despite a few comparative drawbacks, I was hoping that I'd be staying at the Fort Worth jail unit, which had the inmate computers with makeshift email access, several shelves of books available for perusal throughout the day, an actual recreation yard rather than a concrete strip, and otherwise far more space in which to exist than did Mansfield, in addition to the functional law library that could mean the difference between participating in one's own defense and leaving it all to lawyers.

Alas, it was not to be. After my evaluation was completed and it was determined that I was indeed competent to stand trial, I was shipped back to Mansfield. I would remain there for a year.

7

Narcissus v. Leviathan

"They indicted you again," my mom said through the little phone receiver on the other side of the plexiglass. In her hands she held printouts of articles that had appeared in the past two days. She was smiling.

On December 24, 2012, when Jeremy Hammond began posting links, in the main AnonOps channel, to various files taken from the just-completed Stratfor hack, I'd copied and pasted one of those links into the Project PM IRC, where we'd been waiting for the firm's emails for days. Immediately after pasting the link and downloading the file itself, I asked Hammond about the contents, which I'd assumed to be the emails. It turned out to be a portion of the customer credit card data he'd used to make donations to the Red Cross and assorted other charities. Now I was facing eleven counts of aggravated identity theft merely for having copied and pasted a link, even though the transcript showed quite clearly that I wasn't aware at the time that the linked file contained credit card information. Each count carried a mandatory minimum of two years to be served consecutively, meaning I was facing twenty-two years for the link alone. Separately, I faced another ten years for having the document in question on my laptop (although as the government's own forensics people would later admit, I had never even opened the file). This was in addition to the several decades of prison time I already faced from the previous indictment.

I scanned the articles as my mom placed each one up against the glass. Then I smiled, too.

There had been a public case to be made against the government in the context of the threats charges. It wasn't an easy one to make, though, and despite the bits and pieces I'd thrown in so as to direct observers to crucial background information, few reporters were willing to take my points on their own merit regardless of what evidence I'd made available. One might hope the search warrant that had been sitting on *BuzzFeed* since March of that year, when my old colleague Michael Hastings published it in his article about the initial FBI raid, would have been sufficient to give the average professional journalist some sense of what this whole unusual affair was really about. After all, this was the first official, publicly available document regarding my case, written up by the FBI in its own words, and listing exactly what sorts of subjects were of such importance as to merit a predawn raid on a journalist's apartment and a subsequent search of his mother's home. That it didn't mention Stratfor at all, despite the hack on Stratfor having occurred four months prior to the warrant's filing, should have been a tip-off on its own; the FBI can hardly have claimed to be unaware of my involvement with that situation, given that the incident was orchestrated in part by its own full-time asset Hector "Sabu" Monsegur on a laptop that they'd provided him for the purpose—a fact that the agency itself had bragged about to Fox News and since expanded on in various other filings. Even a reporter unaware of these particular facts or of much else of what was already quite public by the time I was charged for the Stratfor copy-paste would hopefully find it unusual that an incident now claimed to be the centerpiece of and justification for a major federal investigation had until recently appeared to be of no interest whatsoever to the bureau.

There is some more perfect universe wherein someone in my situation wouldn't have had to conspire and connive with a few supporters and his soon-to-be-indicted mother in order to nudge the press in the right direction, back toward their own fucking articles, and also away from their own articles that were nonsense. There's an even more perfect one in which some substantial portion of those journalists knew the circumstances quite well and were even party to them, and to whom I'd happily provided background information on some of the very things I was now being prosecuted over in emails that would have done wonders for the public understanding of what was at stake even aside from my expendable self and my expendable mother. But I have been able to deduce from what transpired instead that we had been born into some less perfect world where we would have to conspire and connive, which is what I suspected to begin with. But now, at least, the argument I'd wanted to make on my own behalf, and indeed would have had to by default, was being made for me by the DOJ itself, which had just directed everyone's attention to the fact that I'd been involved in investigating illicit conduct by entities with ties to the federal government. Throw in the DOJ's accompanying over-prosecution for things that weren't even technically crimes, and any half-competent observer was now primed to realize what this was really all about.

And of all the noncrimes the DOJ could have picked in the absence of actual criminal conduct over the period in which I'd been subjected to an expansive investigation, they'd chosen something that was guaranteed to prompt a cross-ideological backlash among the sort of people who could make a backlash stick. In their effort to put me away, the government had tried to criminalize the act of linking. It was a precedent as bizarre as it was dangerous, with implications for anyone who used the internet, but especially for the very journalists and security researchers who would be commenting on my case. It was an opening, and I intended to seize it.

Kevin Gallagher and I had been in touch since our first correspondence after my arrest, and we'd already taken a few steps to bring the situation into focus. With this wonderful catalyst now in play, Kevin began coordinating media activities and fundraising in earnest. Both the legal defense and our propaganda offense would be run like any other Project PM operation.

My thirst for glory and hatred for the state were incompatible with an orthodox criminal defense, in which the limiting of one's sentence is the sole objective. Certainly I wanted to walk out of prison again relatively soon, but I wanted to do so in a stronger position, having publicly confounded my dastardly enemies against all odds, etc., while also damaging the federal government's moral stature in a manner that would perhaps leave some measurable impression on the more attentive segments of the public. So our strategy would center around getting me out of prison at a reasonably foreseeable point in the future without missing any propaganda opportunities along the way. This meant talking to the press about the case, itself a major departure from standard practice.

With all that having been decided, the public defender's office would indeed have to be cut off. Doug Morris himself was actually very competent—one of the few court-appointed attorneys that other inmates actually have nice things to say about—but he was also of a conventional bent. And the PD's elderly lead investigator who kept visiting me at Mansfield, Dan James, was something of a goon. "I met with some of your friends here in Dallas, and Barrett, they were *druggers*!" he told me one day, shaking his head sadly (I never managed to figure out who he was referring to; I had few friends in town, and none who would be described as such, nor did he ever give me any names). Another time he came to warn me that an article *The Guardian* had written about my case had angered the government and that a meeting I'd had with a lawyer I was thinking of hiring was a "mistake" because the angry government could force him to testify about our conversation. This is entirely false except in very rare circumstances, not applicable here, whereby a lawyer is reasonably suspected of being an accomplice to one's crime. I had no idea what James's agenda was and I didn't want to have to spend a lot of time trying to figure it out.

After all, a great deal of my bandwidth was already dedicated to trying to figure out the new judge. Though the magistrate, Stickney, would still preside over any procedural matters in the near future, I'd learned that the case itself would be going to Judge Sam Lindsay. From what I'd gathered from conversations with a couple of lawyers I'd met with, Lindsay was a notoriously dull bird. The most complimentary thing I would hear about him was that he was "careful" or "meticulous"; the broader assessment, which I would gradually come to share, was that he had some apparent difficulty when confronted with unfamiliar subjects and was thus especially susceptible to whatever disingenuous briefings he was provided with by prosecutors. As it turned out, he seemed somewhat adrift even on the fundamentals of criminal law—a quality that would work both for and against me as things proceeded.

Meanwhile, the prosecutor—the inimitable Candina Heath—conveyed to me through my public defender that if I wanted any sort of deal, I would have to cooperate with law enforcement. I refused. Shortly thereafter my mother was charged with obstruction of justice for hiding the laptop, and I was charged with the same thing for having, I suppose, not turned her in. I made sure that this was widely noted in the press; if the government could use my mom as a political football, then, by golly, so could I! (My mom was a good sport about this.)

Gallagher had set up an account on the crowd-funding site WePay to raise money for a private attorney. Heath thereafter filed a motion by which the five thousand dollars that had been raised from the public thus far would be seized and used to offset the government's expenses for the public defender that I didn't really want. The move astonished even veteran reporters and, thankfully, Magistrate Judge Stickney, who ruled in our favor this time, while still taking pains to assert in his written decision that the prosecutor's attempt to seize a legal fund that would eventually save taxpayers from having to pay for my defense at all was merely a good-faith attempt to save the taxpayers a portion of the money on my legal defense (years later, another, more competent federal judge would disagree with this obviously nonsensical assessment, but we are anticipating).

In January 2013, the information activist and early Reddit developer Aaron Swartz committed suicide. He'd been facing a possible twenty-year sentence for having used his MIT network account to make millions of publicly funded research papers available to the very public that had paid for them. This entirely unnecessary tragedy brought national attention to the DOJ's habit of pressuring defendants into pleading guilty to lesser crimes by threatening them with inappropriately lengthy sentences if they took the case to trial. It also prompted focus on its rabid pursuit of those involved in the transparency and information freedom movements; Swartz's assertive brand of advocacy had extended into other inconvenient areas, and indeed my sole interaction with him that I could recall at the time had been when he'd offered to do a Freedom of Information Act request on the entirety of the Pentagon's persona management programs.

Glenn Greenwald, who had by this time moved from *Salon* to *The Guardian*, had agreed to meet with Kevin Gallagher and another Boston-area Project PM volunteer, Lauren Pespisa, to talk about my case, and afterward arranged for a call with me. A few days afterward he wrote a piece pointing out the parallels between Swartz's situation and my own, providing an overview of Project PM's findings, and declaring in summary that "it is virtually impossible to conclude that the obscenely excessive prosecution he now faces is unrelated to that journalism and his related activism." Other articles in *The Nation*, *WhoWhatWhy*, and on the *New York Times* op-ed page summarized Project PM's findings, confirming their significance and thereby bringing into the mainstream the idea that my prosecution was retaliation for my efforts to illustrate the DOJ's own criminality.

Thanks in large part to Greenwald, who'd exhorted readers to contribute to my legal defense fund, we'd now raised enough money to demonstrate the viability of future fundraising. This allowed us to bring on Ahmed Ghappour, a University of Texas law professor with a national security background who'd lately been representing Guantánamo detainees (and the same one that the investigator Dan James had weirdly proclaimed I ought not to have met with lest he be forced to testify), and Charlie Swift, best known for arguing in front of the Supreme Court in *Hamdan v. Rumsfeld*. Both agreed that the case merited an aggressive press strategy, and that I should eventually resume writing as well. More articles began to appear; donations flowed in; documentaries and TV specials I'd been filmed for before my arrest now started airing.

Through it all, I settled comfortably into the traditional role of the imprisoned intellectual as pioneered by Boethius and exemplified by Solzhenitsyn. In Alexandre Dumas's *The Count of Monte Cristo*, the old Abbé tells newly imprisoned Edmond Dantès about the years he's spent locked away, developing his mind, practicing his language skills, writing a treatise on Italian unification using fish bones for quills and blood and wine for ink. Dantès wonders aloud how much else this sage would have accomplished had he been a free man; the Abbé retorts that he would have accomplished very little. This exchange had haunted me since childhood, from which time on I developed a theoretical fascination with the idea of the convict-monk.

Detached now from the endless concerns and addictive pleasures of mundane Western life, and separated even from the minor amenities of an actual federal prison for so long as I remained at the Mansfield jail, I was free to pursue an intensive reading program by which I would eventually take in some four hundred books, mostly history and biography. As a bonus, I managed to overcome the spiritual deficits that had at some point turned me into a horrible anarchist robot whereby I'd been unable to justify reading anything unless it could conceivably be used to win some future debate. The strong possibility that I'd end up doing at least a decade in prison convinced some neurotic, militant portion of my mind to surrender and accept the development of the "soul," or whatever, as a respectable pursuit, and one that at any rate time now permitted. (Incidentally, this supposedly puritan aversion to reading books without some practical objective never prevented me from playing computer games for days on end or smoking crack in the stairwells of housing projects; it only applied to reading.)

The door to an inner life now open to me, I did tai chi exercises in the early mornings before my fellow inmates had woken up; supplemented my reading with games of chess and reenactments of old matches taken from those big chess books that lunatics enjoy; studied the doctrines of sacred geometry; realized that sacred geometry was really complicated and that I should start with a review of regular geometry; studied regular geometry from a textbook until

I found my advancement stymied for lack of a compass, which a couple of inmates tried heroically to construct for me without success; and read Shakespeare, whom I'd rather crankishly denounced as a fraud from middle school on but now managed to enjoy under the circumstances. Later I learned from an old George Orwell essay that Tolstoy, too, had crankishly denounced Shakespeare, whose alleged greatness he depicted as merely a ruse concocted by the Germans; Orwell's theory was that Tolstoy subconsciously realized his own similarity, in the peripatetic and confused latter days of his own life, to King Lear, and revolted against the Bard out of spite. When someone sent me Evelyn Waugh novels, I read them instead of throwing them away, and indeed asked for more. When I came across the autobiography of the late-Renaissance goldsmith Benvenuto Cellini, I read that, too, despite it ostensibly being about art (and was pleasantly surprised to find that it was really more about Cellini getting into disputes with his customers and then stabbing them to death in alleyways). On our sometimes-daily expeditions out to the little strip of concrete, I let the sun drench me with its pagan rays and contemplated the perfection of the triangle, which I had now come to revere in my own vague, dilettantish way.

In addition to secular geometry and chess, I resumed studying Arabic, which I had taken during my brief time at the University of Texas, and which I had been particularly equipped for due to my basic knowledge of Swahili, a mixture of Arabic and Bantu. Watching through the window into the hallway as the mail cart came and spotting the book *Teach Yourself Arabic*, which I'd asked for a few days prior, is one of my fondest memories. After a few weeks of diligent practice with vocabulary flash cards, I came to an aspect of the language of which I'd been wholly ignorant—masculine plural nouns have an entirely different structure from singular ones. Crushed, I cast Arabic upon the imaginary pile of languages that need to get their shit together before I'm going to bother learning them, along with Russian and Chinese. Looking back, I can see how this might have been an overreaction.

I created. Some days I drew modern art in crayon on sheets of notebook paper, which I affixed to the wall by my bunk; eventually it occurred to me that none of the staff cared much about the windowless, graffiti-laden dungeon into which we'd been cast, and I covered the wall itself in golden triangles that I explained to the other inmates as being very sacred; above the doorway of our eight-man cell I inscribed the words *Let no one ignorant of geometry enter here.* I used a pizza box (acquired via one of Mansfield's unusual means of generating revenue from prisoners, which was allowing them to order out on weekdays) to make a board game based on the *Civilization* franchise, and devised a serviceable set of rules and colorful game pieces, although the game itself ultimately lacked balance (but then so does *Civilization VI*). I invented other games as well, including a one-player, randomly generated dungeon crawler whereby the sort of room one enters, the contents lying around, and the presence, attitude, attributes, and actions of any creatures one encounters are all determined by rolling dice and consulting numbered lists. The dice were made by soaking paper in warm soapy water, molding them into cubes using the edges of a metal bunk frame, and letting them harden until such time that they were ready to be marked with the horrible floppy pens that we received each week, consisting essentially of rubber inkwells, which we stiffened by wrapping them in labels from shampoo bottles and the like.

But the soul is a luxury, and one I could never bring myself to care about any more than I would ever aspire to a genuine romantic relationship. Armed with pencils with nothing to sharpen them and pens with nothing to recommend them, I resumed my life as a slightly less horrible anarchist robot, writing always with a view to improving my position and damaging that of the enemy—for the enemy had overextended itself, and the time was ripe for a charm offensive.

My strategy, fleshed out over several months, required that the original collection of generally clueless articles on my arrest be topped over with a layer of newer, better-informed pieces making explicit that the investigation was retaliation for all the great and wondrous things I'd done. Now that Kevin had started the chain reaction, articles I wrote from here on out—so long as they made some brief mention of me being locked up—would prompt readers to look up why I'd been arrested to begin with. Rather than learning from Reuters that I'm best known for threatening to hack the Zetas and for flying a massive Victorian hot-air balloon from Ceylon to Greenwich or whatever the fuck, they'd now be more likely to come across stuff about Project PM—and so would journalists. A new narrative would be composed, and it would become truth. That it was the actual truth was coincidence. That I could now leave the telling to others was essential.

And the new narrative would center around a new character. It's good to have been publicly wronged; it's better to have been publicly wronged on account of one's heroic acts; it's best to be charming. The public would not be won over with stern accounts of state criminality and institutional media failures. The public wants to be entertained. And unlike most wrongfully prosecuted political dissidents the world over, I just so happened to be an entertainer.

I started off with several comedic pieces for *Vice* in which I reviewed Chuck Colson's prison conversion saga *Born Again*, described the television-viewing habits of inmates, and expounded on the foibles of lyric censorship on the radio. Brave Barrett Brown, cracking jokes in the face of decades of prison time! Just a few months inside, I already had more material than I knew what to do with—enough, in fact, that I had the luxury of abandoning all but the most promising topics.

Then Edward Snowden went public, taking with him a vast trove of documents from the NSA and allied agencies in the United States and abroad and providing an unprecedented picture of how our spy agencies are operating. Suddenly I was seeing Glenn Greenwald on television, telling the world of the mass surveillance apparatus described among some of the hundreds of thousands of documents in hand. Illicit intelligence programs were now on the radar; Booz Allen Hamilton itself, for which Snowden had worked as a contractor, was suddenly in public view, at least in outline. Michael Hastings had me call him to discuss the new possibilities inherent to a post-Snowden world and, oddly enough, to recommend that I read Byron's *Don Juan*. Breaking from my all-comedy charm offensive, I wrote an I-told-you-so op-ed for *The Guardian* in which I summarized our prior investigations into HBGary and Endgame Systems and the like while also making gratuitous fun of Thomas

Friedman for having written an anti-Snowden column consisting largely of quotes from the creator of *The Wire*.

With the situation now well in hand, and having finally struck a balance between the casting off of earthly ambitions and the frantic acquisition of earthly influence, or maybe not, I was able to live jail life to full advantage. My mom had set up an Amazon wish list page, and the Free Barrett Brown organization, as Kevin's outfit was now called, made my mailing address highly visible to the public. And so in addition to the letters of support, which served mainly to impress other inmates with my importance, I was in the rare but pleasant position of receiving not only books on any subject I could think of but all sorts of random volumes sent in by the sort of people who send books to imprisoned causes célèbres, a demographic that runs rather jaggedly from the erudite to the insane. Officially, inmates here could possess only five books at a time. In reality, a jail administration can be worn down pretty quickly when they're legally obligated to deliver your mail, and when the process of determining how many books I've hidden among other inmates is an investigative nightmare. Soon they gave in, and with two four-foot-high stacks next to my bunk, I was running my own little library for the twenty to twenty-three men with whom I lived, spreading civilization to the savages like some early Catholic missionary among Germanic tribesmen.

In all seriousness, there were plenty in our enclave who were well equipped to enjoy my offerings. Successful drug dealers of the sort who end up in federal prisons tend to be especially intelligent. And there is a very keen strain of respect for learning among prison gangs, particular to the extent that the knowledge in question translates into actual power. The most popular nonreligious text in the U.S. prison system, as far as can be determined, is *The 48 Laws of Power* by Robert Greene, which is composed mostly of vignettes about various historical figures outwitting their opponents through amoral pragmatism and social manipulation. My bunkie, a very heavyset Tango Blaster in on a meth conspiracy, rather enjoyed *I, Claudius*, which he willingly followed up with *Claudius the God*. Thus it is that somewhere in the federal system, an oafish-looking and seemingly minor figure in a compound's Tango Blast assembly hides his strength and bides his time, waiting for the moment when some latter-day Caligula is jumped by his own captains, themselves now casting about for a seemingly malleable replacement. Or so I like to think.

By chance, the unit I was held in was unusually simpatico, made up largely of Mexican immigrants with a smattering of East African fraudsters and Vietnamese drug dealers. My closest associate, Danny, was a gay Hispanic guy from Laredo or some such place, a bit older than myself and locked up on one of the many complicated instances of fraud he carefully explained to me to no avail, with whom I usually got up early to drink coffee and watch CNN. Best of all, there were rarely any whites held with us, which saved me from all manner of racial social obligations.

The peace of our self-contained universe was occasionally broken. One day the staff brought in a large Black guy with a Cadillac symbol tattooed on his face who went by the name Cadillac, reasonably enough. Cadillac and his uncle had been in the business of robbing the little bank branches they have at Walmart, which I found to be heartbreakingly tacky, and he'd done time in a maximum, or USP, before being released only to be caught with a gun in his car thereafter. He'd been brought to our unit after getting in a dispute with one of his previous cellies, which was a bad sign. Another bad sign was the palpable air of malevolence, as Danny later described it, that forever emanated from his bunk, which was directly below mine. Whether any particular person was in danger was irrelevant; when one is in the presence of a truly wicked person, a portion of one's consciousness is forever taken up by the process of assessing the threat.

Not that Cadillac didn't provide a degree of entertainment as well. I have fond memories of him sitting down on Danny's bunk and having a heart-to-heart about his anger problems. Better yet was the afternoon when he repeatedly called up one of his bitches (for he was a pimp in addition to a robber of Walmart banks) and loudly denounced her for her alleged failure to consistently put money on his books; from his side of the conversation, we were able to determine that this woman had been taken to Taco Bell by some other guy, and that Cadillac's position was that she should have refused the offer of cheap tacos and instead had the guy send the two or three dollars at stake to Cadillac. We made a great meme out of this, trying to imagine how such a request could even be phrased.

Cadillac also expected the rest of us in the cell—which was essentially the non-Mexican cell—to take his side in a running dispute with the Mexicans, this time over control of the television. Naturally we declined—I myself would never take up arms against the Mexican people, even if the cause were just, which this was not—but Cadillac nonetheless pursued this grievance until one day when, after some especially unproductive exchange with the Mexicans (whose strategy here hinged largely on ignoring his menacing gestures and pretending not to understand what he was saying), he banged on the plexiglass window facing out into the corridor and announced to the staff that he was about to "smash one of these hos." So some guards came and told him to pack up his stuff to be moved, and he left our unit.

It would be difficult to describe the sense of relief that set in among the rest of us; prior to Cadillac's arrival, we twenty or so men had been living together almost as a family. The most important asset remaining to each of us was the cheerful and caring camaraderie that can be rare in prison but was here easily achieved by the absence of anyone you could really term a "criminal." It had taken only one person to disrupt all this, and to steal from us the sense of well-being and openness that had developed among us, and to an extent that it today occurs to me I've never experienced in any other situation.

Even better, we soon saw other guards running down the hall in the direction he'd been taken; later we learned that they were taking him to the hole, and that he'd made some spirited objection. A few weeks on, after having been moved to another unit, he tried to intimidate yet another inmate and was promptly beaten down.

In July 2013, when my new legal team entered a routine motion to push back the trial date a few months so that they'd have time to go over all the discovery, Heath took the highly unusual step of opposing this, claiming in a motion to dismiss that we'd had plenty of time to prepare already. My new lawyer, Ahmed Ghappour, responded by noting that the electronic discovery comprised two terabytes of data—the contents of several laptops and phones along with the entirety of my email accounts and text exchanges conducted over two years on IRC, among other things—which they'd only begun receiving from the public defender in June; meanwhile the trial was still set for just two months from now. The forensics expert the defense had retained wouldn't even be done with its initial analysis by that point. And the government, Ghappour added, had not initially provided such basic items as the seven search warrant applications it had applied for to monitor my communications (all of which had been approved, naturally) from early 2011 on, nor the transcript of the probable cause/detention hearings; several weeks after requesting all this, in fact, we'd still only received the warrants. Meanwhile, Ghappour noted, the novel legal aspects underpinning much of the government's case added another element of complexity that would have necessitated more time even if the relevant facts weren't scattered among terabytes of communications that the FBI had been able to comb over at its leisure for up to two years.

The government responded with a claim that the defense had had seven months to prepare, ignoring the fact that this was an entirely different defense team, which had taken over the case from the public defender's office just three months ago, and likewise neglecting to address the fact that we still didn't have access to the bulk of the discovery. Characteristically, Heath included a series of vague accusations of impropriety, which Ghappour dealt with handily in his next response:

> The government also argues that "the current defense team has not meet [*sic*] *in person* with the prosecution team to discuss the discovery, the cases, or the upcoming trials" . . . To the contrary, counsel for Mr. Brown has conferred, corresponded and had telephonic meetings with the government on numerous occasions regarding various case issues, including discovery and other pretrial issues. For instance, on June 25, 2013, counsel emailed the government indicating that he had received discovery from the FPD, that he had catalogued the files that were in an "accessible" format, and requested the search warrants and related affidavits in this case. Again, on July 1, 2013 counsel sent the government a discovery letter. As noted, the government did not reply to that letter until July 12, 2013, and did not produce the search warrants until July 15, 2013. Between July 15, 2013, and the filing date of the motion at issue, July 31, 2013, the defense has exchanged several emails and telephone calls with the government. Undersigned counsel welcomes the opportunity to meet government counsel in person and negotiate additional pre-trial issues, once discovery review is completed.

Rather than explain why they'd just made a series of demonstrably false claims about our access to discovery, outreach to the DOJ, and whether three months was in fact the same thing as seven months, the DOJ instead entered a motion for a gag order.

It was yet another bizarre move, one that would legally bar me, my defense team, and even Kevin Gallagher from publicly discussing the case (the latter on the grounds that he was acting as a journalist because he'd written an article about me for *The Daily Dot*; on the other hand, the DOJ would spend the next year or so arguing that I in turn was not a journalist despite having written for pretty much everything else, though at least one early FBI filing referred to me explicitly as a journalist). Central to Heath's motion was the allegation, never quite pinned down, that I'd made false statements to the press that could hurt the government's case. Worse, we were having an impact on public opinion and successfully bringing in donations: "Barrett Brown and his defense team have demonstrated a desire to encourage and manipulate media coverage to promote Brown's beliefs and his causes, and to enhance fund raising," Heath triumphantly explained.

But just as with the recent attempt to seize my legal fund in order to save the taxpayers negative two hundred thousand dollars, this new stratagem was couched in terms intended to put a noble face on the prosecutor's intentions:

> Perhaps without realizing the prejudicial effects on Brown, the media repeatedly has publicized potentially inadmissible and prejudicial information, such as Brown's (1) incarceration status, (2) anarchist idealology [*sic*], (3) three indictments and potential sentences, (4) admissions of conduct and involvement in Anonymous activities, (5) relationship to other Anonymous figures or hackers, (6) troubled childhood and alternative schooling, (7) declaration that he was an atheist, (8) use and abuse of ecstasy, acid,

> heroin, suboxine [*sic*], and marijuana, (9) lack of steady employment, (10) claimed diagnoses of ADHD and depression, (11) associates [*sic*] descriptions of Brown as a junkie, name fag, moral fag, court jester, (12) self-proclaimed and otherwise assigned titles with Anonymous (spokesperson, senior strategist), (13) receipt of data stolen through hacks conducted by other Anonymous members, (14) use of the stolen data to prank call individuals, publicize personal and confidential information, (15) associates and Brown opining that Brown would end up in jail, and (16) property seized by FBI.

There were times, throughout these years of adventure and turmoil, when something would happen and I knew right away how I'd eventually word my own take on things when it came time to write the story. But I've had four years now to try to figure out where to start explaining everything that's wrong with the above paragraph and all I can think to say is that a more civilized society than ours would have deployed a team of men with tranquilizer rifles to subdue whoever wrote it. So let's give first crack to Ghappour, who pointed out that some of this "potentially inadmissible and prejudicial information" had been "publicized" by the DOJ itself:

> The government has issued two press releases in this case. The government's first press release is an announcement of the 12-CR-317 Indictment. The government's second press release, issued on December 7, 2012, related to the 12-CR-413 Indictment and is titled "Dallas Man Associated With Anonymous

> Hacking Group Faces Additional Federal Charges." Notably, the Indictment does not allege hacking, nor does it allege association between Mr. Brown and Anonymous.

He also pointed out—because this is the sort of thing one is forever having to point out when dealing with this particular branch of the DOJ—that most of the public information they were complaining about didn't depend on our input but was instead based on existing sources, such as the dozens of previous articles, documentaries, and books that had addressed my life with Anonymous, as well as the large volume of TV appearances and interviews I'd done over the past few years; a gag order wouldn't prevent the coming onslaught of international coverage. He refrained from noting that this was of course perfectly obvious to the DOJ itself, which was simply trying to cut off the journalist they'd imprisoned from being able to communicate to the citizenry about what was being done to him and what it all meant.

For my part, I'll simply note that the DOJ's reference to the "property seized by FBI" concerns a tip I was giving out to reporters about the agency's list of evidence seized from my apartment after my arrest, which included a single book: a pocket-size copy of the Declaration of Independence. Presumably this had been taken in vague accordance with an FBI internal memo, made public a few years prior, in which possession of such things as copies of the U.S. Constitution were seriously cited as possible evidence of involvement in dangerous militias.

A hearing was ordered, and once again I was woken up early, snapped into leg-irons, and driven over to the federal courthouse in downtown Dallas to appear in court. I saw that the number of reporters in the galleries had notably increased since my competency hearing a few months back. Aside from being a good sign, it was also an ironic development in light of what the DOJ was claiming to try to accomplish; having already gathered all the allegedly damaging reporting on my case into a public motion that was of course immediately reported on, thereby increasing the number of prospective jurors who might very well learn that I had suffered from depression as an adolescent, the DOJ would now be discussing all of this in great detail while the press took notes.

Naturally Heath didn't really want to go into specifics on the various half-truths and irrelevancies she was allegedly protecting me from; instead she had Agent Robert Smith take the stand and provide an hour-long overview of every conversation with every journalist I'd spoken to over the phone since my arrest. Actually quoting from any of these phone calls wouldn't do; instead, the judge and reporters were treated to Smith's disingenuous summaries, most notably that Greenwald had told me that he planned to "exploit Aaron Swartz's death" in his article on my case. Had I felt any remorse, as opposed to embarrassment, for threatening to ruin Smith's life, and had it somehow outlived the indictment of my mother, it would have dissolved right then and there.

Later, Heath complained again about my article for *The Guardian*, which, as she noted, was "critical of the government." "The tone, too," she added, "is a problem."

This is about the point when Judge Lindsay should have shut down the hearing and dismissed the gag order motion with prejudice. Instead he called both sides to the bench for a whispered consultation. Ten minutes later my lawyers had agreed to a compromise version of the gag order whereby I'd still be able to write and talk to the press, but not about the case. The alternative would have been to let Lindsay make a ruling, trusting in his ability to discern how vastly crazed this whole affair had been.

The struggle continued. As the case hinged almost entirely upon my online activities as recorded in hundreds of gigabytes of discovery materials, my legal team put in repeated requests for me to be given access to a laptop by which I could search through all of this, as had long been common practice with computer-related cases; despite repeated assurances, I never got the laptop, and so would have to rely entirely on my understandably foggy memory when it came to requesting that my lawyers look for exonerating conversations and the like. In contrast, the FBI could dig through all this data for things to rip out of context at will. Meanwhile the prosecution sought a court order to force Echelon2.org's internet service provider to hand over log-in records to help establish the identities of the site's contributors; this move obviously made little sense in light of what the government claimed this case to be about—the identity theft I'd supposedly committed for no particular reason—but was of course entirely understandable in the context of what everyone other than Judge Lindsay knew this case to be about.

Having fired their warning shots, the feds met with my lawyers to make their second "final offer" (the first having been the original ultimatum requiring that I cooperate in exchange for any offer whatsoever). Their new position was that I could plea to just one of the eleven identify theft charges, plus interference with a search warrant and internet threats. If I did, I'd be facing just a few years in prison rather than several decades. I instructed my lawyers to reject it; I'd never sign to anything involving fraud, which I consider an actual moral crime and one that could conceivably be used to discredit me, nor would I help the government establish a precedent whereby others could be held criminally liable simply for linking to content.

Statements of support now came in from Noam Chomsky, Pussy Riot, John Cusack, Birgitta Jónsdóttir, and members of foreign parliaments. Julian Assange mentioned me in a speech from the steps of the Ecuadorean embassy in London, where he'd been holed up to avoid being arrested by the British police and presumably shipped off to the United States on whatever secret indictments had been prepared against him. The documentaries on Anonymous for which I'd been interviewed were released, most notably *We Are Legion* and *The Hacker Wars*, both of which would become staples of Netflix. Reporters Without Borders announced that the United States had plummeted in press freedom rankings largely as a result of my prosecution, and other NGOs followed suit with similar statements. The guitarist for Jane's Addiction auctioned off one of his Stratocasters for my defense fund. The *New York Times* media columnist David Carr came out with a piece sanctifying the DOJ-is-illicitly-persecuting-Barrett-Brown narrative. Each new printout my mom mailed to me added palpably to my well-being.

Through it all, the rhythm of jail life proceeded apace, varying only with the new arrivals who filtered in to the tune of two or three a month. Many of these were ex-cons who had been released to a halfway house, or home itself, only to flunk a drug test or otherwise violate the terms of their probation. The most memorable of these violators to arrive in our tank was a fellow called, for no reason I could determine, Byrdman. Byrdman was quite visibly Aryan Brotherhood or Aryan Circle or Aryan Brotherhood of Texas, or whatever; aside from a rather prominent neck swastika, he also sported a mural of Hitler across his back, along with some text that I can't recall today but that I imagine had something to do with Hitler being good, if not really great. Like some other prison Nazis I'd encounter over the following years, Byrdman actually seemed to enjoy the company of other races, and indeed spent much of his time talking to the Kenyan; from various remarks he made over the course of the next day, it was clear that Byrd believed this African, like all Africans, to be a prolific hunter of wild game—something of a tribal warrior archetype, then, like the Aryan conquerors of yore, and thus a fine fellow in his own way.

Byrdman had done some seventeen years in federal prison before being released to a halfway house, from which he'd been able to conduct expeditions into the greater world. He told us of a trip he'd made to Walmart, where he described being overwhelmed by the sheer variety of goods on display after much of a lifetime spent shopping via checking off boxes on a commissary slip. We were all impressed with the story, which the Kenyan later recalled as "very poignant."

That evening Byrdman revealed to me that he'd managed to sneak in some drugs by stuffing them in a little plastic bag up his ass before the marshals brought him in.

So he, an El Salvadoran drug dealer, and I all "parachuted" some crystal meth, which entails wrapping a portion in tissue and swallowing it, as there was no privacy in which to snort it, and Byrdman possessed the caution of the veteran convict. I spent the next few hours pacing around the unit with a cup of coffee, thinking fondly upon the accelerating success of our propaganda war.

After lights out, we smoked a joint rolled in a page torn from the Bible. Our cell was lit by dim dayroom light that made shadows of the iron bars keeping us in, shadows cast over the Kenyan as we played chess on the concrete floor, and on the El Salvadoran snoring in the corner. The metal, the concrete, the darkness, and the stillness together impressed upon my consciousness something that the whole of the last year had failed to do; only then did it occur to me how sharp were the edges of our civilization.

8

Conclave

I'd built a life for myself, for the first time, both as a prisoner and as a human being. Even at the height of my strange successes over the past couple of years, my position had never really been secure; things had moved too quickly, and jaggedly, for there to be any certainty as to what I would be when things settled down. Now the current narrative was too well established to be easily disrupted. I was a figure, and a figure I would remain. Still, not everything had quite fallen into place, and if certain key aspects were to land correctly I would have to give them a nudge myself.

In a lucky break, I'd been shipped over to Seagoville, a real federal facility like Fort Worth, and in the past months my standard of living had risen dramatically as I enjoyed real outdoor recreation, a vastly expanded pool of acquaintances, better food, and access to the federal inmate email system. This last item was especially helpful now that I was writing regularly again. Tim Rogers, the editor of *D*, Dallas's upscale city monthly, had sent me a letter asking why I was writing for *Vice* and not for them. Having no good answer, I conceived of a regular column called The Barrett Brown Review of Arts and Letters and Jail. In the first edition, "The Poetry of William Blake," I managed to attack Harold Bloom, the U.S. prison system's treatment of the mentally ill, an early-nineties airport novel called *White Ninja*, and the television-viewing habits of white inmates—all through the device of comparing William Blake's incoherent poetic imagery to things we'd overheard from this one bank robber who'd gone permanently nuts after shooting himself up with PCP, an incident that served as a fine segue into the prison system's treatment of the mentally ill.

The resulting column was better received than most anything I'd done prior. And though this was due in some part to the baseline of goodwill one receives when proceeding cheerfully through trying circumstances, the work itself was indeed unusually good and improved over time, thus spurring fundraising and contempt for the state institutions that had persecuted such a charming fellow as myself. But its actual purpose was not to help me get out of prison; rather it was to ensure that the years I spent there would ultimately matter.

The nice thing about being under a gag order was not having to regularly decide between letting some major instance of libel go unchallenged on the one hand—and thereby allowing my credibility to be diminished, and along with it my ability to bring real attention to serious issues in the future—and suffering the vague damage to one's reputation that comes with publicly correcting such things, on the other. It was no longer up to me. Still, I could offset the damage indirectly by taking back control of the narrative. Many knew me largely through the lens of a histrionic YouTube video in which I'd appeared ridiculous, ham-fisted—not so much whistling in the dark as threatening the shadows. And with my actual deficits now having been supplemented in the public eye by a range of made-up incidents and garbled misinterpretations on the part of the press and the DOJ, I would have to present a persona that was charmingly self-deprecating, winkingly narcissistic, comprehensively self-aware—and even candid, in a transparently calculating fashion. If this were to be accomplished to any measurable degree via my new column, the column itself would have to be not only of extraordinary quality but also consistently entertaining, so that it would spread.

This would all be made easier via certain advantages I enjoyed. Being in prison makes it easier to write well; many people believe the opposite, and thus are more easily impressed with anything written under such circumstances; but an inmate, being oppressed, is given wide berth to be "insensitive" or sardonic in ways that allow for more resonant and meaningful humor that would normally catch flak from the sort of person who doesn't really understand the nature of humor; and, by order of the court, I wasn't allowed to harangue people about HBGary, persona management, Romas/COIN, black propaganda operations, or anything else that could be said to relate to my case, which is to say that I was essentially forbidden by law from writing boring think pieces that no one would read anyway.

Oddly liberated by these constraints, and blessed with an editor who smiled upon the longer, more clause-ridden sentences that so many others of his ilk had generally insisted on cutting up and otherwise ruining out of sheer incompetence, I was suddenly free to develop my personal prose style—aristocratic and violent. Over the next couple of years, I went after everyone and everything: Gerald Ford; Axl Rose; ill-conceived prison tattoos; a white prison gang called the Woods; Henry Kissinger; Jonathan Franzen; Lyndon LaRouche; Hegel; Gaddhafi's *Green Book*; the Commission on Accreditation for Corrections; *Time* magazine; the fourteenth-century Islamic historian Ibn-Khaldūn, who thought Alexander the Great dealt with sea monsters that were preventing the construction of Alexandria by diving into the water, drawing sketches of them, and then building statues of same so as to scare them away; Joel Osteen; George Bernard Shaw; Goethe's dad; St. Augustine; a self-avowed Rosicrucian master who wrote a book about time; the New International translation of the New Testament; Thomas Jefferson; Lyndon B. Johnson; Type O Negative; Dennis Hastert; this one guard who forbade us to walk around the upper tier counterclockwise; the Symbionese Liberation Army; some woman Aleister Crowley married in the twenties and who once asked her parents for money for an abortion but really just wanted to buy new clothes; the Discovery Channel; Tom Hanks; my mom's practice of poking my pimples in front of the other inmates during visits; my dad's insistence on relating to me plot developments from a television show called *The Blacklist* whenever I called; Oklahoma; a cellmate of mine known to the press as the "Lunch Money Bandit" because he always robbed banks around noonish, and who spent half an hour trying to convince me that Magic Johnson had only pretended to have HIV in support of a CIA plot, the motive of which escapes me.

Anything put to print could be rendered grist for my mill of self-insistent literary animosity, including signs written and hung up on the walls by Bureau of Prisons officials. I'm never really happy unless I'm mulling over the sort of demented and quasi-literate nonsense that the typical twenty-first-century mid-level state functionary puts out when called upon to try to write something, which was why I was so thrilled by the NSA document leaks. Here at FCI Fort Worth, I had got my work cut out for me. Some examples follow. I'll provide commentary where appropriate, but keep your eye out for such characteristic features as unwarranted belligerence, vague thrusts in the direction of accepted English grammar, and the use of overly formal terminology in the midst of sentences that are themselves broken beyond reasonable hope of repair.

> Beds are to be made military style, blankets tight on top with a 6" collar. A photo of a properly made bed is posted on the bulletin board. Classes will be given by the unit counselor on an as-needed basis one pillow per bed.

Even setting aside the idea, so inherently totalitarian as to actually be kind of charming, that anyone ought to be required to fold one's bedsheets within an inch-based margin of error, as if one were building the Ark of the Covenant and not simply arranging linen, and that this rule is so utterly necessary that a course of instruction should be made available to ensure compliance, and also setting aside the question of where the prison keeps the cryogenically frozen Nazi storm trooper who is presumably thawed out now and again to help the unit counselor teach such a class, I really like how the author of this deranged microtreatise believes that, if a somewhat related sentence fragment happens to pop into his fevered little head, such as something to do with federal pillow quotas, it would be entirely appropriate to just throw it in at the end of whatever sentence he happens to be writing at the moment.

Here's another one that begins reasonably enough by noting that one may check out clothing irons and related accessories by exchanging one's ID card for them at an officer station, and then promptly descends into poorly phrased madness:

> Any of the above-noted items that are found in possession of an inmate without an ID card checked out, will be confiscated and subject to disciplinary procedures.

As an actual American citizen who has spent a total of two months in the hole, I'd hate to see how the BOP goes about punishing a mere iron. Note also the flailing attempt to express the really very simple concept of "items that have not been properly checked out with one's ID card."

> Prior to releasing, turn your chair into staff.

Well, I'm not much of a craftsman, but I'll give it a go.

> There are no unauthorized hooks behind the door or on the walls and they must be removed immediately.

The English language provides countless ways by which one might properly convey the intended idea here, yet this subhuman somehow manages to choose one that fails on its own terms.

The situation was advantageous in other ways as well. Familiarity breeds contempt, while by being absent altogether one risks being forgotten. Having my output limited to painstakingly crafted monthly missives and nothing else constituted the perfect balance by which to develop a more dignified public presence—and, as it turned out, one more capable of appealing to mutually exclusive political groupings.

"You're a cipher," my mother told me during one of her regular trips to Seagoville; in contrast to our daily phone calls, we could speak together in the visiting room without having our conversations monitored and used against us by disingenuous FBI agents. As the DOJ had taken pains to note in the gag order filing, Mom spent a great deal of her time monitoring coverage of my case, up to and including what people wrote on social media, and this intelligence work had expanded to cover the great mass of Twitter commentary that was now appearing in response to my columns, and to my case itself, which became more widely known as new readers sought to figure out why this amusing writer was in prison to begin with. And what had struck her most was the extent to which my new fans had decided that I was a libertarian, a Marxist, a mainstream Democrat, a doctrinaire progressive, even a Republican.

By accident, I now enjoyed the boost to one's potential

fortunes that is typically limited to generals in wartime—the exceedingly rare advantage of being separated from day-to-day politics back home. Just as Napoleon could avoid the perils of revolutionary Paris, and just as Eisenhower was cheerfully obligated by military protocol to absent himself from contentious domestic debates, I was entirely removed from the activist disputes that I would have otherwise been expected to weigh in on, and which tend to have the ultimate effect of alienating more allies than one gains. A longtime U.S. senator creates a paper trail of yeas, nays, and abstentions that may be productively mined by the opposition, fairly or otherwise. In contrast, the returning general is a relatively blank slate onto which each citizen tends to project his or her own views—not altogether without reason, given that Eisenhower, for instance, seriously considered both major political parties before deciding on the Republicans.

And in my case, even a fairly honest person with no particular need to believe that anyone they regard as intelligent and heroic must necessarily share their most fundamental beliefs could be forgiven for thinking I was on their side (especially given the strange new political alliances that were already popping up across the English-speaking world, itself one of the new phenomena of which I would remain happily ignorant for some time to come). There was something in my case for every political persuasion; conservatives made much of the fact that all of this had occurred under Obama and the Holder DOJ, whereas any Democrats willing to overlook this particular detail could frame everything as overreach by the security state set up in large part by the latest Bush.

I knew this couldn't last. Upon my release, I would have to start weighing in again; my agent had already started getting inquiries from publishers just a year after my arrest, and anyway I couldn't carry out my larger plans without defining my views in ways that would alienate many of my new fans. What I didn't know, in those last few years of relative normalcy, was how bad things would really be by the time I got out, and how many of my closest allies would become my most despised enemies.

For now, though, at the peak of my talents and public admiration, I felt happy and secure in the Seagoville jail unit. And aside from the occasional swipes I took at the prison administration in the course of the column, I was content to stay out of trouble. But this turned out not to be possible.

I was in the shower one morning when I heard a voice, pregnant with malice, shout my name from the dayroom. I responded that I would be out momentarily. The voice insisted.

Wrapped in a towel, I came out to find two members of the BOP's Special Investigative Services. One of them, a certain Osvaldo Arellano (whose full name, as with all staff officers, is not supposed to be known to inmates, but then inmates aren't generally supposed to be journalists), had in one hand an envelope of the sort my mom sent me every week, and in the other a printout of a photo, posted on Twitter, of the "Anonymous lawyers" Jay Leiderman and Tor Ekeland standing in a parking lot with a prison fence in the background.

"What the fuck is this?" Arellano asked me.

"It looks like a photograph. My mom sent it."

"So why'd your mom send it?"

"You'd have to ask my mom."

"I don't know your fucking mom. I'm asking you."

"My mom sends me printouts of articles, and, like, coverage of my case. These are two lawyers who came to visit me a few weeks ago along with *Vice*, which was trying to get in to interview me. So she seems to have printed it out along with everything else and sent it."

"You know this counts as an escape accessory? You could use this to plan an escape," Arellano declared, referring to the photo of the same prison fence that I could see outside the window of my cell. "I can throw you in the hole right now for this." Instead he cursed me again and left with the other SIS, who was laughing.

It occurred to me that there is no alternative to conflict.

The opportunity came quickly. The most malevolent of the guards assigned to our jail unit, a certain Hamilton, had made a habit of engaging in threatening behavior toward random inmates, including myself. One day, Earthman—the current speaker for the whites—called a meeting in the little church room that doubled as a more or less official parliamentary chamber for the various gangs. He told us that the elderly man who'd been brought in from California on charges that his legal weed-growing operation had violated some interstate rule or another, and who was well-liked across the unit, had the day before sent an email to his wife asking for several books, including one on astronomy authored by another fellow with the name of Hamilton. Our Hamilton—having apparently gotten into the habit of searching inmate emails for his own name, and seemingly believing the use of it here to be some sort of code—threatened to "put paper on" him (a term referring to the insertion of unspecified negative material into an inmate's BOP file) and pursue other such esoteric measures if he ever mentioned his name—or the name of the coauthor of the Federalist Papers—again.

Upon discussion, it was decided that we would ask for a lieutenant on the following day, before Hamilton arrived for the evening shift, and that we would refuse to enter our cells at lockdown unless we were given some plausible assurance that the matter would be addressed. The meeting was adjourned.

Things went awry when one of our number went to ask Hamilton for his mail, which had apparently been given out during our Caucasian congress. Asked why he hadn't gotten it earlier, the inmate replied that he'd been in a meeting. Hamilton declared that no meetings were allowed without his permission (in fact, the jail staff at Seagoville and many institutions not only allow the races and gangs to meet regularly but insist that they do so and that they elect a speaker; this provides a framework whereby interracial or gang disputes can be dealt with formally, rather than via the mechanism of the riot). Hamilton thereafter either guessed or was told that the meeting had been about him, and took to the intercom to call for us to lock down immediately.

Deducing that Hamilton intended to take the old man to the SHU, we made an impromptu decision to move up our scheduled demonstration to right that second. The Paisas, God bless 'em, agreed to join us, and soon we had some thirty inmates out of the hundred or so housed in the unit standing pat in the dayroom as Hamilton came down the stairs, his face menacing. Arellano and a couple of other staff arrived just then, having apparently been summoned by Hamilton. This was the rank we'd wanted on hand to deliver our grievance, but as Earthman began providing them with an account of events, Hamilton pulled out his mace and started shaking it up in an effort to escalate things. Arellano approached Earthman as if to grab him, changed his mind, and told Earthman to come over to him instead. Earthman declined the invitation. Arellano told us all to return to our cells. We refused.

Ten minutes into the standoff, with the guards mostly just hanging around and one staffer holding a camcorder on us to document who was involved, the prison brought in a middle-aged female officer with matronly hips and indeed a big matronly pelvis. Officer Probably Somebody's Mom walked up, looked up and down the line of outlaw inmates, and declared, with preternatural authority:

"Well, I think you all better go ahead and get up against the wall and put your hands behind your backs!"

Over the course of several confused seconds, looking to one another for cues and finding nothing that might rally us to further defiance, we all indeed went ahead and got up against the wall and put our hands behind our backs. Then we were handcuffed, lined up, made to recite our names and inmate numbers for the camera, and separated into two groups, the larger of which was taken into the little transfer unit right across the hall. The smaller group—shot-callers for the Paisas and whites, plus the old man, myself, and a couple of others who'd been deemed "leaders"—was marched across the yard to the SHU.

And there I remained for a relatively calm couple of

weeks until that day—lovingly described in medias res at the opening of this book—when my Saracen cellmate D declared jihad on our captors.

What happened next would be commemorated in an upcoming column titled "We'll Take the Hole SHU-Bang":

> As D stood there flushing the toilet over and over again, wondering aloud how long he could fill up our cell with water before a guard happened to come by and get wise to what he was up to, I found myself facing an antediluvian dilemma of my own. I knew that if matters escalated past a certain point, the prison's in-house SWAT team would be sent in to subdue us, but first a video camera would be set up on a tripod opposite the door to record the proceedings so as to discourage the cops from beating us up too badly in the process, as is the custom among cops. I figured the resulting video would be pretty hilarious if, while they're storming into our tiny flooded cell and D is fighting them off and yelling, "Allahu Akbar!" or whatever, I would just be sitting up there in my bunk reading the most thematically inappropriate possible book for the occasion, preferably something very erudite or sentimental or both.
>
> The problem was that I couldn't decide on a book. If I'd still had the little personal library I'd managed to store up back in the jail unit, I would obviously have picked *Brideshead Revisited*, with a volume of memoirs by Malcolm Muggeridge coming in a strong

second. Here in the hole, though, my choices were more limited. Although the hardbound collection of works by Thoreau that someone had sent me the previous week would work in a pinch, for some reason it just didn't tickle my funny bone. I also had a copy of *Do Androids Dream of Electric Sheep?*, but then the only thing funny about Philip K. Dick is how awesome he is; in fact, I reflected, one could make a strong case that Philip K. Dick is so awesome that it's not even funny. This led me to reflect in turn on the injustice of a world in which someone like Philip K. Dick can spend much of his life broke and having to borrow money from Robert Heinlein while someone like Orson Scott Card can make a real success of himself, whereas in a more perfect world Philip K. Dick would have been living it up in a gold-plated space station while Orson Scott Card starved to death in a gutter. Then I got back to the task at hand, considering and rejecting several more titles, including *The Decline and Fall of the Roman Empire*, which I dismissed as too apropos.

Finally, I settled on William Shirer's *The Collapse of the Third Republic*, which charts that ill-fated government from its inception in 1871 to its fall to the Nazis in 1940. Though the title was far from ideal for my subtle comedic purposes, I wanted to get back to reading it anyhow, as I had left off at an interesting point; it was that part where the institutions of a free and pluralistic society inevitably come under assault by authoritarian Catholics. Ha ha, just kidding; that's pretty much the whole book. But I really was at an interesting part—the French generals were all agreeing with each other that the military had little use for airplanes or Jews—and it had also now occurred to me that I was putting too much energy into the setting up of a sight gag that would almost certainly be lost on its sole audience of prison officials who review SWAT extraction videos. *Collapse* it would be, then.

Meanwhile, D's watery onslaught against the Decreasingly Great Satan had run into another snag after a passing guard noticed a puddle spreading outside our cell; in the throes of his fanaticism, D had not sufficiently sealed the space under the door. The guard stopped in his tracks and contemplated the puddle for five or six seconds, at which point he seemed to decide that it was unauthorized. After that it was only a few seconds more of investigation before he came to grasp that this particular liquid might perhaps be best understood as merely a portion of some much larger body of liquid, perhaps originating from, say, the nearby cell from which it was clearly originating. And so finally he looked through our door grille and saw the inch or so of water that had accumulated in our cell, saw D standing there muttering in Arabic and repeatedly flushing a toilet, which in turn was visibly clogged by a towel, saw me sitting on the top bunk staring back at him and taking notes—he saw all of this and he said, "Fuck." Then he ran back down the hall.

"You don't need a weatherman to know which way the wind blows!" I called after him, that being the only appropriately ominous Bob Dylan protest lyric I could think of at the time. Then I went back to my book.

"Everybody get yo' shit off the flo'! Imma flood this bitch!" D yelled through the grille for the benefit of the other SHU inmates, whom I could hear rushing to comply with this most practical of fatwas lest their property get soaked.

"You ain't floodin' shit," came the dismissive reply from Mack (the ranking officer who'd started this whole thing to begin with by taking D's Ramadan snacks), who walked up and threw down a stack of blankets in front of our door just as D was pulling the barrier, effectively blocking in most of D's would-be flood (this is the only prison flooding I ever saw but I'm pretty confident I grasped all the mechanics). Whatever water did manage to soak through the blankets was soon taken care of by an orderly with a mop, orderlies with mops being the real victims of most guard-inmate conflicts of this sort. And pretty soon the guards had shut off our water altogether, leaving D with few offensive options.

This was just as well, as he had stopped being angry about ten minutes prior and was now just going through the motions for form's sake. So when the guards came back a minute later to put the "shield" over the door grille—the shield is a rectangular transparent plate intended to deflect any urine that an inmate may decide to toss from a cup at a guard, but which, being transparent, doesn't obstruct the guard's view of the inmate—D felt obligated to at least attempt to knock the thing off the grille. This is tricky, as the grille is laced together rather tightly such that nothing wider than a pencil can be pushed through. Thankfully, Dank—the gangster, pie tycoon, and accomplished SHU insurgent whose own adventures I detailed in the last edition of this column—was already shouting instructions to D from his own cell down the hall. His method involved pencils and pieces of paper rolled up to make a tube by which the pencils can be more easily grasped and then pushed through or something of that sort, which I didn't quite follow as I've always found physics to be confusing and, frankly, kind of suspicious.

Plus I was now distracted with a new problem: I'd decided to provide D with moral support by singing "La Marseillaise," but then I remembered that I didn't know the lyrics in French, or the lyrics in English, or the tune. To clarify, I've almost certainly heard the tune before, but I wouldn't be able to pick it out from among several other tunes that I vaguely associate with France and revolutionaries and whatnot. It really wouldn't do for me to try to start singing what I suspected to be "La Marseillaise" but which would actually turn out to be "L'Internationale" or something by Daft Punk. And, come to think of it, there was no good reason to bring the French into a situation that was already complicated enough. So instead I just shouted, "Down with all human institutions!" in a sort of self-parody.

D finally managed to pry the shield loose using his mystical pencil-paper contraption, and it fell to the floor with a very satisfying clatter. Just then a captain showed up.

"Now, what's wrong, D?" asked this infuriatingly venerable, grandfatherly black man, his face treacherously composed into a mask of understanding and

> earthy good humor that was almost certainly genuine but still enraged me for some reason. D responded with a litany of vague complaints that had nothing to do with his original and quite legitimate grievance, which, naturally, he had already forgotten. In conclusion, he explained, "Sometimes I just need to express myself!"
>
> I swear to God that D actually said that. And apparently this struck the kind old man as a very reasonable answer, because he nodded knowingly and went off to get some more towels with which D could begin to dry our floor. Actually I'm quite fond of the grandfatherly captain, and I like to imagine that he and the handful of other humane and pleasant guards argue on behalf of us inmates in the secretive Council of the Guards, taking our side against the more numerous Evil Guards, who are forever proposing that we all be fed to wild dogs or sold to the Chinese. And the Good Guards are all like, "No, no, let's just give them candy!" It's all very Olympian.

D, who'd been sentenced to five years on a felony-with-a-firearm charge a few weeks back, eventually left for whatever maximum security institution he would no doubt feel right at home in. Later, when the two-month "investigation" into an incident that was not under any particular dispute was completed, I was charged with "refusing an order" (the far more serious charge of "engaging in a demonstration" had been dropped by the regional office in part because the original write-up had failed to note, as required by policy, what it was that we were demonstrating against; the administration wasn't all that interested in going into that particular subject). The formal punishment was a couple of months' loss of phone and visiting privileges; the actual punishment had of course been meted out before, just as it had been with my jail time itself. We ringleaders were returned to the unit.

After the stillness of the SHU, the jail unit was overwhelming. To a greater extent than its Fort Worth counterpart, Seagoville's J-2 detention facility was a hive of activity, much of it economic, fueled by the currency of postage stamps and commissary items.

Aside from the sprinkling of official jobs like laundry, orderly, and food service—each of which pays just a few bucks a month but is nonetheless desirable due to all the de facto perks that can be incorporated into more creative hustles—the unofficial economy of jails and prisons is both vast and ingenious. Even just in jail units, where inmates have little intercourse with the main compound and all of its workshops and training programs and the raw materials that are stolen therefrom, industry is complex and specialized. There are radio fixers, store guys, room cleaners, speaker makers, bauble craftsmen, artists, locker organizers, pen salesmen, lookouts, jailhouse lawyers, phone minute dealers, pie makers, masseurs, and even makeshift doctors who will lance boils or otherwise perform minor surgeries that one may have trouble getting the prison doctors to attend to. People will sell their cells, receive drugs via mail on behalf of others who'd rather not risk it, rent out syringes, write poems, compose allocutions, do tattoos, make tattoo guns, hide contraband, make hooch, rent out locker space, buy extra items at the commissary for others to get around the limits, provide small loans, and draw portraits of one's family or more elaborate scenes, with Jesus if desired, or a nice car, or naked women, and you would probably disbelieve me if I told you that all these elements can be incorporated into a single scene, generally at the request of a Mexican. That's right, syringe rentals.

They'll provide a starched and ironed uniform for your visits, do your laundry, cook your food to order, or sell you pizzas made in a microwave with goods stolen from the kitchen, or anything else that comes from the kitchen (only in prison, though; jail units are served by carts carrying trays prepared in the main compound). They'll acquire an extra mattress and undertake a specialized procedure by which to stuff it into your existing mattress so that your mattress will be more firm with no one the wiser; they'll alter your sheets so that they better fit on your mattress. They'll take your bets—and among the bet takers, you have those who print out rather professional-looking tickets (printed off on the high-tech typewriters that seem to be manufactured exclusively for use by prison law libraries), themselves with brand names like Big Money Ticket.

These tickets constitute the backbone of the economy of many prisons, while still making up only a portion of the gambling activity that prevails altogether. At Seagoville, the most impressive operation was run by the Tangos, who oversaw a poker table during those shifts when the guard on duty wasn't among those who actively banned gambling (which is against the "rules," and thus sometimes not allowed). These being relatively high-dollar games, the Tangos had taken a cue from the casinos and had their younger members serve players with the prison equivalent of hors d'oeuvres—generally makeshift prison pizza re-created from a ramen noodle crust (mixed with hot water in cereal bags and lovingly pounded flat with a heavy object) and topped with commissary sausage—along with lemonade. Had I needed some cash, I might have approached them about doing some stand-up at the table a couple of nights a week; I imagine I could have eventually opened for Dank.

But I was never short on money myself thanks to regular commissary deposits from my mother and other female admirers (many of whom also wrote me letters indicating that they were crazy) plus the money I got from the columns and, eventually, from a more formal support fund made up of public donations. This was lucky for me because the other major component of the prison economy is drugs, and Suboxone had recently become the most popular drug in the U.S. prison system.

I didn't take advantage of the syringe rental service; the universal method had become to snort the dissolved film from a plastic spoon kept for the purpose, in very small amounts at a time so as to reach the perfect balance of synthetic opiate and naloxone, the opiate antagonist that blocks the necessary receptors and thus keeps one from profitably using large amounts. Even at a 500 percent markup, the small quantities that were all that was necessary for a vastly powerful high were within reach of the most humble cell cleaners and locker-space-renter-outers. An increasingly respected literary columnist could afford to get re-addicted. And at the time, the low-quality prison drug tests couldn't pick up Suboxone.

One last aspect of the prison economy requires attention. I had a good friend at one facility who served a prominent commercial and political role at the compound, and who told me of an occasion a few months before when the upper tier of the local convict gentry—ticket men, dope dealers, store guys, shot-callers, and the rest—held a meeting on the rec yard one day to discuss monetary policy. Much of the population was made up of Paisas, themselves largely day laborers with no one putting money on their books from back home, and this had resulted in an economic slump. As with all prisons, compound commerce was driven by postage stamps, each worth its face value of 50 cents, as well as "compound stamps," which were old and unusable stamps stuck together in twos, possessed of some lesser agreed-upon value that might be 25 or 35 cents as determined by each individual compound, or at least by its leading lights—and this is done in the same manner by which nation-states confer value on other nonfunctional pieces of paper, and for the same reasons. This prison's assembled community pillars, comprising a sort of makeshift Federal Reserve through their collective stranglehold over industry and finance and political influence, enacted a compound-wide policy change altering the value of compound stamps, effective immediately. I can't get more specific due to having been told about all this on condition that I don't cite the prison or the exact value of the compound stamps, and also because I really don't understand economics. But I have reason to believe that some insider trading occurred.

Shortly after I got my visits back, my mom came by to inform me that I'd been mentioned several times in the newly released second season of *House of Cards*, the big new binge-drama of the last two years. Gregg Housh, a natural entrepreneur, had become a consultant for the series, which had introduced a hacker and sometime FBI informant character based partly on him. Over the course of two episodes, the character tries to negotiate with his handlers to get his own charges dropped, as well as those of "Barrett Brown," only to be informed that the "Dallas prosecutor won't budge." I pondered whether it might be legally feasible for me to write *House of Cards* fan fiction expanding on the circumstances of the fictional Barrett Brown's case as a dodge around the gag order, which I understood to apply exclusively to this universe and not to an alternate one in which Kevin Spacey is vice president, but presumably my lawyers would have told me to get fucked. They were, after all, busy compiling a series of motion to dismiss filings arguing that each of the different statutes under which I'd been charged was flawed, drawing upon an amicus brief from the Electronic Frontier Foundation on the horrifying implications of the linking charges. Each of our arguments in this vein was pretty solid, but we'd have to wait for the judge to rule on them—and he had the option to wait for the trial itself to hand down his decisions on each separate motion.

In more than 90 percent of federal cases the defendant signs on to the DOJ's first offer. But 90 percent of federal cases don't involve reckless junkie adventurers with a proven disregard for their own future. Two days after we filed our motion to dismiss on the eleven counts of "aggravated identity theft" (or, in human terms, copying and pasting a link to a document that ended up containing credit card numbers someone else had stolen), the government filed a motion to dismiss those counts itself. It was an extraordinarily rare move, one that subjected the DOJ to severe embarrassment as headlines announced the collapse of the centerpiece of its case. Their retreat had been necessary; if the judge had dismissed the charges in accordance with our own motion,

I'd have been able to sue the DOJ under a little-known law that allows defendants legal recourse against spurious prosecutions. And the linking charges had indeed been spurious on several different levels, even aside from lack of intent—credit card numbers aren't government-issued IDs and thus don't constitute means of identification, for instance, as required by the identity theft statutes.

I stood unwilling to plead to anything so long as the remaining charge of actually downloading the file—which, as established by the government's forensics team, I'd never opened—was still on the table. It was essentially a fraud charge, after all, and I wouldn't allow the state to taint myself and my work with the whiff of falsehood. That having been conveyed to the prosecutor, we were asked to come up with another charge that I felt comfortable pleading to, because of course they needed something to justify the original investigation. My lawyer Ahmed Ghappour came up with the idea for me to accept an "accessory after the fact" on the grounds that I'd made the call to Stratfor's executives on behalf of the hackers, offering to redact any sensitive information that could have endangered its foreign informants; we could pretend that this constituted an effort to assist the hackers in avoiding detection, even though that made no sense given that the hackers weren't going to contact Stratfor themselves and anyway could have easily done so without giving away their identities, since of course these guys actually communicate with all sorts of people all day and sometimes break into their computers without there being any means of tracing them.

I was happy with this agreed-on fabrication due to its demonstrable absurdity; it also served as proof, if any was needed, that the federal government's objection to leaking on the grounds that it could endanger people was nothing more than a cynical talking point, given that I would now be punished for having sought to keep such people safe. And so long as I agreed to plea to it, the only other charges I'd have to sign on to were internet threats and interference with a search warrant. Although technically I'd done neither, I don't consider them crimes in a moral sense, as I do fraud, and so had no problem engaging in the requisite Kabuki dance if that was all it would take to avoid a trial in which FBI agents could lie at will. A few weeks later I was taken back in front of Magistrate Judge Stickney and cheerfully pleaded guilty to three counts carrying, realistically, a total of three years in prison, of which I'd already done two and a half. We would be asking the judge to release me at sentencing with "time served," given the totality of the circumstances—the threats to my mother, my going off my medication, and the now universally acknowledged conspiracy that had been waged against me by lawless shadow entities working in conjunction with the very agencies that were now prosecuting me after I'd helped expose their previous crimes. At any rate, my family and supporters could relax; with the plea now signed, the danger of a lengthy prison sentence had finally dissipated.

But it had been a trap. Using a mechanism known as "relevant conduct," which allows the feds to submit an array of "sentencing enhancements" requiring no real evidence, the government managed to convince the court's probation officer to put the linking matter back on the table and even hold me responsible for every additional charge made to the credit cards starting at the second I posted the link to Project PM. In addition to HBGary, Stratfor, and two other firms that Jeremy Hammond hacked and for which I was just as mysteriously deemed culpable, this allowed them to boost my sentence via the "more than two hundred victims" enhancement (although just barely; the chart of credit card fraud activity we were provided listed one victim as having been charged "$0.00," and several others had questionable data attached to them as well). I was also determined to have used "sophisticated means"—presumably the rather bleeding-edge act of copying and pasting a hyperlink—and thus subject to additional punishment.

The probation office's Pre-Sentencing Report contained more than four dozen questionable claims and even demonstrable falsehoods. The officer, Edith Foster, had placed my year of birth variously at 1981 and 1984; claimed not to be able to "confirm" that I had a high school diploma, thereby adding more "custody points" by which prisons determine what security level facility to stick you in; claimed not to be able to "confirm" that I'd been employed by *The Guardian* despite the prosecutor herself having summoned me to the courtroom in shackles to denounce how "critical of the government" my latest article had been; claimed that I'd been a heroin addict for ten years rather than the three years it had actually been, the only source being me anyway; and claimed, in support of God knows what stratagem, that my legal bills had been paid by my parents even though they'd clearly been paid for by the public via the $150,000 worth of donations that the prosecutor had originally tried to seize.

The probation office is permitted to adopt any of the FBI's claims without evidence; judges tend to go with their findings. In this case, the probation officer recommended that I get sixteen years in prison and be held liable for millions of dollars in restitution to Stratfor and other firms, which I would have to pay over the rest of my life.

My sentence had been capped by the plea at nine years. Giving me that maximum, the probation officer argued, would thus constitute a reasonable compromise—an act of leniency, really. We responded with a motion noting that, among other things, she had neglected to mention that the eleven counts of identity theft she referred to in the report had been dropped due to failure to state a crime. She responded that she was happy to make that correction.

The sentencing hearing, conducted in front of a packed gallery under unusually tight security, stretched out over two days and took on many of the aspects of a trial, albeit an unusually ambitious one in which participants sought to define what is and isn't journalism while also deciding if linking to something would henceforth count as "transferring" it, among other matters. We scored an early victory when several of the probation officer's more blatantly crazy findings were rejected by Judge Lindsay on the strength of solid arguments by my local attorney, Marlo Caddedu.

Tim Rogers, the *D Magazine* editor for whom I'd been writing the columns (and who had won a National Magazine Award for his 2011 profile of my activities), was called as a surprise witness to testify that, contrary to the FBI's current position, I was indeed a journalist, regardless of what else I might be. The *Wired* reporter Quinn Norton—as it happens, a former girlfriend of Aaron Swartz—took the stand and pointed out that she, too, had posted the link for which I alone was apparently to be punished, and explained why using this against me would play havoc with the First Amendment; the prosecutor approached the bench and made some noises about prosecuting her as well, and later seemed to imply that Norton was biased against the DOJ merely due to the fact that the agency had recklessly driven her loved one to suicide. Special Agent Robert Smith testified that I was a de facto leader of Anonymous, citing some hundred pages of communications between myself and the movement's more notorious hackers; the defense, contrary to my advice, tried to argue that I was merely a hanger-on and perhaps delusional to boot, which didn't seem to hold up very well against a year's worth of logged chats and recorded Skype conversations with individuals who had already been portrayed in books and documentary films as the movement's key participants and thereafter convicted for hacking-related offenses in the United States and Britain, and who could sometimes be seen deferring to me in these records. Judge Lindsay adopted the prosecution's view, which, though inevitably exaggerated, was closer to the documented reality than the narrative my attorney Charlie Swift had decided to advance even before he'd had a chance to go over the discovery, and despite a year of explanations from me as to what was already public record.

Finally, in a ten-minute speech I delivered from the podium while wearing leg shackles, I pointed out demonstrable inaccuracies in the FBI's sworn testimony and prior filings and denounced HBGary, the DOJ, and the replacement of the rule of law with "the rule of law enforcement." This was all intended for the press, rather than for the judge, who had already made up his mind anyway and promptly sentenced me to sixty-three months in prison (of which I'd already served twenty-eight) and applied restitution of a bit over eight hundred thousand dollars to be paid over the course of my life to my victims—Combined Systems, for instance, a weapons firm that Jeremy Hammond had hacked due to its sales of military-grade tear gas to the Kingdom of Bahrain for use against pro-democracy protesters. As the judge explained, I also gave up my laptops and other items seized as evidence, including one pamphlet-size book they'd apparently found to be suspicious:

> THE COURT: Based upon your plea agreement, you have agreed to relinquish, give up, and waive any legal right, title, or ownership in the property attached to your plea agreement. Are you aware of that list, sir?
>
> DEFENDANT BROWN: Yes. I have a procedural question though, Your Honor. The copy of the Declaration of Independence they took from me as evidence. Will I get that back?
>
> THE COURT: So what are you saying? First of all, let's deal with this. Before we get off track, you asked me about the—I asked you about the property forfeiture. Let's deal with that first.
>
> DEFENDANT BROWN: Right.

After some additional fumbling over fees and technicalities, the judge brought the gavel down and the U.S. Marshals rushed me out of the courtroom as the journalist Alexa O'Brien shouted out a denunciation of the DOJ.

As I returned to the jail unit in a cage in the back of a van, the statement I'd prepared weeks earlier and provided to Gallagher—leaving blank the exact number of months I'd have remaining, to be entered immediately after the sentencing—was already being distributed to the media. As I'd hoped, it led most of the antigovernment, pro-Barrett press accounts that were going up across the globe:

> Good News! The U.S. government decided today that because I did such a good job investigating the cyber-industrial complex, they're now going to send me to investigate the prison-industrial complex. For the next 35 months, I'll be provided with free food, clothes, and housing as I seek to expose wrongdoing by Bureau of Prisons officials and staff and otherwise report on news and culture in the world's greatest prison system. I want to thank the Department of Justice for having put so much time and energy into advocating on my behalf; rather than holding a grudge against me for the two years of work I put into bringing attention to a DOJ-linked campaign to harass and discredit journalists like Glenn Greenwald, the agency instead labored tirelessly to ensure that I received this very prestigious assignment. Wish me luck!

9

A Working Vacation

A month after I'd arrived at Fort Worth's low security compound, where I'd been designated to serve my sentence, I used the CorrLinks prison email service to shoot a message to a journalist I knew regarding a story on BOP wrongdoing that I'd gotten from another inmate. When I checked my email a bit later that afternoon, I was presented with a message explaining that I wasn't permitted to use it.

I tracked down the prison's SIA head, Terrance Moore, in the chow hall. The SIA, which stands for God knows what, is equivalent to a police department's internal affairs division, both in official function and actual nature. I told Moore that someone had taken away my email. He replied that it'd been him.

"You been using it for the wrong thing, Brown."

"Does 'using it for the wrong thing' mean contacting the press?"

Moore nodded.

So it was going to be like that, then.

In 1996, Congress noticed that more inmates were taking their captors to court over due process violations. Rather than ascribe this to the fact that there were now more inmates to begin with, or launch an inquiry into whether these lawsuits might be indicative of widespread problems within the very prison system that legislators themselves are supposed to be overseeing, Congress instead passed the Prison Litigation Reform Act, which prevents inmates from being heard in the courts until they've first exhausted a given prison's "administrative remedy" procedure.

For inmates in the federal Bureau of Prisons system, that procedure entails filing a BP-8, waiting five days for a written response, filing a BP-9, waiting twenty days for a written response, then waiting another twenty days if the prison needs more time, sending off a BP-10 to the regional office, waiting thirty days for a written response, then waiting another thirty days if the regional office needs more time, then sending off a BP-11 to the national office, waiting forty days for a written response, then waiting another forty days if the national office needs more time, and then filing in court.

This would be a cumbersome enough process even if prison officials were in the habit of complying with it. That they would instead work to disrupt it at every turn could have easily been predicted based on two highly relevant things that Congress seems not to have considered important: that this is a process administered by the very institution that has something to lose if it's completed, and that there are no legal consequences whatsoever for failing to comply with it, even in the extraordinarily rare case wherein an inmate convinces a court that the prison interfered to a degree that made compliance impossible. Any alleged missed deadline by the inmate, meanwhile, can lead to the complaint being ruled ultimately invalid.

My own filing process went on for a year. Fort Worth missed three of its own deadlines for response before finally accusing me of using the email service for "criminal activity," though what this might have consisted of was never explained, perhaps out of tact—and although I was naturally curious to learn why it was that I wasn't charged with a crime this time around, I suppose I will go to my grave disappointed. I could appeal to the regional office, they added, in the event that I was left unsatisfied with their libelous and poorly composed reply (I'm paraphrasing a bit). When I did so, a BOP lawyer claimed that I'd missed a deadline (which I hadn't; this wasn't a freelance writing assignment, after all), demanded that I get a written note from prison staff declaring that missing the deadline hadn't been my fault, told me to reduce my complaint to one single-sided page instead of two, and gave me a new deadline for response, including mailing time, that happened to fall on the very next day. When I replied again in a smaller font so as to cram everything onto a single page, along with proof that the prison, not me, had violated the deadlines, and pointed out that the Bureau of Prisons had given me less than twenty-four hours to do several inappropriate things and one impossible one, they demanded three extra copies of the note I'd included explaining these matters. This time, they gave me a deadline of ten days prior to the day I received their response. All of this was even documented via the prison's own "date received" stamps, such that anyone could verify with a glance that the federal officials concerned were intentionally obstructing the legal process. No attempt was made to conceal this.

Not long after I filed my initial BP-8, someone offered me some hooch, which I poured into a plastic mug and placed in my locker for consumption that evening; I'd only drunk a few times since incarceration, back at Mansfield, so this was a rare treat. Twenty minutes later, the unit's case manager and a rookie officer walked into the room I shared with seven other inmates to conduct a "random" Breathalyzer test, something that they'd never done before. Naturally I passed, having not yet drunk anything, but then he ordered us out for a "random" search that, I saw from outside, centered entirely on my locker.

The next day I received my infraction report, which I've cruelly reproduced verbatim below:

> ON JUNE 17 2015 AT APPROXIMATE 8:35 PM DURING A RANDOM BREATHALYZER TEST I DECIDED TO SEARCH INMATES BROWN 45047–177 LOCKER AND FOUND A COFFEE MUG FULL OF PRISON MADE INTHOXICANT. OPERATION LT WAS INFORMED AND INMATE BROWN #45047–177 WAS ESCORTED BY THE COMPOUNP OFFICER TO THE SHU.

Of course, what had actually prompted Officer Tweety Bird here to, er, "SEARCH INMATES BROWN 45047–177

LOCKER" was that a particular snitch had been watching me on behalf of the case manager, something I was able to confirm when a lieutenant came by the hole the next morning to brag to me about it.

This was rather bad timing. Just a few days earlier I'd spoken to Glenn Greenwald, who, since our last conversation a few months after my arrest, had won a Pulitzer Prize for his work on the Snowden documents and gotten what amounted to his own news outlet when the eBay billionaire Pierre Omidyar put $250 million into creating First Look Media, the flagship property of which was *The Intercept*. Greenwald was able to get me $2,000 a column, which, in prison terms, is about $7 million. And of course my work would get vastly increased readership, which meant that I might even have the chance to expose BOP misconduct in a way that would yield discernible results.

The problem with writing columns in the SHU is that one must work with these horrible little eraserless pencils that are handed through the slot along with your soap and envelopes once a week. These can be resharpened only by cajoling a guard into taking your pencils, walking over to the desk at the end of the hall, putting each one in the electric pencil sharpener, and then bringing them back to you; to ensure that this happens on a fairly reliable basis, one must essentially pick out a guard and engage in a long period of grooming. All in all one is suddenly confronted with the mechanical elements of writing (in addition to the apparently busy schedule of a child molester). My rough drafts were jumbles of scratch-outs, rips in the paper, flows of tiny words escaping into the margins and then proceeding into semicircular pathways of ideas I'd just remembered to add. And these drafts would have to be rewritten into something superbly legible so that no words would be misconstrued by the editor (even so, this would happen once or twice a column, on average, ruining some careful phrasing, key point, or crucial punch line).

But in the end, this process actually lends itself to better writing. And it's coupled with the conceptual advantages that are unique to the doubly incarcerated thinker. Being cut off from the world focuses one on those things at hand, with an effect on the mind directly opposite to that of the internet. Not yet having received the titles from the emergency book list I'd provided my mom in case of another SHU visit, I was forced to make do with the horrible paperback thrillers that make up the bulk of prison book cart offerings. One of them, *Holiday in Death* by J. D. Robb, billed itself as "futuristic romantic suspense" and constituted one of a series of novels concerning a female police officer in 2043 who is literally married to the wealthiest man in the world. This was good for several solid paragraphs. My cellmate, a nineteen-year-old illegal Mexican immigrant and cartel affiliate who'd already done time in the state prison for shooting a rival dealer, was good for much of the rest; suffice to say that he made me pray with him to Santa Muerte, the Mexican goddess of death, to request that we receive the prison's rather tasty potato wedges with our Wednesday hamburger rather than the bags of chips that more often accompany the meal. And we did actually get the potato wedges. I rounded out the column with an update on the administrative remedy process, the verbatim text of my write-up for "PRISON MADE INTHOXICANT," and my aforementioned attack on Ibn-Khaldūn for believing that Alexander had to scare away sea monsters from the coast of Alexandria. Take that, Ibn-Khaldūn!

When I was released from the SHU after two months, I found that the administration had switched me to another home unit on the yard, a highly unusual move, and that here I would be placed in a "punishment cell." Officially, the BOP has no "punishment cells." In reality, Fort Worth, being comprised of elderly buildings built to serve some other function, had an irregular array of "alcoves" and "annexes" in addition to more conventional two- and three-man cells lining the corridors. In this case, four double bunk beds had been squeezed into a room so small that they were separated by little more than a foot. It was just one of several significant policy failures—far fewer toilets and less personal space per inmate than is provided for in the standards, for instance—that the American Correctional Association's annual accreditation process had nonetheless waived in favor of Fort Worth, as I'd learned from another inmate's Freedom of Information Act request. Indeed, I'd written a column on the subject and put up a printout on the bulletin board back in the other unit; an officer tore it down and summoned a lieutenant to come question me about it (although nothing came of this). It's also worth noting that around the time I arrived at Fort Worth, the head of the ACA had to resign after being indicted on dozens of charges involving kickbacks and money laundering, and at the time of this writing is serving his sentence at Seagoville.

Rarely did a day go by without some incident. I'd learned

from Alex Winter, the former actor who had since proven to be a talented and remarkably well-informed documentary filmmaker, that he'd sent in a form requesting to interview me; long after the forty-eight-hour period in which the BOP is required by law to respond to such inquiries, he'd received no acknowledgment from the warden's executive assistant (who is also in charge of a given prison's administrative remedy process, and thus a scumbag). The inmate in question is supposed to be informed of any such requests by prison staff within twenty-four hours as well, in writing, via a particular form created for that very purpose; even Seagoville had properly done this, and indeed had accepted such requests from a German reporter and another documentary filmmaker. In principle I was enraged at this latest provocation, but on the other hand, here I was conspiring with the costar of *Bill & Ted's Excellent Adventure* to thwart unjust authority and strike a blow for decency and transparency. It was like one of those dreams you have as a kid wherein the Ninja Turtles ask you to help defeat Shredder and now you're friends with the Ninja Turtles.

Around this same time I was stopped outside the library by an officer stationed at the doorway who seized my notebook, inexplicably deeming it "contraband." The pages were returned to me later by an SIS lieutenant, who questioned me about the contents (aside from notes for the column, I had jotted down testimony from inmates who had come to me for help filing their own grievance forms). I had my editor link to the resulting confiscation report in my next column.

This constant tension took such an emotional toll on me that I did what I would have done anyway and started snorting morphine. I'd gotten off Suboxone involuntarily a month before my sentencing when I was suddenly transferred out of Seagoville to Kaufman County, another local jail facility with a federal contract to house BOP inmates but far, far worse than Mansfield (as usual, the Suboxone withdrawals were especially horrid and took two weeks; the only thing that sustained me under the circumstances was Robert Caro's magisterial four-volume biography of Lyndon Johnson). Doing morphine regularly was dangerous, as I'd been put on random drug testing (contrary to policy, I later discovered; possession of alcohol isn't supposed to trigger any such thing). But morphine goes out of your system in about three or four days, and the tests only occurred once a month, so it wasn't absolutely guaranteed that I'd be caught and thrown in the SHU again, which was enough for me.

Inevitably, though, I happened to get tested not long after one of my thrice-monthly snorts, leaving me in limbo for several days as I waited for the results. Later that week I was out on the rec yard when the cops suddenly locked the gates on us. Watching as a pair of investigators combed the grounds immediately outside the fence, we speculated as to what was going on; someone said that a guy covered with blood had trotted down the stairs leading into the psychiatrist's offices in the basement. Presumably the cops were looking for bloodstains, so as to track the fellow. This made as much sense as anything else.

Twenty minutes later an SIS agent named McClellan, whom I'd encountered a few times before and who handled my drug testing, came to the yard with a cadre of officers and announced that we were to line up to be searched on our way out. Each of us was made to take off our shirt and present our knuckles for inspection, which is standard procedure when a prison attempts to identify those involved in a fight. When it was my turn to be assessed, it happened to be McClellan who did the inspection. And I could tell from the way he looked at me that something was up. I'd failed the drug test.

Walking down the hall past the officer station back at the unit, I heard an insolent voice yell, "Brown!" It was Flores, one of our weekday guards. Flores was best known for having once come across a container in a utility room that he assumed to be hooch, presumably hidden there so that it wouldn't be found in someone's cell. Flores decided it would be cool and funny to take a huge swig of the stuff as a group of inmates looked on. He was rushed to the hospital, for the suspected hooch had actually been bleach. When he returned to work after a few days of undignified convalescence, he found that he was now universally known as Clorez.

Once again I was escorted to the lieutenant's office. After a satisfying argument with the lieutenant on duty, who accused me of having failed to grant him sufficient respect while he read out my infraction report, I was taken to the SHU and placed, to my additional satisfaction, in an empty cell. But a friendly guard whom I knew from my last visit to the hole came by and told me I'd actually be getting a cellie soon, just as soon as the fellow came back from the medical unit. It was the guy whose mysterious beating had prompted this morning's lockdown.

A few hours later they brought him in. He was a small fellow from El Salvador who ran with the Paisas. It was they, he told me, who'd beat him down. This was odd, as the Paisas tended to be relatively amorphous in structure and lax on their rules, which are few; in many prisons they'll even take sex offenders and snitches, so long as they're Mexican or Latin American. He claimed that they'd done it because he'd left the gang. This is something that does regularly happen with, say, the Tangos, who require one to take a beating from a couple of members in order to quit (the entrance requirement is similar), but I'd never heard of the Paisas doing any such thing. At any rate I pretended to believe him.

The Salvadoran and I lived together in a state of pleasant routine. In the mornings, we drank coffee and watched the sunrise through our window, which looked out upon some power lines where birds congregated at dawn. Sometimes we'd see a hawk, and the Salvadoran would say, "There's the hawk!" I'd gotten some surprisingly good graphic novels in the mail and took pleasure in his enjoyment of each one. In the stripped-down simplicity of SHU life, there is a particular satisfaction in helping to put others at ease in the wake of strife.

One evening a notoriously helpful guard came to the door holding a random paperback, opened up the chute, and told my cellie, "Someone wanted you to have this book." The Salvadoran opened it, flipped through, and actually squealed with delight. I didn't ask him what he'd received; instead I secretly watched from my top bunk as he shuffled through the Polaroids that had been concealed therein. Then I understood.

Because Fort Worth is a low security prison with a medical unit, it's been designated by the BOP as one of the institutions where transgender inmates who are currently receiving hormones are placed when possible. There were at least four or five I knew of here. One, a small-framed Hispanic, had taken the name Pocahontas (I can estimate with a strong degree of confidence that at least a third of

U.S. prisons have a gay or transgender inmate called Pocahontas). Another, much rounder Hispanic transgender female answered to the name Pumpkin, and I knew she was also in the SHU at the time, upstairs on the other range. The photos the Salvadoran held now were of Pumpkin, presumably taken before she came to prison. I understood now that his beating by the Paisas had stemmed from forbidden love, now rewarded.

That Friday I was cuffed and taken down the hall for my disciplinary hearing—highly unusual, since such hearings are always held on Wednesdays, and rarely that soon after one is charged. I was sentenced, as expected, to thirty days in Disciplinary Segregation and another ninety days each of phone, visitation, and email loss (although of course my email had already been illicitly seized), and thereafter was taken upstairs to the DS range, where coffee, radios, and (oddly enough) watches are not permitted.

My new cellie turned out to be rather cool and, more important, had smuggled in a bag of coffee. Better still, I received in the mail just then the venerable old Marvel Super Heroes Role-Playing Game boxed set I'd ordered my mother to find on Amazon and ship to me. I'd had this thing back in fourth grade; in addition to the basic texts laying out the framework for the game, the box included colorful maps depicting downtown New York and Doctor Doom's Latvian palace, punch-out cardboard figurines, and booklets filled with background info and game statistics for several hundred old Marvel characters as recorded in the

Reagan era, many of them contemporary to the age and long since forgotten along with so many other ill-conceived products of the artistically uneven eighties. I spent much of the next week on the floor, developing and carrying out another of my one-player custom theater games, this one set in a Weimar-esque yet ultramodern city where fascist and communist street toughs who also happen to have superpowers struggle for political dominance. I used only the most obscure characters.

But in between the running battles between the guy who has a giant whirling blade for an arm but isn't the Grim Reaper and a bunch of other guys of whom I can remember literally nothing because they were conceived by the talentless pseudo-creator Rob Liefeld, I was also plotting again.

Although the column was still intended mostly to play up my likability and otherwise entertain, I increasingly worked in whatever anti-BOP propaganda could be slipped in without weighing it all down. Each surreal new development in the administrative remedy process got its own recap and update; I sent out copies of each new response to be linked to directly from each column; I reported on other inmates' attempts to challenge due process violations as well as on the suspiciously uniform methods by which BOP officials kept them out of court. That my output received vastly more attention now didn't necessarily help; whether the BOP's systematic effort to deny firmly established legal rights to two hundred thousand federal inmates was known to thirty thousand readers or one hundred thousand made no difference to anything other than my own career. Like the great majority of issues that are brought to the public's attention, this one would lead to no actual changes in the policy of our republic unless it happened to hit that threshold of civic-outrage-to-the-point-of-government-action that so many other deserving issues had failed to meet.

This concept of the threshold had become central to my own practical politics, and to my criticisms of American democracy. All other issues, including the ones that so many of us had suffered to pinpoint, were essentially unsolvable except to the extent that the dangerous illusions of mainstream American politics had been abandoned by some capable stratum of the citizenry. I didn't want to focus on surveillance, propaganda technology, war crimes abroad, the drug war, or even prisons. I wanted to make an unanswerable case that the threshold for solving these and an array of other fundamental problems was so high under the current system that no decent person could continue to support the system itself; that the millions imprisoned at home and the millions killed and displaced abroad as a result of our citizens' failures were not, contrary to the vague and unspoken consensus of the degenerate mainstream, morally justified by the fact that a body of voters had in some way authorized it.

And I wanted even some of those who might be generally accepting of our institutions, conceptual and political, to acknowledge the strong possibility that the American republic could easily degenerate into something even they could not support. I wanted others to see what I saw, and then I wanted to recruit them, this time into something that could not be disrupted by the DOJ or anything else on Earth—something designed so carefully yet simply that it could do nothing else but grow even as it refined itself further and further; something that, once set in motion, would ultimately strangle the world's institutions just as so many of their predecessors had been strangled by a thousand other things that likewise began merely as ideas.

But in the meantime I would try, one final time, to be a "journalist." Having compiled dozens of documents demonstrating that high officials of a federal agency were engaging in criminal and unconstitutional conduct on a vast scale, I would present these findings in an op-ed for one of the major newspapers and even conclude with a reasonable solution that could be immediately implemented so as to alleviate at least some of the abuses: that President Obama sign an executive order requiring the BOP to allow inmates to conduct their administrative remedy procedures on prison computers that would automatically require adherence to deadlines on both sides and provide a record of all such things for courts to consider when determining whether an inmate's attempts to secure his own rights should be thrown out on procedural grounds.

Prison reform, after all, was now on the table. Congress had even instituted several productive measures as of late, including a broad reduction in drug sentences and redefinitions of sentencing enhancements deeming certain individuals to be "career criminals" on spurious grounds. Obama had just recently ended the practice of placing children in solitary confinement (and it's worth rolling around in one's head for a moment or two that this was something that actually had to be done by a twenty-first-century American president). Eric Holder had given a speech signaling that DOJ prosecutorial overreach had gone too far. And here was a circumstance unlikely to be repeated—a journalist with a growing audience made up to an unusual degree of other media professionals, with a continual spotlight on his adventures and a case against an indefensible practice that was so solid as to approach absurdity. If even under such circumstances as these, nothing came of a bid to correct a massive wrong that could be addressed with so little effort, then it would at least help to illustrate the larger case that all these institutions were broken, along with American journalism itself.

I was informed that I was to be shipped out on the next bus. My latest infraction had caused an increase in custody points, which, coupled with the BOP's ongoing failure to acknowledge my status as a high school graduate, now designated me as a medium security inmate. I wouldn't learn where I was headed until I was on my way. From what I'd gathered about the various mediums in the region, my new home would be either relatively laid-back or one of the perpetual war zones where everyone opts to be awake, alert, and strapped into their work boots by the time the doors open in the morning lest they be caught sleeping by an enemy. The array of questionable circumstances suggested that Fort Worth was actively trying to get rid of me as a matter of policy, and breaking more than a few laws in order to do it. Later I was able to confirm this with their own documents, which is always nice.

In shackles, I rode a bus with two dozen other inmates from the area up to the outskirts of Oklahoma City, where the BOP maintains its extraordinary central transfer facility, made up of several dozen jail units plus a bus station and even an airstrip. During my weeklong stay, I tried for the third or fourth time in my life to read the *Lord of the Rings* trilogy, the only decent offering from this unit's book cart, but as usual found that my awareness of J. R. R. Tolkien's sociopolitical obnoxiousness cast a pall over my moderate enjoyment of his intellectually thin Anglo-Luddite meta-parable. This is a man who was too much of a dumb-fuck Christian reactionary even for C. S. Lewis, whom he actually stopped speaking to after the latter married a divorcée.

It turned out I'd been designated to Three Rivers, a medium security prison near the Mexican border (and, incidentally, not far from the horrible little town where my mom grew up). When I arrived after a twelve-hour bus ride in shackles and handcuffs, I discovered that I'd gotten lucky. This being a medium, there were few of the sort of supernaturally obnoxious cops one regularly dealt with at a low or minimum. But it wasn't so much of a medium that I'd have to worry much about the inmates, either. Within twenty minutes of arriving at my new unit, I'd made friends with the shot-callers for both the whites and the Tangos and had a free piece of Suboxone, which was ubiquitous on the compound.

My first full day began pleasantly enough, if rather bizarrely, as I headed out to the rec yard with Shannon Long, a hyperactive former meth kingpin, and "John Deer," his de facto intern. Somehow Long had acquired two small turtles, which he'd been keeping in a cardboard box in his cell, and it was time, apparently, to take the turtles out to the big sandbox used for whatever that game is where you roll a ball across the sand and try to get it to either hit another ball or not hit another ball. After dropping the turtles off, Long and

I headed over to the concrete picnic tables so I could meet with other pillars of the white community. Later we discovered that one of the turtles was missing. John Deer was promptly blamed for having failed to sufficiently monitor the creature's whereabouts, and then we found that a Mexican had taken it. It looked very much as if my second day at a medium security prison would involve a race riot over a stolen turtle, but things were smoothed over.

The next year was taken up largely by baroque goings-on of this nature, with much of the rest spent reading, writing, and creating increasingly elaborate experimental meta-narratives out of pen-and-pencil role-playing games. Occasionally I played with other inmates, as I had now and again at previous facilities, but my real passion was the development of fleshed-out worlds that would proceed largely of their own accord, with dice and stacks of notebook paper covered with numbered lists serving to determine the psychological attributes of the characters and the nature of the world, and only the occasional narrative nudge from myself. Here at Three Rivers, at the height of my artistic journey, I used the eighties cyberpunk RPG Shadowrun as the template of my saga, for which I rolled up two hundred reasonably multidimensional characters via my precious lists of personality aspects (although I gave thematic direction to those belonging to Tango Blast, which in my customized Shadowrun future has become a multinational corporation while still making proud use of the symbolism and customs of its humble origins). I also established expansive yet versatile mechanisms for determining the odds of encountering cops, bandits, civilians, or corporate freight while traveling down I-35, the exact nature of the mutated animals and unaffiliated elemental spirits characters might run into if they veered off the highway, and the results of ongoing industrial espionage campaigns among regional commercial powers like Texas Instruments and Tango Blast Ltd.

To supplement all this I cut up boxes of the low-end prison tea I drank all day into pieces of various sizes that I painstakingly illustrated with colored pencils to depict and make recognizable each individual character as well as vehicles, robots, creatures, dumpsters, and the exteriors of buildings. By the end, my metal desk had been fitted with taped-down paper depicting a network of streets and alleys, upon which I maintained elaborate bird's-eye-view city scenes with dozens of civilians and even tiny stray cats. Above it all, I'd rigged a sort of pulley with strings hanging off it on which to tape individual helicopters, drones, and flying monsters and keep track of their exact position by way of the makeshift tape measure I'd affixed to the wall. My evolving theater was the chief attraction of the entire prison; guards would come from other units to pretend to search my cell, but really to examine, transfixed, each superbly rich new iteration of the living world I'd set in motion, as I watched with the sort of pride that less imaginative men reserve for their biological children.

One evening I got on the phone and called up a radio station in Houston to do a live interview they'd scheduled some days prior. An hour later I was called to the lieutenant's office and thrown in the hole for, I was told, an "investigation," which according to policy can continue for six days without anyone having to write down, even for internal use, what it is that the inmate is suspected of having done. This worked out well for whoever had ordered me locked up, since I'd violated no rule. Aside from the large number of print journalists I'd spoken to on the phone since being locked up, I'd also done live interviews with a couple of other outlets, including the Canadian Broadcasting Corporation, and even the unusually scummy staff at Fort Worth hadn't thought to lock me up for it. The BOP's policy on inmate communications with media was clear that such interviews were not at all prohibited.

The SHU at Three Rivers was shockingly bad, with what appeared to be black mold on the upper walls of my cell (and at least several others, as I was later able to determine), and our window having been for some reason painted over from the outside. My cellie was a headstrong and slightly obnoxious drug dealer from Portland who mentioned he'd gotten to see scenes from the just-released new *Star Wars* film the day before when he happened to be in the medical station down the hall while a guard watched a pirated copy on a computer in the officer station. This led to a conversation about *Star Wars* in general, during which I happened to note in passing how horrible *The Phantom Menace* had been and how I'd skipped the rest of the prequels on account of it.

"Man, *Phantom Menace* was awesome! With Jar Jar Binks and all that?" he responded.

Thereafter I became rather cold to him.

Exactly six days after my illicit detention began, I was released. A sympathetic prison staffer informed me that the "investigation" had been ordered by the executive assistant to the warden, Thomas—the very person I'd written up over his failure to follow policy and respond to Alex Winter's press application.

Upon returning to my unit I learned that a few days prior I'd won the National Magazine Award in the category of commentary, for the first three columns I'd done for *The Intercept*. While I'd been racked with opiate withdrawal and airborne mold spores in the course of retaliatory captivity, I was being applauded at a New York awards ceremony as my editor accepted a little glass bauble on my behalf. As an added bonus, one of the columns for which I'd won—titled "Please Stop Sending Me Jonathan Franzen Novels" and constituting a rather virtuoso takedown of the author's middling new novel, *Purity*, on both ideological and stylistic grounds—was listed by name to the crowd, which included Franzen himself, on hand in case an article of his that had been nominated in the category of travel writing was chosen to win. It wasn't. Had I actually felt one way or another about Jonathan Franzen rather than merely having found him to be an easy target, this would have been sweet indeed.

What was actually satisfying was the fact that any further instances of BOP misconduct would be perpetrated not against some ambiguous anarchist outlaw who also happened to have written for a bunch of outlets but against someone who, having won one of the most prestigious awards in American journalism, was now clearly a journalist (or alternatively someone who, despite not actually being a journalist, had beaten out someone at *The New Yorker* to win one of its top honors, which I kind of liked better). That I'd won the award was known to the prison, which obviously monitored my calls and letters closely. In theory, my higher stature would protect me from any further such incidents.

With the honeymoon now over, I began pursuing my new enemies in the administration in earnest, increasingly with the assistance of disgruntled staff members, such as the two officers who had separately tipped me off about Thomas having given the order to throw me in the SHU. Others acted on a combination of interest in my history and contempt for the BOP; Thomas, for instance, had failed to do his job in such a way that it caused serious difficulties for a particular guard, who told me about the document that staff at every prison must review once a month with names, photos, and backgrounds of inmates deemed most worrisome. I was on this prison's list, described as a "hacker."

Other figures were more ambiguous. The head of the local SIS had a grudging admiration for me (apparently based in part on the mistaken notion that I was somehow involved in an ongoing Anonymous operation against ISIS), eventually restoring my email and putting into writing that there had been no documented reason why it should have been taken away in the first place. When I inquired why my emails were often delayed for several days, which wasn't the case when I was in the jail units, he explained in writing that I had been designated by the BOP as an "Inmate of Greatest Concern," requiring local SIS to manually approve every single email that went in and out of my account. Still, he was SIS, and had signed the order for my "investigation" upon being asked to do so. Regardless of all the praise I received from guards over the years, some of whom ardently believed I was a crucial fighter against whatever configuration of government overreach they happened to oppose based on their own haphazard political understanding, there was not a single one who would have taken anything other than the most negligible risk to thwart the unconstitutional adventures of the people who oversaw their jobs. Many of them were ex-military; that rare sort of American veteran possessed of individualistic moral courage, rather than mere collective physical courage, tends not to seek employment in the prison system, and wouldn't last long in such a context anyway. After a great deal of stonewalling, the BOP finally responded to a Freedom of Information Act request I'd had my editor at *The Intercept* do for all files related to me. Of the 170 documents yielded, the bureau had entirely redacted a third of them for vague reasons of "security." But even with the most incriminating evidence thus concealed, several items that would have appeared innocuous without necessary context made it past the censor.

There was, for instance, my quarterly report from Fort Worth, produced by the strange little fascist who managed the unit I'd been inexplicably sent to after getting out of the SHU, a fellow named Gutierrez, and my case manager, Suzanne Vanderlinden. The document commended me for my "good sanitation," continued monthly restitution payments, and participation in GED courses (which I'd been required to attend since I was not a high school graduate in the eyes of the DOJ and thus also of its subsidiary, the BOP). I had a copy of this report already, and had even considered sending a copy to my mom to hang up on her refrigerator.

But I hadn't seen a separate document composed just twelve days after that glowing review and signed by the very same two corrupt officials—which had been submitted to the regional office in support of Fort Worth's request that I be shipped to another prison immediately. Suddenly, Vanderlinden and Gutierrez had decided I'd actually shown "poor institutional adjustment," "poor program participation," and even "poor living skills." Naturally I was never supposed to see it, lest I be able to prove that a federal agency had falsified information on an official document in order to retaliate against a journalist for working to expose its misconduct, as if any of this mattered.

One day I walked over to the row of inmate phones on the wall of my unit and dialed up Alex Winter. For the last few months, I'd been calling in to his office each Monday for another fifteen-minute recorded audio interview to serve as material for a short documentary he was doing on my case.

Before I'd reached the phone, the unit officer, Gonzalez, called me over.

"They want you over at the assistant warden's office," he said.

"I've got a phone interview right now," I replied, "but I'll be over there when it's done in fifteen minutes or so." He nodded and went back to the officer station to relay the message, and I went back over to the inmate phones to call Winter.

"Well, we've got an interesting development here," I told him when he'd picked up. "The administration wants me to go talk to them, I guess about your application."

Like Fort Worth, the Three Rivers administration had ignored Winter's application, contrary to policy. They ignored the one after that, too. Then they ignored the dozen or so inquiries I'd made over the prison staff request system and printed out for my records. Finally I'd filed a formal grievance against Thomas, the executive assistant, and Yates, the assistant warden, noting that policy had been repeatedly and willfully violated. The five-day deadline for their reply had already passed—fairly typical, as I'd noticed in prior attempts to file grievances—but now they were at least calling me in for a meeting.

We'd been on the phone for a few minutes when Gonzalez came up to me and whispered, almost apologetically, "They said for you to go over there now."

"I told them I'd go when I'm done here," I replied, having put the phone aside but speaking loudly enough to be picked up and recorded on Alex's end. "And really, it's inappropriate for Yates to insist on a meeting with an inmate who has an active grievance claim filed against him."

"Actually," said Gonzalez, "it's Thomas that's over there."

"I have one filed against him, too. It's the same grievance. And it's about their failure to follow policy on letting in the press. This guy I'm doing this phone interview with right now is seriously the same guy they've refused to answer for seven months. The very same guy. Neither of them is in a position to make any demands right now. Tell Yates if he wants to talk to me he can come over here."

Gonzalez shrugged and walked away.

We continued with the interview. Soon Winter was asking me about the spate of police shooting incidents that, having been caught on film, had dominated the press cycle in recent days. "Yes, we have a problem with racism in America, but overlapping that we have another problem that's more fundamental. We have a cop problem," I explained, endlessly entertained by my own rhetoric.

"Now of course," I continued, "the president is unable to say what needs to be said about the matter, for two reasons." But before I had a chance to decide what those reasons were, a very large lieutenant by the name of Tarango appeared beside me.

"Hang up the phone," the pig demanded.

"I've gotta go," I told Alex. "Looks like I can't talk to the press anymore. Tell Roger Hodge." Then I hung up, satisfied that Winter would now call my main editor at *The Intercept*, who would in turn announce that I'd been interrupted by prison staff during a media interview and presumably placed in the hole.

Two officers escorted me across the compound over to the SHU. And for perhaps the dozenth time in my four years as a federal prisoner, I watched as one of the door slots was unlocked and fell open, and as some unknown person stuck his wrists through, palms up, to be handcuffed. Once cuffed, the other inmate stood to the side, as protocol demanded, while the guards then unlocked the door, opened it, and ushered me into the room. The other inmate stood against the opposite wall, as ordered, his hands likewise cuffed behind him. Then the door was shut and locked behind me. As was my custom, I stepped away from the door, nodding to it, inviting my new cellie to have his handcuffs removed first. And as he was attending to this, backing up to the slot for this procedure—this cuffing-up process that must be done whenever the door is to be opened and is one of those constants of SHU life that one gets used to surprisingly quickly—I introduced myself: "Sup. I'm Brown." Then he gave his name, and then we were friends.

It had taken me a while, in the early days of forced pairings, before I realized what it was they reminded me of: It was like when you're a little kid and your mom has a friend who has another little kid and so she drops you off at their house. And suddenly you and this other kid, having been designated as playmates by the mysterious dictates of momdom, are thrown into each other's presence, with no preexisting social delineation on which to rely. But you're essentially in the same boat—you've both been partnered with some previously undiscovered child and told to play, and really, to play together does seem to be the most reasonable course of action, regardless of what you might think about the institutions that brought you together. So you play.

And so it was here, too. My new cellie, a drug dealer whom I'll call Simon Bolivar, went through the usual introductions, the two of us relating in turn what we were in the SHU for, how much each of us got at sentencing, at what other places we'd done time; then we'd determine who we might know in common back on the compound and exchange gossip on the subject of gang relations and the doings of particular ho-ass cops.

Bolivar, twenty-five, had been raised in Houston and immersed from childhood in the city's gang culture. When an elementary school project called for him to bring in a family role model, he chose his uncle, a prominent local Crip. When Bolivar was twelve his father caught him storing guns and drugs in his room (which he'd been keeping safe at the behest of neighborhood gang members) and threw him out. Eventually he ended up in the Texas state prison system, which I'd come to know by reputation from the other federal inmates I'd met who'd done state time.

The Texas Department of Corrections had been the subject of my first real work of journalism, back in 2004, when the rape of a female inmate by two state prison guards had made the news. Shortly afterward, the state prison board met to enact a new policy—one that would make it harder for journalists to interview inmates about life in Texas state prisons. Even so, I was consistently shocked by the things

I'd been told by my fellow inmates who'd previously done time in Texas state prisons.

Now, as we paced our little cell, Bolivar gave me a cheerful summary of the arranged fights between individual staff and gang members, something one inevitably hears about from both guards and inmates. After he held his own against one affable guard much larger than himself, the fellow brought him a meal from Burger King—a story that immediately reminded me of when the tentacle-faced alien hunter in *Predator 2* presented his human adversary with an antique pistol in recognition of the latter having put up a commendable fight.

Bolivar also told me of a youngish female guard who once offered to let him fuck her in a utility closet for one hundred fifty dollars. She also asked for cash to get lunch afterward, presumably to make everything more classy, so he gave her twenty dollars and told her to go get a steak at a restaurant he knew to be nearby whereas I gathered that other males in those circumstances would have sent her to Burger King and that she had expected nothing more. Afterward, he got in some trouble with his own girlfriend when he called her on a cell phone and told her to send the money to this particular officer, who had a clearly female name. He told his girlfriend it was to pay the woman off after she'd caught him with weed, but she didn't believe him. It didn't help that for some reason he'd also decided to note that he'd given the cop some cash for a steak.

"Why you gonna buy that bitch a steak?" his own bitch had inquired. And of course he wasn't in a position to admit that he'd fucked the cop in a utility closet and that the dictates of good taste required that a steak be involved. But the point here is that inmates and staff both tend to share basic assumptions about life and social conduct, such as the presenting of gifts of fast-food items as a means of commemorating significant interpersonal interactions.

Much of Bolivar's time here in the SHU was given over to the acquisition and consumption of synthetic marijuana, generally referred to as K2 for the same reason that all gelatin is known as Jell-O. Contraband makes it into the SHU via methods I'm not at liberty to discuss (I feel about the secret ways and means of drug activity much like an NSA director feels about national security), but the way in which these things are transferred from cell to cell is not a secret to the authorities, and at any rate it's more interesting.

The two other SHU units I'd inhabited, at Seagoville and Fort Worth, were constructed in such a way that the cell doors reach the floor (though not so closely that one can't still flood the range, Allah be praised). But here at Three Rivers, as at many other prisons, the doors in both the main units and the SHU corridors left sizable gaps under them. This inch-plus gap allowed for the pursuit of one of the most remarkable phenomena of prison life: "fishing."

To "shoot the line" is to slide a small weight, such as a battery or toothpaste tube, across a hallway so as to allow for the transfer of objects to and from other inmates. The weight is attached to a long piece of string, itself usually produced by ripping up clothing or sheets; when the weight is successfully shot across the hallway into another cell, the receiver can then pull the string to get whatever the sender has tied to it that he means to provide. Or he can tie his own object to the end that's just come under his door, then have the original sender pull it back into his cell. Often, both of these things will happen. Bolivar, for instance, will shoot his line over to his homeboy's cell down the hall on the other side by expertly kicking it at just the right angle. Timed properly, the weight will shoot straight under the target cell door, and the connection is established. Back on our end, Bolivar has tied a note to the length of string, and now yells through the crack in the side of the door, "Pull!" The homeboy in question pulls his end and the note slides along the hallway with the string until it reaches his cell. Homeboy takes off the note—in this case, a request for a double-A battery, which many inmates have for use with their radios and which may be bought from the SHU commissary cart each week. The note will read something along the following lines:

> Yo dawg wat you up to over there me I'm just chillin wit my cellie its that white boy Brown he's like a hacker or sometin hey lemme get one of those double A's so I can smoke I'll get you back on that and that other thing next week okay gotta go.

The homeboy sits at his wall-mounted metal desk, with its little blue stool that extends out from one of its legs, and ponders the merits of the proposal, taking into account some wide range of factors—he himself is Valluco, a gang made up of Hispanics from the Rio Grande Valley, and he knows little of Bolivar, who just got to this compound a month ago; but he will have heard Bolivar shouting back and forth to his other homeboys down the hall, people he does know by reputation, and so can deduce that he's a solid guy. And anyway, he has plenty of batteries, plenty of money on his books with which to buy more next week. Besides, Bolivar, like most gang members, can be expected to be true to his word. There's a small chance that he'll be moved to another corridor or something before he gets a chance to pay him back, of course, but in that case he can just send stamps via the orderly, who's let out of his own cell every day to clean the halls and, being himself a solid guy, also brings items back and forth from corridor to corridor.

Having gone through some thought process along these lines, our across-the-hall homeboy puts a double-A battery in a mailing envelope along with the original note, upon which he's written a reply:

> sup man yeh I can give you this one just to help you out thats cool you gotta hit that deuce I got ya not much to do in here get me back tho okay cuz my cellie smokes too and he's on comsary restriction so I been letting him use my battries too its no big thing hey were you over in jim wells unit do you know that pistolero from Uvalde I want to see if they shipped him thats my boy okay peace

Note that while all of this is going on, the string is just sitting there in the hallway, running from our cell to homeboy's, easily seen should any guard happen down our corridor. But the stealth of the guards is hampered by the huge, perpetually jingling sets of keys they wear; furthermore, as each of these corridors is set off by a sort of gate that must itself be noisily unlocked, the inmates generally have time to pull the line back into one of the two cells before a guard might become aware of it. Still, the risk exists that a guard will manage to grab one, seizing at the very least a line that's taken time and effort to fashion out of sheets; worse, he may get it while a note with specific, actionable intelligence is attached, or perhaps contraband. And even if the guard doesn't manage to catch it, if he's so inclined he can call in backup, order the inmates to cuff up, pull them out, and do a cell search. In fact, this is exactly what happened to Bolivar a few days later, and thus he lost his extra clothes and "hoarded" juice packets and all the other little items that every SHU inmate has but that can technically be seized by staff, particularly if they're mad at you, and of course he was lucky not to have had any serious contraband in the cell at the time—all because Bolivar and so many other young gang members are in the habit of just leaving their lines stretched across the corridor while they and their homeboys sit at their rusty little wall desks, leisurely writing each other letters as if they were fucking Jazz Age poets catching up on their transatlantic correspondence at a Parisian sidewalk café rather than prisoners living in a dungeon with guards running around looking for people to oppress.

Eventually one of the lieutenants arrived to give me my infraction sheet, known colloquially as a "shot." We went through the cuffing ritual again and my cellie was taken down the hall for the duration so that the officer could read me my infraction report and get any statements I might have for him to put down, in privacy. This officer, a reasonably personable fellow named Johnson with whom I'd had no prior dealings but whom I could nonetheless reasonably expect to be either personally corrupt or a moral coward and thus regularly complicit in the corruption that surrounds him, like most Americans, told me that I'd been charged with "refusing an order." The institutional party line held that Gonzalez had given me a direct order to go to the meeting at the assistant warden's office. I provided a statement to the effect that I'd not been given any order at all, that in fact the whole exchange had been captured on the prison phone that had of course been recording when Gonzalez came up to me during my interview and that this could thus be verified very easily, and that at any rate the request had itself been inappropriate for several reasons, all of which I'd articulated at the time, again in such a way as to have been recorded both by the prison and by Alex Winter. The lieutenant wrote down some conveniently abridged version of this explanation, left me a copy of the original infraction sheet, and withdrew.

Bolivar was brought back in and I regaled him with an analysis of my infraction proceedings up to this point and how they might play out in the near future. Actually this promised to be an uninteresting case, as the infraction itself was of a low severity ranking—a 300 series, as it's known, with such things as possessing hooch and stabbing people being classified as 100 series—and thus they wouldn't be holding me in the SHU in advance of a formal disciplinary hearing where I'd be able to call witnesses and make a pest of myself. Rather, my counselor and case manager back at the unit would look over the infraction report, consider my statement, and then decide on some relatively minor punishment, likely entailing loss of phone or commissary privileges for a couple of weeks; in any event, I'd be let out of the SHU as soon as they'd gotten this done, probably within a day or two. I offered to leave Bolivar the bag of coffee I'd ordered from commissary, assuming that the cart would come by the next morning before I was let out. I was vastly relieved that I'd be back in the unit before Suboxone withdrawal kicked in in earnest.

The next morning my acting counselor, Musquiz, appeared at the door and motioned me over. I didn't know the fellow very well, as he technically worked the unit next to mine and was only handling my case due to ongoing staff changes, but from reports I'd gotten from other inmates I knew him to be about as decent a fellow as one can expect to come across within such an entrenched de facto criminal bureaucracy as the BOP. My only interaction with him had occurred a few months earlier, when he told me he'd seen *The Hacker Wars* and asked me what Weev was really like. I'd explained that Weev was an amoral racist weirdo but that some of his early pranks were highly amusing.

Now, Musquiz had brought me a copy of the results of the mini–disciplinary hearing he and the case manager had conducted; they'd given me two weeks commissary and visiting restriction but suspended the sentence pending two weeks of good behavior—the prison equivalent of probation. "What's right is right," he said, having been made aware of the actual circumstances of the incident (though not from the infraction report itself—I noticed that Johnson had refrained from writing down any of the key points I'd stated to him the previous evening in my own defense and had instead merely written that "inmate says he would have gone after the interview"). But even without having my full side of the story, Musquiz and my case manager had deemed the shot to be without merit; even Gonzalez's own description of events, which recounts how the officer "then went and ordered Inmate Brown he needed to go now," was awkwardly phrased enough as to be clearly the end result of some pragmatic attempt to shoehorn the requisite direct order into the incident lest he himself be found guilty of disobeying the order from Lieutenant Tarango, who in turn was merely acting on behalf of either Thomas or Yates. But none of that mattered now for my purposes, since I'd be getting back out to where the Suboxone was before the withdrawals had really kicked in. "I'll go ahead and tell them to kick you out of here, so you should hopefully be released this afternoon," Musquiz told me.

"Okay, great, thanks."

"But here's the thing. Yates really had his feelings hurt about this. So that might end up being a problem."

That was to be expected; although Gonzalez's written account didn't include my several reasonable objections to breaking off in the middle of a scheduled phone interview with a media representative who'd been wronged by the prison so that I could go meet with the very official who'd wronged him by ignoring both of our inquiries for seven months but who all of a sudden just had to discuss the issue right then and not twelve minutes later, he did see fit to write down the following quote from yours truly, which, if not word-for-word accurate, did at least capture the gist of something I did actually say at the end of my monologue: "No I am giving a interview you tell Yates he can come and talk to me over here if he wants to speak with me." At any rate, I'm fairly sure I used commas and perhaps even a semicolon in the real exchange, if only in spirit, and obviously I would have distinctly pronounced the *an* before *interview*, for do I not stand fast against the encroaching darkness?

But I had indeed forced Yates to lose face with my dismissive response, which had promptly been reported to him, making it all the more noble of Musquiz to have nonetheless given me probation whereas many other counselors would have gone further in the hopes of staying on a vindictive assistant warden's good side. So I thanked him again as he left, and then I set about preparing for my departure.

Naturally I offered to Bolivar to take with me any messages he might have for his buddies on the compound (I knew he probably didn't have any, being fairly new around here, but one always asks out of politeness).

Time passed, and still no one had come to get me, whereas kick-outs, as they're lovingly termed, are generally done after lunch at the latest. Over the next few hours, as I queried passing officers about the prospects of getting this show on the road, the replies got noticeably less cheery, more vague. Then an officer came by to explain that Yates had told them to simply keep me back there. I explained that this was illegal. He said he knew it was; being possessed of good manners, he apologized for having to violate the Magna Carta at the behest of his liege lord, though I'm paraphrasing. I asked for the lawyer call that was constitutionally guaranteed to inmates at any time. I never got it.

Up until that point I'd still had one illusion left about the nature of the American republic. Each criminal or otherwise illicit thing that had been done to me had nonetheless been perpetrated within the channels of policy, supported by at least a layer of plausible deniability, even if such things convinced no one and didn't have to. Each new move against me, or against my mother, or against my contributors and supporters, had come complete with a thin veneer of legality and a nod to the rule of law. That was always reassuring; it indicated that even the boldest elements of the state-corporate axis were themselves mindful of lines that couldn't be safely crossed, and this meant that I still had rights and thus that I'd need not fear, for instance, being locked away, incommunicado, without even falsehoods to justify it all.

Over the next two weeks, suffering from withdrawal and rage, I sat quietly in my dungeon.

When I was released back to the unit, I learned from staff that I was to have spent the remaining months of my sentence in the SHU on Yates's orders; only repeated calls from lawyers had caused the warden some concern that his assistant might be getting him into unnecessary trouble.

I wrote up the op-ed on the administrative remedy issue and sent it first to *The New York Times*, which immediately accepted it for the print edition. Perhaps nothing would come of it, but I was satisfied that I'd done my duty to my fellow inmates; indeed I'd done my duty as a citizen of a republic, having gone to some considerable lengths to operate within its own framework so as to prompt that change and achieve the justice that, we're told, is simply a matter of patience and persistence. And perhaps the incrementalists had a point. Perhaps the citizenry would come to focus, in coming years, on the institutional rot that plagued not just the prisons but also law enforcement, the intelligence community, and other fundamental mechanisms of the state that had gone effectively unaddressed.

A few weeks after I got out, *The New York Times* informed me that they'd killed my piece. It was too late to take it to another paper in hopes of prompting action; Donald Trump was about to take office, having been elected president with the assistance of my chief enemy, Palantir founder Peter Thiel, and my chief ally, Julian Assange.

SYNTHESIS

10

Synthesis

Alex Winter had arranged to interview me one last time, on the day of my release, during the long drive from the South Texas prison to the Dallas-area halfway house where I'd be spending the next few months. Up front, my dad drove and my mom handed out snacks; in the back, with Alex and his documentary crew, I spoke darkly into the camera of things to come.

At some point during the ride we received a message via the Courage Foundation from Julian Assange and his longtime second-in-command, Sarah Harrison, congratulating me on my release and promising a surprise. This turned out to be the HBGary emails, restored and searchable once again after years of sporadic hosting, and now on WikiLeaks itself, along with the Stratfor emails that I'd never gotten around to reading before going to prison over them.

A few years prior, while awaiting sentencing, I read through a dozen-volume set of George Orwell's correspondence, personal notes, BBC broadcasts, and published magazine work. From scattered footnotes found therein, I pursued the narrative of the mid-twentieth century through dozens of related lives—Malcolm Muggeridge, Alex Comfort, Kim Philby, the Mitford sisters, Evelyn Waugh, Samuel MacGregor Mathers, Kingsley Amis. This was an age wherein the queen sent her valet to the nearby anarchist bookstore to pick up a copy of *Animal Farm*, written by an atheistic socialist anti-imperialist in an attack on the Stalinists; wherein that same socialist had gone to Spain to fight for a republic against the fascists, who would shoot him in the neck, and in alliance with the Stalinists, who eventually tried to finish him off; wherein English conservatives would cheer the sinking of a British-chartered ship by Francisco Franco, accomplished with the help of the Gestapo; wherein the Indian nationalist Subhas Chandra Bose praised Japanese imperialism as a foil against British imperialism, while Gandhi recommended mass suicide as an alternative to both.

One may come to understand the era well enough via a single narrative thread that begins in 1939, when Nazi Germany and Soviet Russia signed the Molotov-Ribbentrop Nonaggression Pact. Previous to this, English communists and their counterparts abroad had been among the most reliable bulwarks against fascism. Now, prompted by Moscow, they discovered that Nazism existed under some previously unknown category of economic development that was in fact somewhat redeemable, and at any rate less of a threat than imperialism, capitalism, and the patchwork array of social democracies and constitutional monarchies that still dominated much of the West. Some two years later, when Hitler invaded the Soviet Union and the latter turned to England and the United States for help, the line changed anew, and English communists would now speak fondly of Winston Churchill, who himself had hailed Mussolini not long prior as "the greatest lawgiver among men."

"Jailed since 2012 for his investigations, #BarrettBrown has finally been released from prison," Edward Snowden had written in a tweet I found reprinted in a copy of the *Dallas Morning News* at the halfway house. "Best of luck in this very different world."

In fact, I recognized this world all too well.

The BOP's standard early release conditions require that one seek employment, and the column seemed not to count any more than did the book deal I signed a few weeks after getting out. So I got a job at *D Magazine* reporting on city politics, taking notes by hand at city council meetings on account of the bureau's warning that I would be returned to prison if I used any device that could conceivably connect to the internet, up to and including a video game console—a condition that was to last for the duration of my six-month "supervised release" period. The judge had actually ordered only that my internet use be monitored by software installed on my laptop for the two-year period of my probation, and a friendly DOJ reentry staffer who visited the halfway house each week tried to clarify this to her BOP counterparts, to no avail. At any rate, my city council pieces won the Folio Award for "Best Local Coverage," which would have been far more difficult had I actually refrained from using a computer at work, and far more impressive were the Folio Awards not total bullshit.

By the end of April, I'd been granted home confinement at my mom's house and was approaching the relatively happy status wherein my direct oversight by the Bureau of Prisons would finally end, to be replaced by a less onerous period of supervision by the DOJ's probation department. It was at this time that the regional BOP director Luz Luhan learned of interviews I was scheduled to grant PBS and *Vice*'s cable channel over the following week and conveyed to me that not only was I required to get written permission from the BOP to speak to the press at all, but I would also have to convince the journalists in question to seek her personal approval as well. Since the BOP's own publicly available program statements on media policy make perfectly clear that no such rules exist for incarcerated inmates, much less those who've been released, and that media outlets are never required to seek permission for anything other than the ability to enter an actual BOP facility to interview prisoners, I informed Luhan that I would be disregarding these and all other illegal attempts to impose prior restraint on the press, at which point she hung up on me. Naturally I'd recorded these two phone conversations and had them made public via the Courage Foundation (of which more later). Then I went on the same Houston radio program that I'd been thrown in the SHU for talking to back at Three Rivers Medium, summarized this latest instance of unconstitutional interference with basic press freedoms, and had the host call Luhan's office number to solicit an on-air comment.

The next morning I was arrested by two U.S. Marshals whom the BOP had told to seize me on the grounds, as one marshal told me, that I'd "refused an order." They placed me in the same Seagoville jail unit where I'd spent 2014, which at least gave me the chance to catch up with a few old friends who were still around. This time, the BOP didn't even bother to write up an infraction sheet, either before my arrest or afterward, although these and other documents are legally required to confine an inmate or even take away their commissary for a week, to say nothing of actually arresting someone. No documentation seems to have been generated at all, in fact, nor was there any disciplinary hearing when I arrived at the jail. Throughout my stint in the BOP, the regional administration had learned the same lessons I had about the real extent of state power, even against the press, which they now viewed with such accurate contempt as to feel comfortable imprisoning me without even the legal fig leaf of a falsified report to back it up.

In any society where the rule of law is lacking, money and connections make a fine substitute. I was released four days later after the *D Magazine* publisher Wick Allison paid eleven thousand dollars to the high-powered New York law firm Haynes and Boone to call the bureau's national office and threaten to take the matter before a judge. By this point only a month remained until my period of BOP jurisdiction finally came to an end, which was fortunate, since Allison only had so much extra money lying around to buy me due process.

The problem was that my six months of BOP-supervised release was followed immediately by two years of DOJ-administered probation. And the DOJ had a new and very personal reason to misuse their remaining years of control—for Kevin Gallagher, head of the Free Barrett Brown defense fund, had filed suit against my prosecutor Candina Heath and FBI Special Agent Robert Smith in federal court in San Francisco just a few weeks prior, and the judge had already signaled that it would be allowed to go forward.

Gallagher and I had been coordinating on this move in the year or so since he'd discovered that, in the course of Heath's attempt to seize the legal defense fund Gallagher had created on my behalf in 2013, her office had subpoenaed the fundraising site WePay, demanding all available information on everyone who'd donated. Given that such information was obviously irrelevant to Heath's stated purpose of simply determining how much money was there so as to seize it for the taxpayers, and taking into account her broader pattern of behavior before and after, this was obviously an attempt to identify and scrutinize supporters of a cause that the DOJ found inconvenient—much as the Palantir employee Matthew Steckman and the HBGary Federal CEO Aaron Barr had planned to do to those who had been found to have made entirely legal donations to WikiLeaks or to have spoken out against the U.S. Chamber of Commerce. Remember that? Yeah, you remember!

The DOJ's real intent here was plain enough that a respectable law firm took the case on contingency, filing a due process claim on behalf of Gallagher and an anonymous donor on the grounds that Heath and friends, along with the DOJ itself, had violated the well-established First Amendment right of citizens to donate to political causes anonymously, as well as the Stored Communications Act. And it was obvious enough to Magistrate Judge Maria-Elena James of the Northern District of California that she refused to dismiss the case despite several lengthy motions to dismiss filed by a crack team of DOJ lawyers brought in from Washington. As Judge James summed it up in an early ruling, "Defendants have failed to articulate any facially reasonable explanation for requesting donors' identities." Amusingly, the DOJ had sought to defend itself on that central point by citing the fact that Judge Stickney, though having denied Heath's unusual motion to seize a defendant's legal fund, had nonetheless taken pains to declare in his ruling that her attempt had merely been a good-faith effort to protect the taxpayers. But Stickney's credulousness carried no weight in this other, more competent district. Threatened by the prospect of the case proceeding into the discovery phase, whereby Gallagher's legal team could demand relevant documents that themselves would almost certainly reveal further wrongdoing, the DOJ could only argue its case on procedural grounds of legal standing, jurisdiction, and the like. The result was a case in which the defendants ultimately wriggled out of any measurable legal consequences, but in which no one concerned believes them to be innocent of the underlying conduct—a sort of mirror image of my own case.

More harassment naturally followed, with *The Intercept*, my agent, and my new publisher all receiving subpoenas over the coming months, ostensibly as part of the DOJ's broadly defined right to collect my $890,000 of court-ordered restitution via garnishment of wages, in addition to the

10 percent of my income I was already paying directly. As always, the technically valid core demand was accompanied by all manner of little extras, such as their initial demand for all communications between myself and my editor at *The Intercept*, and, later, their order to my publisher to stop paying me the scheduled advances I was living on until some "further notice" that turned out to be ten months away, which is quite further indeed. And so on and so forth.

From the inside I'd managed to get a sense of a country in visible decline, its culture growing over with new layers of sordidness and its politics increasingly baroque, fractalized. I spent the first few days at the halfway house on the phone with old contacts so as to get a sense of how deeply the system had wounded itself over the course of the last election. And then there was the question of the strange new realignments that a shift in the basic questions of national politics had made possible. The various elements of the Net-focused world from which I myself sprang had cracked and re-formed into strange configurations that, like those occupying the national stage, were revealing and sometimes amusing, and at any rate would complicate things.

Anonymous had succumbed to itself, having finally become little more than the "idea" that some always held it to be; today it consists mainly of a few thousand Facebook pages and Twitter accounts with comparatively little to show for themselves. The AnonOps IRC had been in decline since late 2011, in part over rumors, apparently true, that the server itself had been compromised by the FBI; the hodgepodge array of similar networks either were all gone or might as well have been. The cultural uprising that had made the media its consistent tool was over.

None of this was inevitable. Had things proceeded such that people of a particular caliber had continued to pour in and serve as the human nodes necessary for a network with no structure, as had happened over and over again in Anonymous's history, it would have continued as always and perhaps even gone on to greater successes. Some savvy band of online adventurers could perhaps reanimate it even today; but revived, the creature that resulted would still be a jellyfish.

Nature, or its online equivalent, had given birth to a new sort of animal, itself born of the same fertile jungles as Anonymous. The alt-right had gone much farther from its incubation grounds at 4chan, and toward formal political power, than had its largely left-libertarian predecessor, which itself was always too intrinsically anti-institutional to receive anything other than masked tributes from Polish parliamentarians and sprinklings of assistance from assorted Establishment dissidents. That Anonymous was known almost universally as a "hacker group," and thus fundamentally criminal, had also prevented it from making the same institutional inroads as the alt-right, whose tendency toward violent street confrontations was insensibly eclipsed by its habit of engaging within the system itself, and indeed embracing large portions of it; such is the usual pattern of fascist movements: they mix revolution with institutionalism and thus enjoy the support of the police. To the extent that what was happening was new—and indicative more of the future than of the past—it was most fully embodied by the fact that white grievance and twenty-first-century meta-irreverence had found expression and unity of purpose in the form of a stray 4chan meme, that of Pepe the Frog.

The situation was telling in other ways. The degree to which 4chan—and even some of the more backwash-y elements of Anonymous—had given direct rise to the alt-right remained unclear to me until a writer for *The Atlantic* called to ask for background but ended up mostly having to bring me up to date. All I could think to note was that this dynamic, wherein the same raw material gives rise to mutually exclusive and opposing movements, is not at all unprecedented. Marxists and Nazis both cited Hegel as their ideological predecessor (which is what happens when you write vague, fraudulent nonsense that can mean anything at all). The various anticapitalist movements of the early twentieth century did involve some limited overlap, with such figures as Mussolini and Goebbels migrating from left to right while others moved in the opposite direction, as the broad and undifferentiated caucus of Opposing the Current State of Affairs gradually sorted itself out into specific factions advocating increasingly distinct ideals. It's a natural process that had likewise occurred among proto-Protestants and thereafter their more established denominational successors. The chief difference today is that these broad alliances and odd reconfigurations can now proceed at a pace so frenzied as to fundamentally alter the game itself, and make nonsense of our attempts to predict humanity's future or even grasp its present.

A more explicitly outré network of self-avowed neo-Nazis had also emerged, overlapping with the alt-right and sharing some of its postmodern symbology while also incorporating it into the more traditional imagery of white supremacy; a digital poster for the Charlottesville Unite the

Right rally depicted a row of Pepes marching in Confederate gray under a sky run through with Nazi emblems. I was only partially surprised to find that Weev, who'd been a drug-addled troll with no identifiable political views during our shared time at Encyclopedia Dramatica back in 2007, was among the network of young men who had made all this possible. Weev had taken full advantage of the well-intentioned but naive hero worship available to each of us veteran "hacktivists" when he was unjustly indicted and imprisoned for notifying *Gawker* of a vulnerability in an AT&T website that made customer info visible to the public; this had been sufficient to land him a key role in the documentary *The Hacker Wars* alongside myself and Jeremy Hammond, and to prompt praise on the *New York Times* op-ed page alongside the same incompatible company. That Weev had never been any sort of activist didn't matter in this environment. Now possessed of the social currency that is positive press, and having learned many of the same lessons as the rest of us as to what the internet can be made to do, he promptly built himself into a figure of the Nazi resurgence, working to oversee its major propaganda node the Daily Stormer from his new base of operations in Eastern Europe.

At some point in my absence, the underground had emerged to combat the mainstream, and had at least temporarily overrun it. Never again could one seriously deny the internet's potential to produce sudden and dramatic change. And no one could any longer maintain that the American republic was essentially sound, its institutions capable of upholding themselves against whatever the future might bring.

But one wants institutions to fall in the right direction.

In a phenomenon just as indicative of the times as the Molotov-Ribbentrop Pact, the DOJ and FBI had suffered unprecedented assault, but on largely partisan grounds in which both sides were partly right and partly wrong, and generally right only for the wrong reasons. The weeks before the election brought the spectacle of the two major parties alternating between admiration and criticism of James Comey based on each new development in the Clinton investigation. I watched with other inmates as the earnest-looking FBI director told Congress that the bureau treats everyone the same, or words to that effect but more awkwardly phrased, somehow. There followed the even more extraordinary realignment, whereby much of the right had little choice but to seek to discredit the law enforcement and intelligence communities, while some large preponderance of Democrats were compelled to defend such things as a bulwark of liberty and decency. No real reform could be expected to emerge from such an obscurantist ballet.

Perfectly encapsulating the missed opportunities of this new era was the widespread introduction and rapid devolution of the term *deep state*. The underlying concept of "deep politics" had been introduced and fleshed out over decades by the essentially left-wing former Canadian diplomat, author, and Berkeley professor Peter Dale Scott. Starting in the sixties, Scott wrote extensively about the CIA and its dramatic Cold War growth beyond its legal confines (and well beyond the intent of President Harry Truman, who denounced the agency he himself had created in a remarkable newspaper op-ed published shortly before his death). More broadly, Scott was interested in the manner by which the visible and official aspects of a state may be undermined and partially controlled by the more opaque elements that exist beyond effective oversight. The value of his work is perhaps most efficiently conveyed by noting his identification of Frank Sturgis as a figure to be watched years before he became known to the public via his role in the Watergate burglary. Moreover, Scott's terminology and findings would gradually be adopted by academics in Latin America to describe the networks of military and intelligence officials whose machinations were ultimately more relevant to the politics of a country than the state's visible surface; just a few years ago, in publications like *The Economist*, one could find references to Egypt's "deep state" of entrenched bureaucrats so powerful that even a dictator would have to contend with them in order to achieve basic reforms. It was a vastly useful concept, descriptive of phenomena ranging from the palace eunuchs who at times effectively controlled the Byzantine Empire to the networks of anti-communists, oil men, and intelligence assets who remained loyal to Allen Dulles well after the more "structured" portions of the government had relieved him of his official leadership of the CIA. And then, suddenly, these things were incorporated into the conceptual toolkit of people like Newt Gingrich and madness descended upon the land.

The jujitsu surrounding "fake news" was even more horribly appropriate, and most fully embodied by *The Washington Post*'s declaration that the website PropOrNot would clarify what was and wasn't propaganda and its subsequent admission that perhaps it wouldn't clarify anything at all. The legacy press obviously does a great deal of good work of the sort that otherwise wouldn't get done, and in certain other respects competes well with many of the alternatives, but it collectively overreached in its attempt to make of all things its province and to give a name unto every animal it found thereupon. That the outlets we've inherited were unable to effectively reassert themselves as the natural arbiters of the truth is only partially a result of the bad faith and outright fabrications now routinely deployed against it; like many of the other institutions now having a hard time of it, the news media opened itself up to disingenuous attacks by first opening itself up to legitimate ones.

More fundamentally, each of these institutions has failed because the people have failed. Much of what goes wrong in the United States simply doesn't happen to any comparable degree within the borders of other Western democracies. Certainly, the American people do some things very well. But if time reveals that its latter generations were ultimately unable to govern themselves within the demanding framework of a constitutional republic, historians will not have to search terribly hard for causes. It would be enough to note that there was no particular reason why things should not have gone wrong. Every society rests ultimately upon the qualities of its people, particularly to the extent that its institutions are representative of the public will. That much of the American public is wiser and more humane in many respects than previous generations isn't necessarily enough to ensure that it will also be collectively capable of overseeing the vast and complex apparatus that has grown up in its name. And contrary to the unspoken assumptions that once seemed justified by recent history, and that helped to justify in turn a basic premise of American democracy, there was never any reason to expect that the well-informed and basically decent percentage of the citizenry should have ultimately tamed and neutralized the other, more dangerous portion that was always present, and is now ascendant.

Central to each of these issues—cause and symptom, promise and peril—was WikiLeaks.

My connection to WikiLeaks had always been rather indirect. I'd never communicated with Assange himself; during my incarceration, he released several statements in my defense, including one especially detailed document that appeared on the day of my first sentencing hearing in which he reminds all concerned of the bizarre fact that a major piece of evidence in my prosecution was a call for murder delivered by a Fox News "analyst" against Assange himself that I had merely quoted in disdain. Not long after, Gallagher's Free Barrett Brown fundraising apparatus was rolled into the new Courage Foundation, founded in part by Assange and Sarah Harrison to assist whistleblowers and activists. Naturally I'd continued my yearslong offense against his most ill-equipped detractors—Jonathan Franzen, for instance—in my column and the occasional phone interview.

I'd had no problem with WikiLeaks' release of the various Democratic email sets, regardless of how they'd been acquired, or by whom, or to what end; indeed, to have not released these plainly newsworthy materials would have been a betrayal of the organization's original mission. That WikiLeaks was now most fiercely championed by a sordid array of right-wing figures from Trump on downward was, while disheartening, not necessarily a sin of commission on Assange's part. Even taking active advantage of this support, as he was now openly doing, wasn't a deal breaker. Given the degree of blatant persecution that Assange continued to endure, as well as WikiLeaks' continued role as a clearing-house for valuable leaks such as the series of CIA documents it put out in 2017, the urge to forgive Assange his faults was strong and, I think, largely justifiable. When Randy Credico, the New York comedian and longtime radical-left activist, asked me to do a regular segment on his WBAI program and appear opposite Assange for a special fundraiser, I had no problem doing so. I even appeared in a videocast with Kim Dotcom, a close Assange ally for whom I'd developed increasing distaste as I learned more about his views (and on whose behalf Anonymous had knocked down a couple of law enforcement websites in protest of the DOJ's campaign against his piracy business, Megaupload, back in the day).

At the same time, it was becoming plain that a public break was inevitable. Too much of what Assange now did and said was of such a character that I would have attacked anyone else for it. And to make even constructive criticism was to court conflict. I'd already heard of the July 2016 incident in which Edward Snowden had written, "Democratizing information has never been more vital, and Wikileaks has helped. But their hostility to even modest curation is a mistake," prompting the official WikiLeaks account to retort, "Opportunism won't earn you a pardon from Clinton & curation is not censorship of ruling party cash flows." It was an ironic line of accusation in light of what would later be revealed about what Assange himself had been up to around that same time.

Even had I been comfortable dissimulating for a worthy cause, there loomed the question of whether this cause remained worthy. History is strewn with examples of relatively benign entities that, knowing themselves to be better than the enemy, feel themselves justified in adopting increasingly immoral tactics so as to prevent the devastating results that would come with the enemy's victory; indeed, this is one of the major patterns of institutional development that can be seen in any society and on any number of scales. Sometimes this works out quite well, and the entity achieves some considerable good in the world. Other times, the entity becomes worse than the original threat. And on still other occasions, the entity remains morally superior to the opponent, but loses so much of its own credibility in the process of fighting as to give up the advantages that come with credibility, and thus it ultimately loses anyway. This happened to the Democratic Party in 2016 and is happening to WikiLeaks now.

It wasn't just that WikiLeaks was no longer viable as a focal point of the sort of global reform coalition that I wanted to see established; in many ways, it had become part of the problem. When CNN put up an article reporting that Paul Manafort had been wiretapped in conjunction with an FBI investigation well before the time when he became Trump's campaign manager, and then for a second period after he'd left the campaign, Assange took to his Twitter account to make the bizarre claim that CNN had just reported that Trump himself had been wiretapped—and thus Trump was vindicated on the matter of various strange accusations the president had himself made to that effect some weeks prior on his own Twitter account. But what Trump had actually written was:

> Terrible! Just found out that Obama had my "wires tapped" in Trump Tower just before the victory. Nothing found. This is McCarthyism!

> How low has President Obama gone to tapp my phones during the very sacred election process. This is Nixon/Watergate. Bad (or sick) guy!
>
> Is it legal for a sitting President to be "wire tapping" a race for president prior to an election? Turned down by court earlier. A NEW LOW!
>
> I'd bet a good lawyer could make a great case out of the fact that President Obama was tapping my phones in October, just prior to Election!

The only true element of any of these specific allegations was that a wiretap had occurred, whereas the falsehoods included (1) that Obama had ordered this (2) to be done to Trump (3) during the election (4) outside the legal process (5) only to find no wrongdoing whatsoever—but that was all quite irrelevant to Assange, who saw fit to characterize the matter thus:

> TRUMP: I was "wire tapped"
> CNN: Haha. That idiot @realDonaldTrump thinks he was wiretapped.

Six months later . . .

> CNN: Trump was wiretapped

This came, of course, after a long series of other dishonest and self-defeating utterances that there was no reason to believe was ever going to stop. So I criticized Assange publicly for the first time. Shortly thereafter he reached out through a mutual contact to make arrangements to speak to me directly, but then seems to have changed his mind.

Not long after that, *The Atlantic* published a series of Twitter direct messages between the official WikiLeaks account and Donald Trump Jr., beginning a few months before the election and proceeding well into his father's term of office, indicating that WikiLeaks had actively aided the campaign despite its public claims of neutrality. I put out a brief statement explaining why this had not been the correct thing to do, except with more profanity. For one thing, Assange had clearly lied to the public and his own supporters about a matter central to its operation and purpose; in a November 2016 "Ask Me Anything" forum on Reddit, "Wikileaks staff" responded to a question on the subject as follows: "The allegations that we have colluded with Trump, or any other candidate for that matter, or with Russia, are just groundless and false. We were not publishing with a goal to get any specific candidate elected."

As Assange refrained from offering anything other than broad explanations for the Trump Jr. communications, his defense fell largely to close supporters and associated social media accounts like WikiLeaks Task Force, who collectively maintained, chief among all, that this had been an entirely typical exchange between a journalistic outfit and a "source." It was a plausible enough defense to the extent one avoided dealing with the actual content of the communications, which began with WikiLeaks providing Trump Jr. with the password to a soon-to-be-launched anti-Trump PAC; asking "you guys" to "push/comment on" a report that Hillary Clinton had once spoken of sending a drone after Assange (an unsourced claim, probably based on some truth, that first appeared on the rather scurrilous website True Pundit);

proposing that they provide WikiLeaks with Trump's tax returns and laying out why this would be advantageous to both parties; suggesting that Trump should refuse to concede if he lost on election day and instead "spend time CHALLENGING the media and other types of rigging that occurred"; requesting in the weeks after their victory that Trump call for Assange to be made Australia's ambassador to the United States; and finally offering a method by which Trump Jr. could minimize the fallout from a set of emails that *The New York Times* had obtained—the ones between Trump Jr. and the publicist who'd set up the Trump Tower meeting with a Kremlin representative who was supposed to be offering dirt on Clinton—through the stratagem of having Trump Jr. release them himself (which he promptly did).

Since the majority of this was hard to defend as typical "journalism," Assange's proxies focused on the tax return gambit, which to the extent that one refrained from actually thinking about it could be presented merely as an attempt to get newsworthy info into the public eye. Even the fact that Assange had couched the proposal entirely in terms of mutual convenience—that it would forestall the possible release by "the most biased source (e.g. NYT/MSNBC)" and meanwhile "dramatically improve the perception of our impartiality"—could be dismissed as mere social engineering for the ultimate purpose of tricking the Trump people into transparency. Indeed, this is the tack that Assange himself settled on, stating that "WikiLeaks appears to beguile some people into transparency by convincing them that it is in their interest."

The problem with this scenario is that it doesn't make any goddamn sense. Had Trump actually "leaked" his tax returns to WikiLeaks, as WikiLeaks proposed, and had

WikiLeaks thereafter published them, they would have had to make clear that, contrary to all prior practice and the very point of WikiLeaks, this particular "leak" of material had actually been provided by the institution itself, rather than by an anonymous leaker intent on subjecting that institution to scrutiny for its misdeeds. Rather than "improve the perception" of WikiLeaks' impartiality, this unprecedented voluntary leak would have done quite the opposite. But then there was another possibility—that WikiLeaks would have published the tax returns without making it known how they had received them, thereby deceiving the public and gaining for itself plausible deniability as to its preference for the campaign it had secretly been providing with advice and information.

Had this all occurred in a vacuum, it would have been possible to give Assange the benefit of the doubt and take him at his word that his engagement with the Trump campaign was not actually conducted in an effort to assist that campaign. But by this time Assange had been promoting the work of pro-Trump alt-right figures like Mike Cernovich and Jack Posobiec, both notoriously prone to putting out demonstrable nonsense, while saving his ire largely for non-Trumpian news outlets—and from time to time putting out his own contorted defenses of Trump for things that merited no defense whatsoever. Those who still wanted to believe Assange was speaking truthfully when he wrote, in a public statement released on Election Day, that WikiLeaks' activities had not been influenced by "a personal desire to influence the outcome of the election" could still believe this if they really wanted to. Indeed, they could continue to believe it even after February 2018, which saw the release of a huge trove of leaked private Twitter messages from Assange in which he'd told a group of confidants before the election that "we believe it would be much better for GOP to win" and explained in detail why Clinton had to be kept out of the White House at all costs.

At any rate, my detailed and unkind analysis of Assange's behavior—coming from a former ally who'd gone to prison in part "as a direct result of his journalistic work on our Stratfor materials," as Assange wrote at my sentencing—was a significant break in its own right, and indicative of the larger fracture within the original transparency coalition that had occurred while I was away.

The Trump Jr. emails widened the chasm beyond repair. The Freedom of the Press Foundation, founded in 2012 by Daniel Ellsberg and run by a board that would eventually include Snowden, had assisted WikiLeaks in receiving hundreds of thousands of dollars in donations during the U.S. economic blockade that had begun in late 2010. Not long after WikiLeaks' collaboration with the Trump campaign came out, the FPF announced that it would no longer be providing that support, though it cited the end of the blockade as the reason. Assange responded by posting on Twitter a picture of rats drinking milk from a bowl and labeling it "Picture of @FreedomOfPress board meeting."

Over the course of getting up to speed on everything I'd missed in prior years, I gradually formed a clearer picture of the extent of the rot. There was the Seth Rich affair, whereby a murdered DNC staffer was supposed to have leaked the party's emails only to be assassinated thereafter by Clinton's agents. In the context of modern history, such a thing was hardly impossible, and the Washington, D.C., police department reports upon which rests the mainstream view of a mugging gone wrong ought not be taken as gospel, given the source; it's even quite possible that Rich was indeed personally targeted for some reason. But Assange, despite intimations to the contrary, never believed that Rich was the source. I know this based on separate conversations with people close to the situation (and who I have reason to believe will eventually speak publicly on the matter), but it's clear enough from the public record anyway. It was Assange himself who first popularized the notion in an interview with Dutch television:

> ASSANGE: Our whistleblowers go to significant efforts to get us material and often significant risks. There's a 27-year-old, works for the DNC, who was shot in the back, murdered, just a few weeks ago, for unknown reasons as he was walking down the street in Washington.
>
> HOST: What are you suggesting?
>
> ASSANGE: I'm suggesting that our sources take risks and they become concerned to see things occurring like that.

The sordid exchange continues for a full minute, during which Assange continues to deny having tried to associate the murder with the leak while also struggling to explain what legitimate purpose such a reference could have if that had not been his purpose. In the months to come he limited himself to such slightly more ambiguous gambits as putting out a reward to find Rich's killers. Those in his circle could be more explicit; Dotcom thrilled the more credulous portions of both the right and the anti-Clintonian left by announcing he'd be putting out important new information on the subject, though this turned out to be a statement claiming that his lawyer didn't want him to talk about it lest he get in trouble.

Later still, when the Rich-as-leaker hypothesis had become clearly unviable, WikiLeaks sought to insulate itself from charges of ghoulishness by claiming that neither Assange nor anyone else involved in the organization could have attempted to associate Rich with the leak because WikiLeaks has a policy of never identifying leakers. "Source identities never emerge from WikiLeaks and are not even shared within WikiLeaks. Nor does WikiLeaks give 'hints' as to sources," wrote the official Twitter account in August 2018—the same account that had tweeted out, "We have strong reasons to believe, but cannot prove, that Aaron Swartz was a WikiLeaks source" in the days after Swartz's death.

Naturally my attacks on Assange led to some complications in the form of strained relationships with other figures whom I would have liked to have involved in my ongoing plans. This was to be expected, but it was the nature of the criticisms I was getting that told me the most about the current environment. To take issue with Assange, I learned, was to side with the CIA and American imperialism and war. "Nice to see you on the same page as Clapper," ran a typical comment from Randy Credico, referring to the former NSA chief. In some cases I was able to maintain a civil relationship—as with Credico himself, whom I privately interrogated about his alleged involvement in helping his old friend Roger Stone coordinate operations between Assange and the Trump campaign, even as I agreed to advise him on how to deal with the congressional subpoenas he kept getting (although the only useful tip I could offer was to stop messaging me about that stuff on fucking Facebook). This was the exception, though. When Dotcom, in accordance with the current party line, promoted the claim that it couldn't have been Assange talking to Trump Jr. because he'd been cut off from the internet at that time, I made public his prior messages to me in which he'd personally admitted that it had indeed been Assange (who had of course skirted Ecuador's attempts to keep him off the internet, which was long known to both U.S. authorities and many in his circle). Rather than address this latest discrepancy, Dotcom denounced me as "emotionally unstable," which is true but rather beside the point.

Finally, Assange himself attacked, writing in a tweet that the project I'd established upon getting out of prison would be fraught with "censorship," and claiming that I was purging people simply for "supporting" him. Frankly I wish I had been, given how obnoxious his remaining boosters tended to be; what we'd actually done was kick out Suzie Dawson—head of the Dotcom-funded New Zealand Internet Party—when it became clear that she was somewhat delusional. Later, a WikiLeaks volunteer released a huge cache of messages between Assange and some of his core supporters in which Assange himself had admitted concern over some of her writings, such as a blogpost in which she accuses President Obama of stealing her ideas. She would manage to top this by suggesting that the recent deaths of two Freedom of the Press Foundation board members might be a bid by the deep state to prevent her from discovering how the org had been taken over by its agents. As of this writing, she remains a major figure in the WikiLeaks orbit.

But Assange's dwindling retinue wasn't all Dotcoms and Dawsons, and still included a few people of great worth, intent on helping to protect his legal rights against the states that, after all, had started their pursuit of the man in response to his virtues, not his vices. Like them, I hold that Assange must be protected from U.S. prosecution lest it set dangerous precedents for journalism; this is a fairly standard view among the various press advocacy orgs, including those he's represented with photos of rats drinking milk from a bowl, and it doesn't require one to believe that Assange has always acted as a journalist or even as a decent human being.

In August 2018, I received a call from the new director of the Courage Foundation—the widely respected English activist Naomi Colvin, who'd taken over the role from Sarah Harrison earlier that year—in which she informed me that Assange had summoned her to the Ecuadorean embassy some time back and complained about my ongoing criticisms. Now, acting at his direction, the board of directors had ordered her to remove me as a "beneficiary," and thus she felt duty bound to resign. I thanked her but explained that it was no particular skin off my nuts if they did remove me, since I'd agreed to the foundation's request a few weeks after my release to allow donations intended for me to instead go into the common pool for use by others. Of the $13,000 that had been donated to help me pay the $890,000 I faced in restitution in the years since Courage had taken over from Free Barrett Brown, I'd received about $4,000. The rest went to the use of those still facing charges, extradition, or further prison time, such as Jeremy Hammond and the British hacker Lauri Love—and Assange himself, who had left the board and was now receiving benefits. I was confident that, severed from such an unusual arrangement, I would someday manage to pick up the pieces and move on.

But Colvin was disgusted with Assange's conduct as well as the board's and insisted on resigning via a public statement to be delivered after the weekend. Meanwhile I took the story to the *Daily Beast* national security reporter Spencer Ackerman, whom I'd met recently when he interviewed me onstage at a conference in New York. The resulting article was headlined, "Julian Assange Went After a Former Ally. It Backfired Epically." WikiLeaks declined to comment.

A few weeks later, Colvin joined my project as a board member, where she serves alongside the former member of Iceland's parliament and early WikiLeaks volunteer Birgitta Jónsdóttir.

Julian Assange has done more than anyone else to clarify what is possible in an age such as ours, where any sufficiently clever person has the world at his or her fingertips and the levers of power may be reached from anywhere. WikiLeaks struck at institutions that have committed such vast crimes against such a preponderance of the world, with so little real debate among the citizens who claim these governments as their own, that only a truly psychotic moral calculus could have found fault with its original mission of showing the public how such a system operates—particularly as it did these things via methods that were entirely legal, and pursued in partnership with traditional press outlets across the world. This is not the place to recount the array of crimes that were directed against WikiLeaks and its supporters by the federal government and its private-sector partners from at least 2010 onward—we have seen sufficient examples in previous chapters even apart from what was done to me—or to attempt to understand what it's like to have politicians and media personalities routinely call for one's murder in public statements. Assange bears responsibility for his own actions. So does Henry Kissinger. That only one of these two men will face any consequences, and that it will not be the one responsible for millions of unnecessary deaths, is as good an argument as any as to why the United States has no moral authority to condemn Assange, much less to prosecute him.

But I condemn him, because there is nothing to justify him. If one abandons all principles, one had better have something to show for it.

When I learned of Trump's victory, over a little pocket radio in my darkened prison cell in the early morning after Election Day, I experienced the same visceral terror as any vague-minded, historically illiterate Democratic Party centrist or incompetent neocon commentator would have felt, but for somewhat different reasons. I wasn't especially concerned about large-scale death and destruction, given how much of this Trump would have to accomplish in order to compete with Johnson or Nixon or Bush or even Bill Clinton, who happily presided over the sanctions that left so many young Iraqis dead to no particular end. Having the presidency occupied by a likely de facto agent of Russia was not much more worrying to me than having it occupied by de facto agents of Saudi Arabia, as it had been for a third of my life. To the extent that Russia had "interfered" in our elections—and it was clear even during the campaign, from what I was hearing from contacts outside, that they had at least attempted to do so—this was hardly something that anyone who identifies with the American federal government and shares the mainstream reverence for its past could complain about with any justice (which is to say that many of them did, over and over again, on the sort of cable news programs wherein phrases like "Iran in 1953" tend not to be heard). And it wasn't as if I were personally threatened by any of this; I'd spent half of the last, "legitimate" administration in prison as a direct result of political activities that weren't even illegal, conducted against pro-government types whose actual crimes were either ignored or actually rewarded. But I was terrified nonetheless; it is one thing to predict that things will deteriorate, and indeed to count on it, though quite another to see it happen.

But the fear faded quickly, to be replaced by optimism over the pessimism of others. The disturbing implications of Trump's victory, I reasoned, would shake the Establishment press out of its careerist inertia, and the nation's producers and editors would begin to take seriously their role as the central nervous system of a complex postmodern imperial republic. The arguments that had solidified over the course of my adult life—about the overemphasis on access, horse-race political coverage, TV news personalities with contracts in the tens of millions—would be decisively concluded in favor of reform. Mothers sending their children off to journalism school would tell them, "Come back with your shield, or on it," and should they later discover that their twentysomething graduate had taken a job with some NBC morning "news" show, they would rend their own garments, blacken their faces with soil, and proceed through the town square bearing a coffin, all the better to wallow in their shame.

What the major press outlets actually did was spend the first few weeks focusing on their collective failure to predict the election results, as if this was a legitimate function of any news apparatus to begin with. Thereafter the cable show producers started booking anyone at all who claimed to be an expert on Russia and its machinations abroad—up to and including a deranged ex-member of the British parliament, Louise Mensch, whose assessments were so consistently nonsensical and her predictions so routinely failures that the invitations soon dried up and she lost her press-appointed "expert" status, which not even William Kristol had ever quite managed to do. Kristol himself was rehabilitated along with George W. Bush and so many others of so little worth that it's a wonder Tom DeLay hasn't been given his own MSNBC morning show. Others still were deified; reporting from John McCain's funeral, Dana Bash of CNN looked to the skies for signs that the gods had received him into their number: "The angels were crying. Here at CNN—just a few blocks away—no rain. Just there."

It was inevitable, though not as inevitable as it should have been, that many otherwise intelligent and well-informed people would look upon this civic religion of mediocrity and war and decide that it must be as wrong about Trump and Russia as it was about Iraq and Afghanistan and America itself—or that even if its adherents happened to be right this time around, they must never be seen to have been vindicated lest they parlay the victory into renewed public authority and resume their blind and bloody march across the world. The image of Michelle Obama and George Bush laughing and eating candy and setting aside the old debates on exactly what form American military-intelligence preeminence should take at home and abroad can only be pleasing to the extent that one has no conscience; and in a time of vast and varied obnoxiousness that ought to have overwhelmed the moral sense into disuse, I can still work myself into a frenzy of bloodlust and visions of American cities aflame when I see James Comey tweeting out Bible verses about God's swift furious sword of justice or whatever the fuck.

But the truth of a matter is not determined by the character or the competence of anyone involved, nor is it eroded by virtue of being accompanied by falsehoods. That many of those who subscribe to the general theory that Putin and Trump have an illicit connection are also ill-informed on what exactly is alleged to have happened and what evidence exists for it tells us nothing about the theory itself. It's no black mark against the theory of evolution that untold millions of laymen who acknowledge it to be true think that it tells us that humans evolved from monkeys. And if evolutionary science is used to justify social Darwinism or the sterilization of undesirables, this is not a valid argument against evolution, nor reason that it must be opposed, much less disbelieved. This is a strange thing to have to put into writing, but a necessary one in the context of a debate that is so rarely argued on its factual merits and so commonly fought in terms of its implications.

11

Conspiracies of Convenience

It is especially appropriate to an age marked by confusion and role reversal that someone like Glenn Greenwald should have denounced suspicions about Russian activities during the election as "outlandish conspiracy theories"— and not just because his own contrary position requires a rather intricate conspiracy on the part of key intelligence and military elements of the United States, Britain, the Netherlands, and much else besides, or because the term "conspiracy theory" was a favorite phrase of the FBI chieftain J. Edgar Hoover that would later be shown to have been promoted by the CIA. Greenwald himself, you'll recall from an earlier chapter, was once floated as the chief individual target of a cutting-edge black ops propaganda effort planned by several firms with close links to the intelligence community, which was itself thwarted by an international team of dadaist outlaws united under the long-discarded symbology of seventeenth-century English Catholic terrorism. Not long afterward he was summoned to Hong Kong to meet with the fleeing U.S. intelligence defector who'd single-handedly pulled off the broadest intelligence coup in human history, and would go on to spend the next couple of years of his professional life reviewing secret documents detailing a vast, illicit surveillance and disinformation apparatus overseen by the NSA and GCHQ. It is a stubborn intellect indeed that can nonetheless go on to denounce "outlandish conspiracy theories" in the comparatively less baroque context of Russian influence operations, which shaped much of the twentieth century in ways that would remain poorly understood until the fall of the USSR and the opening of the Mitrokhin archive.

More appropriate still is the insensible recent shift of the mainstream political press into its new and unfamiliar role as a forum for speculation on conspiracies. The sussing out of conspiracies is a practice that even the most pseudo-skeptical mediocrity of a political reporter does on an ongoing basis, given how much of politics consists of behind-the-scenes agreements whose nature must be determined indirectly. But the average journalist does not consider himself a conspiracy theorist just because his work involves theorizing about conspiracies; rather he accepts the vague notion that a "conspiracy theory" is a silly thing indeed, but would be unable to articulate any principle by which to distinguish such things from his own, clearly serious work.

Alex Jones, when I first learned of him in 2000, was merely one of a handful of local cable access hosts in Austin, and by no means the most compelling (that would be a Calvinist preacher called Reverend Rick who wore a toilet seat over his head for reasons he was cheerfully reluctant to explain). Jones wasn't even the most fun to prank call when you and your friends were stoned (that was Reverend Rick) or to debate with when you were just drunk (that was Reverend Rick). A few years later, when Jones had expanded to AM radio, he was sufficiently known among believers and smart-asses alike that a small national outlet agreed to pay me to write a profile of him; he was still sufficiently obscure that they changed their mind after I'd already interviewed him in person. My impression was of a raw and candid man who knew enough history to disregard the conventional view of the present, but who lacked the intellectual rigor to paint any alternative reality with anything other than the broadest brush, and also he wasn't terribly fond of Mexicans. That we've since proceeded to a point where such a man can influence an American presidential election is not an aberration; it was inevitable. When the Establishment press simply absents itself from a large and clearly important body of issues, it leaves a vacuum to be filled by others.

The mass declassification that followed the end of the Cold War confirmed two things. First, the U.S. intelligence community and its counterparts abroad, having been run by brilliant eccentrics playing for unimaginable stakes, had gone far beyond what even well-informed observers might have expected. Second, the major news outlets were routinely infiltrated by those intelligence agencies (or, as in the telling case of the *Time* magazine founder Henry Luce, the outlet was simply made available for their use). The subsequent rise of the internet allowed any inquisitive young person to learn of these things, and then to wonder why they hadn't learned of them elsewhere. Then they came to wonder why they likewise had to learn about still-extant subjects like the Bilderberg Group and the Council on Foreign Relations and the Trilateral Commission and Bohemian Grove from low-end websites and excitable AM radio hosts.

And they can be forgiven for concluding that this was by design—that the news media's widespread silence on matters of such obvious and legitimate interest only makes sense if the media itself is complicit. It takes years of direct experience with the press to grasp the real extent of its failures, to recognize the patterns of incompetence, laziness, careerism, and cowardice that may be easily confused with complicity, given that the end result is the same.

Yes, there are instances where elements of the press are consciously allied with the obscurantist figures that they're supposed to be reporting on, and actually aid them in deceiving the public. Luce and the CIA is a good example, but somehow less instructive than that of Judith Miller. As noted earlier, Miller received from Dick Cheney's chief of staff, Scooter Libby, information seemingly intended to discredit the war critic Joe Wilson, whom Miller deceptively described in the resulting article as a former Congressional aide rather than a chief architect of the war at issue. It would seem she concealed her "source" not out of journalistic principle but rather in order to launder her involvement in a conspiracy to deceive the public into supporting a war that she happened to believe in. Later, as she fought a subpoena, Libby wrote her the following letter:

> You went into jail in the summer. It is fall now. You will have stories to cover—Iraqi elections and suicide bombers, biological threats and the Iranian nuclear program. Out west, where you vacation, the aspens

> will already be turning. They turn in clusters, because their roots connect them. Come back to work—to life.

To their credit, some number of mainstream journalists came to the obvious conclusion that Libby's obnoxious little poem thing referred to the Aspen Strategy Group—a neocon outfit both belonged to, and that had held a conference in 2003 wherein participants hammered out a "Grand Strategy for the Middle East" centering on what should be done about Iraq. Miller was not the only heavyweight journalist to be a member, incidentally, nor even the only one from *The New York Times*; she just happened to be the one who got caught up in the sort of highly publicized circumstances that are generally required for an event-driven media to examine anything at all.

It is just as well that all of this centered on the Aspen Group and not, say, the Bilderberg Group; Aspen is sufficiently obscure to have escaped the attention of Alex Jones and his colleagues. And so when the institution did come into view, it came pure and unadorned, with no vague associations in tow. Now contrast this with the Bilderbergers or the Trilateral Commission. To the extent that most people have heard of these, it was likely from Jones or someone like him—perhaps even David Icke, the former English soccer player and Green Party spokesman who popularized the concept that the British royal family and random other luminaries are fourth-dimensional lizard people. To the extent that someone is an absolute fool, he will accept everything the conspiracy theorist says as true. To the extent that someone is only a half fool, he will disregard it all as untrue. The great majority of working journalists, editors, and producers are half fools; they have heard of the Bilderberg Group from someone who claims it to be a subset of the Illuminati or what have you, and they determine that it must be one of those silly conspiracy things that are not worth looking into at all.

This vicious cycle builds on itself over time. The Trilateral Commission, a private group founded by David Rockefeller in 1973, would promptly receive the degree of ongoing press attention appropriate to an organization from which Jimmy Carter picked much of his cabinet. Figures like Noam Chomsky criticized it for its stated goal of achieving a "greater degree of moderation in democracy" via "indoctrination of the young"; conservatives quickly recognized it as an essentially globalist project incompatible with their own vague brand of nationalist religiosity, and at any rate a creature of the same centrist Establishment Rockefeller crowd who had opposed them for control of the Republican Party for a generation prior. These debates were important, and worth reporting on. But as time went by and the Commission fell from its peak of influence, the mainstream discussion naturally turned to other matters. The resulting vacuum was filled by rhetoric from groups like the John Birch Society, which presented a considerably less nuanced picture of the group and its aims, thereby tainting the subject. The next generation of editors and producers would know it mostly through this lens, and thus disregard it.

This is actually an unusual example in that the topic received any sustained mainstream attention to begin with. More common is the dynamics surrounding such phenomena as the Bilderberg Group and Bohemian Grove, which might as well not even exist as far as much of the press is concerned. Both receive an occasional mention, but neither is subjected to the scrutiny that is obviously appropriate to regular, secretive gatherings of formidable individuals representing various state, industrial, financial, and media power structures, collectively equipped to influence public policy in key respects, with goals that may only be guessed at by the citizens of the democracies involved, and doing that influencing via means that are plainly at odds with the concept of informed consent (or even with good taste, in the case of Bohemian Grove, which operates under traditions dreamed up by early-twentieth-century artistic types of dubious talent). One need not necessarily take issue with the policies formulated, or even with the practice of formulating them outside of public view, to understand why such phenomena merit discussion in the press. And one need not agree with the worldview that holds these organizations to be uniquely powerful factors in the affairs of nations. But they are at least as important as the array of other somewhat opaque institutions, from the Democratic Congressional Campaign Committee to a state governor's mansion to the board of directors at Google, whose doings political analysts will happily speculate over on national television—with or without evidence, and well past the point of diminishing returns.

The sin of commission here is not that the press disregards these subjects as unimportant but rather that they almost always do so without having performed the basic research necessary to make such a determination (Richard Nixon gave what he considered his best speech at the Bohemian Club, which should be enough to prompt serious interest in the group's annual events; he also called it "the most faggy goddamn thing you can ever imagine" in a tape-recorded conversation in which he went on to declare that he "won't shake hands with anyone from San Francisco"). Intelligent people of a relatively logical and skeptical bent are subject to the same unconscious, unvoiced mental heuristics that every human being is prone to allow to manage one's system of understanding except to the extent one examines each one. As throughout history, there is nothing today inherent in being educated or even possessed of real native intelligence that guarantees one immunity to being prone to the most demonstrably crass brand of magical thinking in ill-conceived service to skepticism or reason or sheer decency. The most deleterious of these, at least for the purposes of establishing a cogent and self-aware civilization, is also nearly universal to the jumped-up postmodern yokels who run our civilization's informational and political infrastructure. It goes something along the lines of, "If I have heard of some version of a claim that is crazy or unreliable, then any other version of the claim is crazy and unreliable, and there is no need to examine the claim, even to the extent that further evidence is presented that points to some version of the claim being true."

There's nothing terribly wrong with focusing on those things that are more likely to pan out; this is how a pretty good journalist operates, and the end result is pretty good journalism. But when such a heuristic is widely followed within media, the result is that the citizenry is never apprised of a certain category of actual facts and events, including those things that are important enough to obfuscate by one or more of the countless entities that draw upon specialized and poorly understood scientific disciplines in order to do that exact thing. Such a press corps, possessed of blind spots that may be identified and acted upon by anyone privy to the truth of matters reported otherwise, is prone not only to being nullified as a threat to large-scale misconduct but also to being coopted to misinform in service to same. It will also prove unable to contend with the broader and more eclectic set of truths that are no longer secret or never were to begin with; and this includes most of the very things one ought to know about the subject before deciding how the world does and does not work.

And so some great preponderance of the press are unaware, for instance, that the former CIA director John McCone was found to have concealed evidence from the Warren Commission and that the CIA itself now admits this; or that the United States actively sought to provoke the Gulf of Tonkin incident as a means of escalating involvement in Vietnam. They are unlikely to know that the U.S. military's chemical weapons division sprayed pathogenic and carcinogenic materials over various U.S. cities in the fifties and sixties to test such things as dispersion rates; that they did so with the assistance of firms like Monsanto; and that they in some cases sprayed the chemicals directly onto schools, from station wagons with mounted nozzles, in broad daylight, claiming it to be a "test" of a "smoke screen," which in a way it was: aside from chemical warfare doctrine, military and intelligence officials were also learning how much they could get away with, literally in plain view.

There is nothing about being a journalist, or anything else for that matter, that entails automatic knowledge of what is and isn't established in the public record, or of what theories have and have not been seriously addressed in the "serious" outlets. This is why *The Economist* ran a short piece on the fiftieth anniversary of the JFK assassination asserting that the book *Case Closed* had "painstakingly debunked the various alternative theories," only to have a professor of history at the University of Arizona send them a quote from *The Economist*'s own 1993 review of the book, castigating its author, Gerald Posner, for "smugly slant[ing] every piece of disputed evidence in favour of the lone-assassin theory" and concluding that it "no more closes the case than the many volumes inspired by conspiracy theories over the past 30 years."

How, the mediocre journalist will ask, could operations of massive significance be kept secret for so many years? The answer is that they do not have to be kept secret; they need merely be prevented from reaching whatever threshold of attention and certainty that would cause the project to fail. This should be clear enough given the known history of the Manhattan Project, or the unprecedented movements of men and machinery that the Allies routinely managed to conceal thanks to the imaginative stratagems of eccentric English turncoats and outlawed Polish aristocracy throughout World War II—or the fact that the Turing machine was publicly billed as merely an abstract thought experiment for well over a decade after it had actually been built. Now that this latter secret in particular has ushered in a new age defined largely by information, one could object that similar secrets would be more difficult to conceal. And one would be right. The most fundamental scandal of our age is how little this has tended to matter.

During the run-up to the 1988 presidential election, *The Nation*'s Joseph McBride discovered a 1963 memo from J. Edgar Hoover noting that "Mr. George Bush of the Central

Intelligence Agency" had been briefed by the FBI about how anti-Castro Cuban exiles were reacting to Kennedy's assassination. When asked for comment, the Bush campaign suggested that it must have been some other fellow named George Bush, and certainly not the one who would be appointed to lead the agency as an "outsider" after the scandals of the mid-seventies and who was now running for president. Soon thereafter the CIA announced to inquiring reporters that they had identified the former employee in question, while also claiming that they couldn't locate him. Given that this other Bush now worked as a claims representative for the Social Security Administration and that McBride was able to find him immediately, this should have struck the press as suspicious; instead most outlets repeated the CIA's claim as fact, and continued to do so well after McBride wrote another article detailing other discrepancies in the story and noting that this second Bush had been a low-level photographic analyst who obviously would never have received a briefing from one of the most powerful men in Washington. But the press had moved on.

There is a mechanism in the federal court system that inmates term "ghost dope"; it allows prosecutors to charge those caught selling, say, ten ounces of cocaine as if they had been caught selling, say, a thousand ounces, so long as they can convince a judge that the accused has been dealing for some period of time. It's a stratagem that's ripe for abuse, but it's based on the entirely reasonable notion that if you come across someone selling drugs, or singing a song, or doing a cartwheel, or overthrowing a democratic government, or studying the methods by which the public may be distracted from things that they might prefer to know, this someone has likely done it before and likely intends to do it again.

In 1974, *The Washington Post* published an article about a Pentagon spy ring that had illegally monitored the Nixon White House for some time. The piece was written by Bob Woodward and Carl Bernstein, and readers could be forgiven for taking it as a reliable account, given the preeminent role that the two young journalists had already played in bringing Watergate to public attention. And so the article's suggestion that a low-ranking officer by the name of Radford was "apparently the central figure" in the operation, and not the two admirals to whom Radford was regularly providing stolen documents, was widely accepted—and so were assertions by "informed sources" that "it was never clear who in the Pentagon set up or benefited from the unauthorized pipeline." Had readers known then that one of the admirals in question, Robert Welander, had been Woodward's commanding officer just a few years prior when Woodward was still a navy communications officer, and that the two had been good friends, they might have wondered whether this might not have informed the reporter's odd emphasis on the enlisted man who physically took the documents and not the high-ranking officials who'd ordered him to do so. A self-professed skeptic might ask why Woodward would have worked to break such a story had he been inclined to protect one of those involved. The answer is that he didn't; Seymour Hersh had been investigating the spy ring as well, such that the principals were aware that the whole affair would soon be made public anyway, and the young journalist's piece in *The New York Times* appeared on the same day as Woodward's, though with a focus on

Woodward's old friend Welander. Woodward's sources, meanwhile, "said Welander was removed from his National Security Council post only because Radford had worked for him." Hersh doesn't mention Radford at all, not having any reason to do so.

Today anyone can discover Woodward's relationship with Welander on Woodward's own Wikipedia page, where the two are briefly described as "close" based on a 2005 *San Diego Union-Tribune* obituary for Welander that notes this in passing. Likewise, one may now learn that Woodward denied having any relationship with the key Watergate figure and Nixon chief of staff Alexander Haig when he was first asked about rumors to that effect in the early nineties by a pair of researchers, that he challenged the two of them to find anyone who would say otherwise, and that they promptly found three people, including the former secretary of defense Melvin Laird, who each told them on the record that Woodward actually briefed Haig at the White House in 1968 and 1969 as part of his navy duties. Tape recordings of those interviews are now housed at Texas A&M University, maintained as part of the Colodny Collection of research materials on Watergate. The books and articles and scholarly papers that have drawn on these materials since 1991 have nonetheless been ignored by "serious" journalists who write for the major outlets even in cases where such materials are written by their very own colleagues with bylines in the very same outlets. Such is the natural consequence of the sentiment, almost universal to editors, that if a story of great significance has occurred for which public evidence has long been available, then it will have been picked up by some other outlet—and that if it hasn't, the evidence must have been lacking.

This was the American press on the eve of the 2016 election.

Its authority was opposed by both the highly informed and the poorly informed, counting as their constituency those who lie in between. Now the poorly informed had gained a champion, and the White House. The press responded by doubling down on its own legitimacy and reasserting its monopoly on the means of determining the truth. They denounced conspiracy theorists, and then they denounced the president as a Russian agent put in place, they theorized, via a conspiracy. And when large portions of the public rejected even that evidence that was public and historical, and in many cases failed to even examine it, Beltway reporters were perhaps more astonished by this than they had any right to be.

The early resistance to the story was not entirely the fault of the press. Many would have ignored the compelling case that Trump is illicitly engaged with the Russian kleptocracy even had they lived in some alternate dimension where the major outlets had no long and documented history of being infiltrated by the intelligence community, and in which that intelligence community had not been repeatedly caught lying about Russia in particular and everything else in general. But it was inevitable that the most visible portions of the news media would promptly muddle matters, being confused about some of the most relevant matters themselves. This extended well past the usual difficulties in deciding who was and wasn't an expert on any particular matter and whether Louise Mensch might perhaps qualify. Worse, the story would come to hinge on the issue of intelligence contracting and internet propaganda methodologies, a subject that every major outlet had mishandled in 2011. Worse still, most of the reporters who'd be covering these topics this time around had forgotten whatever narrow lessons they'd managed to learn from prior events, and often the events themselves.

Palantir had only increased in power since the 2011 Team Themis scandal, when they'd been caught serving as a senior partner in a trans-corporate black ops sabotage boutique whose specialties included intimidating journalists, setting up activists on fraud charges, and spying on children for leverage. In subsequent years the firm expanded into an array of new and impressively disturbing industries like "predictive policing," confident that its recent and indefensible history would prove irrelevant even to the extent that anyone recalled it. In March 2018, when the former research director of the "consulting" firm Cambridge Analytica, Christopher Wylie, revealed to the British parliament that an employee at Palantir had assisted them in harvesting the Facebook data of fifty million U.S. voters, the resulting *New York Times* story made no mention at all of the plainly relevant Themis affair that the *Times* itself had covered (or at least summarized after a week of headlines elsewhere). Perhaps the authors of the Cambridge Analytica story just didn't consider Palantir's 2011 scandal relevant to understanding this latest one. Let's dive into an excerpt, concerning a staffer whom Palantir blamed as the sole participant, and see if we might find cause to differ:

> The Palantir employee, Alfredas Chmieliauskas, works on business development for the company, according to his LinkedIn page. In an initial statement, Palantir said it had "never had a relationship with Cambridge Analytica, nor have we ever worked on

> any Cambridge Analytica data." Later on Tuesday, Palantir revised its account, saying that Mr. Chmieliauskas was not acting on the company's behalf when he advised Mr. Wylie on the Facebook data.

If this sequence of events feels somehow familiar, it's because it's virtually identical to what happened in 2011. "Palantir did not participate in the development of the recommendations that Palantir and others find offensive," the firm had stated then—right before the discovery of emails showing that employee Matthew Steckman had actually helped craft those very "recommendations," at which point the firm put him "on leave pending an investigation" and then quietly promoted him after that investigation concluded that no one was still paying attention. This was only fair, since Steckman had been working on Themis with fellow employees Eli Bingham and Ryan Castle, themselves both included in emails concerning the proposals, and with the demonstrable knowledge of several other Palantir staffers, and under the direct oversight of the same Palantir general counsel, Matt Long, who was telling the press how saddened they all were—for all these employees were cc'd on the other Themis threads that *The New York Times* apparently couldn't be bothered to search through themselves even when Anonymous put them on a searchable, linkable archive that other, more with-it journalists were using to document their stories. The Palantir president Alex Karp himself is noted in one such email to have approved Themis, which the firm explained away as mere bluster.

Of course none of this would have sounded familiar to those who get their news from the *Times*, which had run its belated and somewhat garbled take on the matter in a

February 11, 2011, article inexplicably headlined "Hackers Reveal Offers to Spy on Corporate Rivals." Over the next few days the extent of Palantir's lies became increasingly public, but *The New York Times* had already deemed the matter concluded.

The next time the paper of record looked into Palantir, the result was a piece titled "Unlocking Secrets, If Not Its Own Value," in which readers are given the unfortunate news that the firm might not be making as much money as it really should. As the lead photo caption explains, nobility comes with a price: "Alex Karp, chief of Palantir Technologies, has resisted calls for it to go public. Despite a growing number of private clients, he says an I.P.O.'s emphasis on stock price would be 'corrosive to our culture.'" A hilariously sanitized version of the Themis incident is provided later in the piece, where the plot against Greenwald and other journalists is characterized as involving "misinformation" rather than the campaign of intimidation that was actually proposed in emails and presentation slides ("ultimately most of them if pushed will choose professional preservation over cause, such is the mentality of most business professionals"); no mention is made of the fact that one of the *Times*' own reporters was also listed in the presentation as a potential target. The article presents the firm's original public statement that this was all the result of a lone employee's poor judgment as if this were fact, rather than a demonstrable lie that was immediately exposed as such. Anyway, the reporter reassures us that "the idea fizzled," which is true in the sense that many of my adolescent attempts to sneak out of the house to smoke pot often "fizzled" when my mom caught me climbing out my bedroom window. He notes Karp's apology to Greenwald, though not the portion of that apology in which he vowed to fire anyone involved—which is lucky for Palantir, since Steckman's continued role at the firm as of 2014 actually gets noted later in the article (though his promotion doesn't) and the discrepancy might have occurred to the reporter. Or maybe not: "We really learned that we do work in areas where we come into contact with bad actors. We have to be vigilant," the Palantir recruiter Ari Gesher explains, probably as his entry in some office-wide contest to see who can get this guy to print the quote that bears the least possible scrutiny (the real winner was the reporter himself, Quentin Hardy, who would later be hired by Google to serve in some vague company managing editor role on the apparent grounds that he wasn't the kind of journalist they'd have to worry about).

Perhaps the actual reason Palantir was reluctant to take itself public was that to do so would make it vulnerable to the one force on Earth that could truly damage the firm and subject even its executives to the consequences of their actions: wealthy investors. And since the firm always had to seek outside capital beyond what Peter Thiel had put in and the $2 million it got from the CIA investment arm In-Q-Tel in its early days, wealthy investors constituted a threat that could never be entirely avoided. Thus it was that after skating through an indefensible scandal that struck against the very basis of democracy in 2011, and then skating through an indefensible scandal that struck against the very basis of democracy in 2018, Thiel and his man Karp met their match in early 2019 when the fund manager Marc Abramowitz convinced the Delaware Supreme Court to order them to turn over to him any potentially relevant emails. That Palantir had fought this particular outcome tooth and nail was perfectly understandable. They were no longer dealing merely with Congress or parliament or *The New York Times*, but with competent men who insisted on results; the subject was no longer the firm's conspiracies against democratic institutions but whether someone's investment should have by this time been worth more than the $60 million at which it was estimated to be valued. A line had been crossed.

In all seriousness, Palantir will do just fine; just a few days after the court order, the UN announced that it was giving the firm access to the data of millions of food aid recipients so that the relevant programs could be better organized. And just a few days after that, *The Wall Street Journal* ran an article headlined "Peter Thiel's Secretive Data Giant Palantir Finally Raking In Cash." No mention was made of Themis or even the Cambridge Analytica election scandal, but it was announced that the firm had decided to do the IPO after all, no doubt after a long period of fasting and prayer by which to harden Karp's staff to the temptations of the secular world. Indeed, even Matthew Steckman, who took upon his brow the collective sins of his colleagues, has not found the weight to be particularly burdensome; several of those colleagues have lately moved on from Palantir to run the Facebook veteran Palmer Lucky's new startup, Anduril Industries, which in turn seems to have modeled itself on its spiritual predecessor: aside from also being named after fantasy nonsense from *Lord of the Rings* ("Palantir" is some magical bullshit thing, while "Anduril" turns out to be a mighty sword of valor), and aside from likewise being founded by some vaguely sinister nerd with ties to Trump, Anduril Industries also now employs Steckman in the same basic role to which he'd been promoted at

Palantir: head of corporate and government affairs. It even shares Palantir's focus on providing the most unaccountable forces in the modern world with comically dystopian innovations; its first major project involves advanced drone AI by which to catch immigrants crossing America's southern border, a technique for which all manner of exciting additional applications will no doubt be found in the decades to come. Palantir also signed a $40 million contract with ICE around the same time.

It is indicative of how futile were our efforts to alert the public about these matters back in 2011 that Palantir was not the only one of our old adversaries to have later come up in connection with the various data mining and disinformation campaigns that permeated the 2016 election; it wasn't even the only one to have done so in tandem with Cambridge Analytica. Archimedes Global—which one may recall from an earlier, wonkier chapter as having teamed up with HBGary Federal and TASC to win a bid for the complex Romas/COIN apparatus funded by the U.S. military—would go on to assist Cambridge Analytica's parent company, Strategic Communications Laboratories, in developing the methodology that made the 2016 operation possible. The Obama State Department gave the two firms their big break years prior, when Archimedes was contracted to run Operation Titania, a massive disinformation effort targeting the Yemeni public, and brought on SCL to assist. The Archimedes vice president and "behavior change analyst" Kirsten Fontenrose would eventually start working directly for Cambridge Analytica over the period of its U.S. election operations—and then directly for Trump himself, as National Security Council senior director for Gulf affairs. To its credit, Politico caught on to this aspect of the story despite steps Fontenrose had taken to hide it, and even mentioned Archimedes itself in passing. But it was left to the irrepressibly left-wing Max Blumenthal to dig up Titania, which led him to Archimedes, and then to my long-ignored piece on Romas, and thus to my revelations that Apple and Google had met with these firms (and Aaron Barr himself) to discuss how they might assist them in developing the same dangerous technologies that would later be redirected against the American public. Blumenthal called me for details, published a thoroughly researched two-part article that also recapped my previous work and cited the documents connecting Apple and Google, and was ignored. Thus it is that those in the press most ideologically inclined to take the Trump campaign's illicit election activities seriously are nonetheless so ill-equipped to handle the subject that much of the story had to be pieced together by the biggest Russophile to have written for *The Nation* since the magazine stopped chartering yachts for editorial cruises down the fucking Volga.

In October 2018, *The New York Times* ran a piece on the discovery that an Israeli firm called Psy-Group had offered the Trump campaign the use of its army of convincing fake online personas with which to manipulate RNC delegates, though the campaign was believed to have turned down the proposal. No mention was made of the larger problem of this practice, which even *The Atlantic* had found sufficiently important to summarize back in 2011, though not so important that it need be remembered. A more in-depth piece by Ronan Farrow in *The New Yorker* revealed that the firm had been more successful in drumming up business elsewhere, such as by working to "embarrass and intimidate activists on American college campuses who support a movement to put economic pressure on Israel because of its treatment of the Palestinians"—the first specific, documented example of when and where the broad use of what was previously known as persona management has actually been used outside of CENTCOM's implied targeting of the Arab world as a whole. But even this article made no reference to anything that might convey that this was not merely the one-off escapade of a colorful Israeli fixer whose firm had by now gone into liquidation. The body of knowledge that had begun accumulating with its notice by an individual user at *Daily Kos* and then fleshed out via the crowdsourced adventures of Project PM before being solidified into mainstream acceptance by *The Guardian* and other outlets—all of this might as well not have been done. The problem in this instance may be as simple as the firm's reliance on terms other than *persona management* in its materials, since it appears in neither article (and is anyway increasingly used to refer to a mundane aspect of server administration, such that a search for the phrase would yield little of relevance). But then Palantir is still called Palantir and its documented history is just as lost to the press, even as it has continued into the future. It is not the Information Age we envisioned, nor the worst of what is to come.

Speaking of naivete, I watched the 2017 hearings on Twitter propaganda bot activity and its influence on the last election with some expectation that even a single congressman would ask the assembled national security types whether their own agencies might perhaps have contributed to the problem they now proposed to address. That

U.S. Central Command had encouraged the proliferation of this phenomenon by putting out "requests for proposals" for persona management software in 2010, such that every intelligence contractor and foreign intelligence agency on the planet that watches for these nonclassified RFPs would now be thinking through the possibilities themselves, was not even "secret" in the sense that Romas/COIN is still a secret—that is, in the sense that it might as well be a fucking secret as far as the non-Blumenthal press is concerned; even *The Atlantic* had run a couple of paragraphs on persona management in the months after the HBGary heist. But at least the topic was getting discussed, even if limited to the comparably unsophisticated spam bots that weren't designed to bear much scrutiny, and that Russia had deployed in such vast numbers that they wouldn't have to worry about the inevitable mass bannings (this is also how Russia won World War II).

But even this conveniently stripped-down aspect of the problem of automated online propaganda was too much for the likes of Congress and CNN to handle without fucking it up. For one thing, many of the bots operating in the context of various Western referendums and disputes were wrongly identified as Russian by those wrongly identified as experts by those wrongly deemed credible journalists. Prior to the subject going mainstream and ideological, Twitter bots had been studied by a handful of dedicated researchers using data visualization and other appropriate tools to determine patterns and attribute campaigns to particular actors. The American writer and researcher Erin Gallagher began looking at the problem in 2014, when she first came across bots operating in "real time" in the context of various Mexican political controversies; soon she came across the work of Alberto Escorcia, a resident of Mexico City who'd begun graphing out the visible relationships of these bots since first writing about them in 2011 (and who had naturally been targeted for online harassment ever since). By the time the American press had determined it needed experts on the subject, Gallagher was among the most qualified in the English-speaking world, in part due to her long familiarity with Latin America.

Unfortunately, the expertise that matters most is branding. "Meet the Indiana dad who hunts Russian trolls," runs the headline that's appeared in various forms since August 2018, when CNN sent a camera crew to interview the systems analyst Josh Russell, described as one of a "growing network of online sleuths" who've taken it upon themselves to fight online propaganda. "Russell's work in particular has helped journalists at CNN, NBC News, *The Daily Beast*, and other outlets cut through the lies and disinformation," notes one of those journalists, CNN's Donie O'Sullivan. This might be a good time to cut in and note that CNN had previously held up Louise Mensch as an expert on the exact same subject matter until she posted a tweet declaring that Putin had killed Andrew Breitbart, though without offering proof that this had actually occurred or that it would even be such a terrible thing that couldn't perhaps be forgiven. To be fair to CNN, it was *The New York Times* that actually went so far as to run one of Mensch's op-eds (three years after she declared on Twitter that anyone who uses the term *Zionist* is an antisemite, was asked whether this included Theodor Herzl, and replied in the affirmative). But then Mensch's qualifications were always vague, whereas Russell's were made more bizarrely explicit in CNN's own profile piece: "I had been consuming alt-right news for three or four years without knowing. Someone had been lying to me." By the end of the article, Russell has assured CNN that he responds to "death threats and stuff like that" by sending his online antagonists "a photo of [my] gun."

As CNN described Russell in their parody of a profile piece, "No matter his interest, be it videogames [*sic*] or miniature figurine board games, he always wants to be the best." Apparently there aren't many miniature figurine board games in which the objective is to refrain from getting caught up in an embarrassing scandal that discredits your work in a highly public manner, because Russell had managed to involve himself with a rather unusual outfit called New Knowledge, which among other things had been providing the Senate with data for its official reports on Russia's social media disinformation operations. Like countless other researchers who came to the propaganda bot story in the late second act and promptly cast themselves as narrators, Russell saw no reason why an oddly constituted for-profit private intelligence firm headed up in part by an unreconstructed ex-NSA officer might not be the best approach to defending the informed electorate. More to the point, he still didn't see any such reason after internal documents were leaked to *The New York Times* in December 2018 revealing that the firm had interfered in a U.S. Senate election by—well, let's not let good copy go to waste: "We orchestrated an elaborate 'false flag' operation that planted the idea that the Roy Moore Senate campaign was amplified on social media by a Russian botnet."

The *Times* report prompted an apology from the firm's founder and a call for a federal investigation by Senator Doug Jones to determine the nature and extent of the conspiracy to connect his opponent to Russia. Facebook even suspended the personal account of CEO Jonathon Morgan, who during the election had personally published a graphic on Twitter that he claimed was data accumulated by his firm's bot-hunting spinoff #Hamilton68 proving Russian bot activity in support of Moore, but that were of course his own bots, deployed for the purpose. And then, less than two months after the firm's immaculately indefensible fraud against the voting public had launched a news cycle that would conclude with this unprecedented array of consequences, NBC News put out its own report.

According to an investigation and evidence provided by outside "experts," NBC's reporters said, Russia was considering a "possible campaign of support" for Tulsi Gabbard in the 2020 Democratic presidential primary. This may well have been true, based on the previous month of coverage by several Kremlin-linked outlets, which NBC summarizes for us thusly: "Gabbard was mentioned on the three sites about twice as often as two of the best known Democratic possibilities for 2020, Joe Biden and Bernie Sanders, each with ten stories. Kamala Harris and Elizabeth Warren had fewer." But then Gabbard had declared her candidacy toward the beginning of that monthlong sample period whereas these other figures had not, and lesser-known candidates do tend to generate more coverage for the very reason that so much about them is unknown. We'll have to take NBC's word for it that "the other contenders were treated more critically than Gabbard"—and we probably should, given Gabbard's relatively pro-Moscow stances—but it's also worth remembering that Bernie Sanders is someone NBC singles out as a Kremlin target, which may or may not reduce the frequency by which NBC commentators and other slapdash types single him out as a Kremlin stooge. Even NBC seems to have realized that this was pretty weak stuff for a news article, particularly given the lack of any comparison with coverage by non-Russian outlets, so they threw in some equally compelling evidence. Unfortunately, this evidence consisted of comments posted to the newfangled alt-right board 8chan about how a strong Gabbard run might help split the left, or at least characterizations of those comments provided to NBC by its expert source, New Knowledge, with additional corroboration by its other expert source, Josh Russell, whose name NBC managed to misspell. No mention is made of the widely covered and indefensible scandal for which New Knowledge was now best known, or even of Russell's current gamer status. But we are treated, just for fun, to the father-of-two's own evidence, or at least NBC's characterization of what any such evidence might supposedly consist of—"a few clusters of suspicious accounts that retweeted the exact text about Gabbard, mostly neutral or slightly positive headlines."

In his memoirs, Henry Kissinger made note of Richard Nixon's tendency "to make proposals in such elliptical ways that it was often difficult to tell what he was driving at, whether in fact he was suggesting anything specific at all. After frequent contact I came to understand his subtle circumlocutions better; I learned that to Nixon words were like billiard balls; what mattered was not the initial impact but the carom."

In a different way, and for different reasons, American political rhetoric could now be described similarly. In any partisan environment marked by disputes unmoored from principle, every facet of discussion becomes important not for what it is but for what direction it appears to be heading in. In the current environment, this has become not merely noticeable but fundamental. This is the nation of the carom, in which no opinion on any matter at all can be easily divorced from which faction could conceivably benefit from it. To criticize WikiLeaks is to support the NSA; to criticize Clinton is to support Trump; to declare that the Russians manipulate elections is to excuse the Americans for having done so; to point out that the FBI is not always reliable is to defend Russia and Trump; to report on connections between Kremlin kleptocrats and the White House is to play into the hands of the neocons and thus foment a nuclear war that will end the world forever.

Is dishonesty such a terrible thing that we must rail against it as if we were Hebrew prophets? The Bolsheviks from Lenin on down spoke in open contempt of the bourgeois morality that compelled their enemies to at least pretend to stay true to their word; unrestrained by convention and justified by the crimes of the institutions they opposed, they scored victory after victory against reactionaries and revolutionaries alike with tactics that would have scandalized an Italian pope, and killed so many for so little purpose that they might have impressed a Spanish one. Now the fascists had their own justification, and kind words from Churchill. When the fascists themselves became too great a threat, the Allies found it convenient to pretend that the Soviets were not actually starving and enslaving large masses of people and that the British Empire was something other than an extortion racket and that an alliance between them would constitute a crusade for "democracy." After the fascists were defeated another, longer crusade for "democracy" would be carried out, this time with the help of Nazis, some of whom came willingly with the knowledge that they would be safest in the arms of American intelligence officials, who spoke in quiet contempt of the "idealism" that compelled their countrymen to fight for democracy by democratic means; unrestrained by the Constitution and justified by the amoral totalitarianism of the state they'd previously been allied with against the regime whose amoral totalitarianism had produced such impressive scientists, they toppled democracies lest these prove too democratic to be of use against the dictatorship that threatened democracy. Now the Soviets had their own justification, and kind words from young and idealistic Westerners, who knew their elders couldn't be taken at their word about the Soviets or anything else. And it became necessary that dozens of nations be crushed and quarantined, and that tens of millions die on top of the hundred million lost in the prior war. And as the Soviets emptied the gulags and filled Afghanistan, the Americans built more prisons and sold arms to the Iraqis, and there followed another war that was necessary to reestablish the territorial integrity of two theocratic monarchies. Over the next ten years, the United States would be directly responsible for the deaths of well over a quarter million other children in Iraq, itself one of the key bipartisan accomplishments of the 1990s, and billed by our first female secretary of state as "worth the price." This was the Golden Age, the End of History.

Yes, dishonesty is indeed such a terrible thing, and we should be prepared to punish it as severely as we are able. And we must start with the press.

12

A Republic, If You Can Fake It

In September 2018, a white Dallas police officer named Amber Guyger shot and killed her Black neighbor, Botham Jean, in his own apartment unit, under circumstances that could only be guessed at—unless you worked at *The Dallas Morning News*, in which case you could repeat various bare assertions by Guyger, police union officials, and anonymous law enforcement sources as factual, even when these contradicted each other in significant respects and were internally incoherent to begin with. The Texas Rangers' arrest warrant for Guyger, issued a few days after the shooting, looked like something that had been written by the defense—the crime is designated as manslaughter, in contravention of statutes that the city's legal professionals universally noted called for a murder charge, regardless of the circumstances; and Jean's apartment is rather astoundingly characterized as Guyger's, perhaps by right of conquest. More important, the account of Guyger's actions leading up to the killing is substantially different from that presented in the Dallas police search warrant issued a few days prior for Jean's apartment. Nonetheless, a *Dallas Morning News* reporter assured the public that some detail from the second document was "what happened"—although it was perhaps better described as one of the major conflicting accounts provided by a suspect in what would soon clearly be a murder case. Another *DMN* staffer reported as fact a claim by the president of the Dallas Police Association that Guyger had received threats on her phone while going on to describe as "misinformation" any other claims made beyond the sacred confines of the Ranger indictment (except for the search warrant that contradicted it). Naturally, I wrote a piece for *D* attacking both the Dallas Police Association and the press, which garnered considerable attention given the sheer sordidness of the circumstances documented.

Neither the police nor the *News* took it well. By the time things had settled, I'd been publicly denounced in vague terms by the *Dallas Morning News* managing editor Mike Wilson, several longtime *DMN* reporters, and the Dallas Police Association president Mike Mata, who'd also written to my longtime editor at *D Magazine* to claim that my focus on supposed irregularities in the handling with Guyger's phone was mistaken (I've reproduced his words out of cruelty to everyone concerned):

> Mr. Brown-
>
> The only time law enforcement seize a persons phone is when the suspect refuses to allow the agency access to the information on the phone.

> So the agency will seize the phone obtain a search warrant to pull the information of the ph.
>
> In this case it wasn't necessary because the phone was willing handed over so the information off the ph was dumped with permission. The agency doesn't want the ph they want the information off the phone, once they get it the agency gives you back your phone.
>
> Eric I appreciate your help in this matter and again please give Mr. Brown my number I know you can attest to my willingness to have a positive conversation when asked.

If you've been paying close attention to this story, you're likely to recall two things. One of those things is that I love having positive conversations, too, and if the other party agrees to it as well, then, all the better! So I was disappointed when Mata proceeded to duck my calls and texts for a year until I finally called him from my girlfriend's phone and posted the resulting conversation on YouTube, as is my custom. The other is that I actually had a few run-ins with the law myself in my younger days, and also in my slightly less younger days, and have since been employed largely in documenting and redocumenting that story in order to present certain truths about our civilization and point the way toward possible solutions to the problems described, and also to be entertaining because people enjoy that. And so I just happened to know that what Officer Mata told me and my editor Tim Rogers and some guy named Eric about how I was mistaken on this point about how cops always ask you for your phone before seizing it or knocking it out of your hand or shooting you because it might be a gun was, oddly enough, not entirely accurate, in regards to either actual statutes or de facto practice (and these can differ).

If it feels like I'm setting the bar kind of low here, it's because there's a small chance that you are my former editor Tim Rogers, who initially forwarded me Mata's entirely false grammatical black hole of a fucking email with the following message appended:

> BB: Looks like I'll need to add a correction to the post. See below from Mata.=

With some effort, I was able to make Rogers understand that this would not be the correct thing to do, journalism-wise.

But a few weeks later, when a man using his own name threatened to blow up the magazine if it continued to publish my articles and Rogers notified the Dallas FBI office and the Dallas police, which told him to keep it quiet, I was less successful in getting him to agree to talk to the Freedom of the Press Foundation head, Trevor Timm, or any of the lawyers Timm had offered so as to supplement the advice Rogers was getting from the Dallas police (which, it turned out in the trial, had indeed allowed Amber Guyger to delete evidence from her phone after she shot and killed her Black neighbor, and that Mata himself had presided over the police's handling of the affair. Oops!).

So I went ahead and made public the bomb threat over my articles, along with the fact that two law enforcement agencies whose malfeasance I'd been documenting in those articles had immediately convinced my editor to keep it quiet, because one can really only set the bar so low.

What followed would be commemorated in a handful of articles that appeared in the months to come as I released new evidence obtained, including audio recordings I made with unsuspecting cops as I spent some portion of the following months investigating my own bomb threat and the subsequent police/media coverup. I released the resulting audio of ranking Dallas police officers telling unconvincing and contradictory versions of why all this might be occurring.

FEBRUARY 20, 2019

> Early this morning, the Dallas Police Department and the Dallas Mayor's office received an email from Barrett Brown containing a secret recording of a phone call, a copy of which was released today by Distributed Denial of Secrets and is embedded below. In this recording, a Dallas police officer claims that the Assistant Chief of Police lied to a city councilman about an investigation of terrorist threats made against the City of Dallas and against Brown's publishers in retaliation for their publication of his work . . .
>
> In the recording, *D Magazine* editor Tim Rogers explains his confusion. "Yesterday, I got an email from you saying 'we have not arrested him.' I get that there's a difference between arresting someone and taking them into custody, but when I get that and then a couple hours later, I'm reading on Twitter the words of Lonzo saying that he was taken into custody . . . I'm like, 'what's going on here?'"
>
> In response, the police officer explains that it's

"because it was not true. Not everything was true that was presented there. It's still ongoing and things didn't happen the way they were presented, truth be told."

Rogers quickly followed up, asking "so what Lonzo told Philip Kingston is not true? Because that's really important."

In response, the unnamed police officer attempted to end the phone call. "Look, see, here you go again. I guess we're done here. It's just that you're getting very dated information and the investigation has changed. You're sitting here asking questions and you're gonna spin it the way you spin it."

The officer declined to offer an explanation for the apparently false information given to the city councilman except that "the investigation has changed."

—Emma Best, Distributed Denial of Secrets

MARCH 7, 2019

On Feb. 24, 2019, Brown sent assistant police chief Anderson copies of more evidence he had dug up on Taylor—screenshots of Facebook messages that Taylor had sent to Brown's girlfriend asking about him, and photos from Taylor's Instagram page that shows him posing with a gun. He also posted the photos and screenshots on Facebook and Twitter. In response, a former DPD officer left a comment saying that Brown "has a smug, punchable face."

On Feb. 26, Brown spoke with Sheldon Smith, a DPD sergeant overseeing the investigation, about the current status of the case. In the conversation, which Brown recorded, Smith told Brown that the DPD investigated the bomb threats against the Dallas library and *D Magazine*, but ultimately determined that there was not enough evidence to charge Taylor.

"Initially, we believed that we would have enough information to file those charges on the individual that we're talking about, just based on the preliminary information," Smith told Brown, according to a recording of the conversation. "But after we conducted a thorough investigation, we didn't have the elements needed in order to actually file the offense for that."

Smith offered two explanations for why charges could not be brought against Taylor. First, he said, Taylor had never said that he would personally blow up *D Magazine*'s building, just that "someone" could.

"He didn't say that he would," Smith said, according to the recording. "And the element we needed was if he had said, 'I'm going to blow the building up.' But when he said 'someone,' that's why we couldn't physically charge him."

Brown pointed out that this explanation couldn't account for the decision not to charge him for the bomb threat against the Dallas library, which contains the explicit statement, "I'm gonna blow your fucking library up."

To that, Smith offered a second explanation for not charging Taylor. The problem, he said, was that the police could not be sure that Taylor was actually responsible for the threat posted from his Facebook account.

> "We did extensive research on his Facebook account and we could not confirm that it was actually him that said that," Smith said, according to the recording. "It may have been him, but we weren't 100 percent sure that it was him."
>
> On Nov. 26, shortly after Brown tweeted out excerpts of Anderson's email, *D Magazine* published a post about the bomb threat. A few days later, the post was abruptly deleted without any explanation. Rogers told the Tracker that he could not comment on what had happened.
>
> —Peter Sterne, Freedom of the Press Foundation

Later it turned out that Taylor was a violent felon who had been arrested for offenses ranging from trespassing to assault with a deadly weapon.

In giving talks at conferences and universities in the last two years, I've usually refrained from introducing myself, instead listing a series of mutually exclusive characterizations that one could find on me in the major outlets. I'd done a similar thing in my first column for *The Intercept*, and with much the same background objective in mind:

> Back in the go-go days of 2011 I got into some sort of postmodern running conflict with a certain declining superpower that shall remain nameless, and shortly afterwards found myself in jail awaiting trial on 17 federal criminal counts carrying a combined maximum sentence of 105 years in prison. Luckily I

got off with just 63 months, which here in the Republic of Crazyland is actually not too bad of an outcome.

The surreal details of the case itself may be found in any number of mainstream and not-so-mainstream news articles, from which you will learn that I was the official spokesman for Anonymous, or perhaps the unofficial spokesman for Anonymous, or maybe simply the self-proclaimed spokesman for Anonymous, or alternatively the guy who denied being the spokesman for Anonymous over and over again, sometimes on national television to no apparent effect. You'll also find that I was either a conventional journalist, an unconventional journalist, a satirist who despised all journalists, an activist, a whistleblower, a nihilistic and self-absorbed cyberpunk adventurer out to make a name for himself, or "an underground commander in a new kind of war," as NBC's Brian Williams put it, no doubt exaggerating.

According to the few FBI files that the bureau has thus far made public, I'm a militant anarchist revolutionary who once teamed up with Anonymous in an attempt to "overthrow the U.S. government," and on another, presumably separate occasion, I plotted unspecified "attacks" on the government of Bahrain, which, if true, would really seem to be between me and the king of Bahrain, would it not? There's also a book out there that claims I'm from Houston, whereas in fact I spit on Houston. As to the truth on these and other matters, I'm going to play coy for now, as whatever else I may be, I'm definitely something of a coquette. All you really need to know for

> the purposes of this column is that I'm some sort of eccentric writer who lives in a prison, and I may or may not have it out for the king of Bahrain.

My favorite instance of flawed reporting on the escapades of yore hadn't been included there, but I used it quite regularly when I spoke: this was the Reuters piece from after my SWAT raid explaining that I, Barrett Brown, "a self-professed leader of the computer hacker group Anonymous"—demoted from the wire service's own headline, wherein I'm described as a genuine "leader"—am "best known for threatening to hack into the computers of the Zetas, one of Mexico's deadly drug trafficking cartels." It listed a total of four contributors, and one of them was Joseph Menn.

When Aaron Barr had gone looking for a journalist willing to publish his public relations coup about having supposedly discovered the "founder" of Anonymous, he found Joseph Menn. In the weeks and months and years to come, the fact that Menn had published the demonstrably false claims of a man whose own emails and notes showed him to be a consistent liar would be related over and over again in every new telling of the HBGary hack, not least by me. This doesn't seem to have done much to damage Menn's career, since, as I came to remember, the *Financial Times* not only continued to run his stories but even allowed him to write about that same incident and the people most closely involved. Naturally, Menn got it wrong.

"The article set off a small panic," Menn wrote in a piece on Anonymous in September 2011—a relatively harmless face-saving fib about the reaction at the AnonOps IRC server that Barr had "infiltrated," intended to imply that those of us therein were not, say, writing comical press releases within hours of Menn's February piece appearing. But the revisionism escalates quickly, such that artful phrasing cannot confine it from growing into a lie that cures the villains of their villainy, robs the antiheroes of their justification, and blinds the public to the lesson that Menn would prefer them not to learn: "When the hacktivists subsequently discovered that many of Barr's identifications were off-base, they published them, devastating the security company and forcing Barr's resignation on February 28."

Obviously we had already known these would be off-base given the particular absurdity of what Menn himself had deemed credible enough to publish as news, though we did confirm how much else was incorrect upon publishing Barr's notes and hearing from the various random people he'd wrongly identified by name as having anything to do with Anonymous, such as Benjamin de Vries, a San Francisco man he'd decided was Commander X (Barr had in turn wrongly identified X as "the leader"; he was in fact an aging vagrant so widely despised among key participants that he'd been banned from the AnonOps server some weeks prior and had written me an email asking me to intervene on his behalf).

But of course it hadn't been Barr's errors in identifying Anonymous participants that led to his resignation, as Menn conveniently claimed, but rather the various possible crimes and other indefensible acts he'd plotted against journalists like Glenn Greenwald, activist groups like Codepink and Stop the Chamber, and the children of labor leaders, including one child he'd dug up info on in order to prove his utility to the U.S. Chamber of Commerce. And even if Menn had somehow failed to catch any of this when it was described in *The New York Times* and dozens of other outlets, he definitely knew of it after February 14, 2011, when at his request I emailed him the extensive notes my volunteers had compiled on Palantir's involvement in these various crimes against democracy.

Menn's piece for CNBC described me as "Barrett Brown, an Anonymous member who has admitted to roles in other operations," without himself admitting that my most celebrated and consequential role had begun with embarrassing him personally. Still later, in an article published after Hector "Sabu" Monsegur was revealed to have been turned by the FBI months prior and Jeremy Hammond and others were arrested, he described me as "a past Anonymous spokesman who knew Monsegur and was interviewed by the FBI during a search on Tuesday." In the same article, he describes Jennifer Emick as "a former Anonymous activist who began working against it when it started attacking the U.S. government," a demonstrable falsehood given that Emick had begun working against Anonymous after a sordid conflict with other participants in the 2008 operation against the Church of Scientology. In a long and dubious profile published in Gizmodo in June 2012, for instance, Emick is depicted as having "spent the last two years battling Anonymous and it [*sic*] sympathizers," with no mention of any attacks on the U.S. government, which would not occur until well into 2011 in the course of the running battles against HBGary, her most prestigious client, and its close partner the FBI, for which Emick was an admitted, compensated informant. Another contradictory version of Emick's virtuous stand against the activists who had helped to establish the democratic revolution in Tunisia had appeared in the 2011 profile piece on yours truly that had won Tim Rogers his National Magazine Award. Still another was provided by Emick herself when she spoke at DEFCON and revealed that she was indeed "Asherah," the moniker she had used for some time, with the justification that she feared retribution from Anonymous were her real name ever to become known (as it had been to most everyone she'd come to pursue for years, which is why it's listed in the *D Magazine* piece), and if she were to ever come into their violent and "terroristic" reach (as she was then, onstage, in an auditorium where Anons booed and catcalled but somehow refrained from engaging in violence against the woman who stood smiling before them all, before going on to chat briefly with Gregg Housh, whom she'd publicly accused for years of trying to "swat" her—just as she'd once accused me of doing, prior to the FBI making the same claim at my bond hearing).

Some of Menn's deference to HBGary may perhaps be explained by this 2010 email from Menn to the firm's CEO, Greg Hoglund:

> Hi Greg, I haven't heard from you yet. Things are looking good for the book, I expect really good coverage. I need to finalize a cocktail party-style book talks for Black Hat DC on Feb 2 and at RSA March 2. If HB Gary would be interested in co-sponsoring for a grand or two and speaking there, please get in touch with me or [redacted] in the next day.

I began publicly asking Menn about these and other indiscretions via Twitter after getting back on the internet in 2017. His responses ranged from vague to nonexistent to obviously nonsense, which is to say he was more responsive than most. Then, at the very end of the torturous process of writing this fucking book, Kevin Gallagher informed me that Menn had sought and obtained from him the portion of an earlier draft I'd passed around for comment that dealt with Menn himself, who had explained that he needed to check it for accuracy lest I end up libeling him.

That other piece on Jennifer Emick from June 2012 was titled "This Is What Happens When Anonymous Tries to Destroy You," and had been written for the *Gawker* property Gizmodo by a hobbity-looking fellow named Sam Biddle. That he'd repeated the informant's latest narrative even where it contradicted her own past statements in addition to the public record was somewhat egregious given how little Googling would have been required to determine she was lying. Arguably worse is that he should have known much of it was false, having reached out to me for comment via an email to which I replied with some of my growing collection of evidence that Emick was engaged in an FBI-sanctioned campaign to deceive the press and public about matters of national consequence while also doing the same exact things to activists that Biddle would soon ascribe to those activist targets. Among the things I sent him was an IRC transcript in which Emick justifies looking into the teenage daughter of a woman I had a romantic relationship with on the grounds that the mother retweeted Anonymous materials on OpTunisia, as well as correspondence hacked and released a few months prior in which Emick deals directly with the HBGary executives Jim Hoglund and Jim Butterworth in the wake of the Themis scandal and was slated to be paid for her efforts. In both cases Emick had acknowledged the authenticity of the documents, as I also noted to Biddle, who neither replied to my email nor made any note of what I had sent him. Among those of Emick's tormentors whose threatening language via Twitter and IRC chats was presented as the meat of an article about what happens to people when Anonymous tries to destroy them was Emick's own longtime partner, an ex-military fellow whom she'd regularly sicced on her activist targets and their loved ones before the two of them split in a sordid puff of recriminations some months prior to the article. The handful of other events portrayed as making up this newsworthy and unconscionable Anonymous terror operation consisted of tweets from accounts that Biddle never quite gets around to connecting to Anonymous by even the most conveniently broad definition. One threatening cyber adversary described as a "rival hacker" was in fact another documented and self-admitted FBI informant with whom Emick had also had a falling-out, as is her wont. The article has been viewed several hundred thousand times, and remains in place today.

I found another of his old Gizmodo pieces, "The Former Face of Anonymous Is Going to Prison" ("Face of Anonymous" being the term *Gawker*'s Adrian Chen had granted me via the mechanism of the half-dozen articles he wrote about me between 2011 and 2013, later to be replaced by "self-proclaimed Face of Anonymous"). This one had been written to commemorate my sentencing in early 2015, by which time the press had concluded I was perhaps a worthwhile person who had overseen some worthwhile things at great risk and sacrifice and at any rate was not someone whose suffering and further captivity were any sort of desirable outcome, or even a neutral one. Biddle was the exception: "Way back in 2011, things were going very well for Barrett Brown, a hacker groupie-cum-journalist who'd made some friends in Anonymous, the once-fearsome online collective. Today, he was sentenced to 63 months in prison after aiding them in their reign of crimes and bullshit theatrics."

Biddle has since become a staff writer at *The Intercept*, where he worked on the Reality Winner documents that the whistleblower would shortly be arrested for having revealed, and is bylined on the article alongside another reporter, Richard Esposito, who would go on to become a spokesperson for the NYPD.

I'd quit *The Intercept* in 2017, had come close to quitting even before that, while still in prison. But I'd maintained a friendly relationship with many there, and had gone on Jeremy Scahill's flagship podcast, *Intercepted*, on the occasion of my initial conflict with Assange. I'd even been relatively civil with Greenwald, although I'd come to resent him more in recent months, partly because I'd now had the chance to look more closely at our correspondence leading up through my first FBI raid.

Early in 2018, *The Intercept* closed down its Snowden archive and laid off much of the research staff who had maintained it. *The Intercept* itself refrained from putting up any sort of explanation on its website; instead Greenwald released a statement asserting that the cost was too great, and that anyway other outlets possessing portions of the documents had mostly stopped reporting on the contents.

And then I learned that Laura Poitras—the *Intercept* cofounder who'd been the one Snowden went to next after Greenwald initially brushed him off—had been excluded from the decision, and that Snowden himself hadn't been consulted or even told. I reached out to Laura to get a sense of what was going on and ask if there was anything I could do to help. She gave me an overview and then sent me some documents.

It turned out that a couple of people did want to talk, which is how I got a copy of the nondisclosure agreement that outside researchers had to sign before accessing the Snowden archive; this was mostly notable for the high-flown language, in the form of a preamble to the effect that such things as are contained therein were made available at great risk and sacrifice and meanwhile the republic is always served best by transparency, and not secrecy. In September 2020, documents from an internal investigation into the handling of the Reality Winner incident were leaked to *The New York Times* by a former *Intercept* staffer. *The New York Times'* Ben Smith noted that Betsy Reed, the longtime *Intercept* editor in chief who'd accepted my National Magazine Award on my behalf, "had assigned the investigation to Lynn Dombek, then *The Intercept*'s head of research, who reported directly to her . . . Ms. Reed's oversight of the investigation, [*First Look* cofounder Laura] Poitras wrote, was an attempt 'to cover up what happened for self-protective reasons.' It was, Mr. Greenwald agreed privately, a 'whitewash.'"

13

The Things That Should Have Been

The collaborative system that Project PM had originally been intended to put out back in 2009 would now go forward, in a greatly improved form drawing upon the lessons of digital organizing and online activism, under the name of Pursuance, and it would be quite a neat little thing, allowing huge numbers of individuals and existing organizations who've agreed to a basic set of commonly held beliefs to self-organize and achieve wonderful things, from crowdsourced research to philanthropy to political engagement. But I hadn't come this far just to offer up a salve or a supplement. And although Pursuance would incorporate the mild-mannered and the incrementalist into its ranks, probably as the majority, and would indeed be used in large part to help reform rather than to revolutionize, I wanted it clear that I was presenting something that was intended as a sort of alternative civics, ultimately destined to challenge the existing structure of power. There was a segment of the public that was ready for such a thing, even in 2016; the intervening years have only served to emphasize the need for this or something akin to it.

Things were well in motion by the time of my release, with my media push kicking off twenty minutes after I'd walked out the gates at Three Rivers. Alex Winter had brought a camera crew to film in the car as my parents drove me from the prison to the halfway house I was required to check into within seven hours or face rearrest; the resulting short documentary, done for Laura Poitras's new film company, would appear a few weeks later. This wasn't the right format to bring up Pursuance; it had to be introduced by someone other than me, and anyway I was carsick for much of the shoot because smoking lots of Marlboro Reds after abstaining from smoking for four years turns out to be ill-advised.

But Winter had struck a deal with *Wired* to make the film available first through them, embedded in an accompanying article for which Andy Greenberg would be interviewing me in the coming weeks. By then, I would have to have something in place to anchor the plan, and myself, in reality. It was also crucial that I project a trajectory of future success; the awards I'd won for the column would not be sufficient. I'd spent the last year of prison writing by hand a fifty-page book proposal, and we had a deal in place by the time Greenberg called me on the Samsung flip phone I'd bought off one of the seven drug dealers with whom I'd shared a room.

"Anonymous' Barrett Brown Is Free—and Ready to Pick New Fights," was the *Wired* headline a week later.

> Since leaving prison, he's wasted no time in resuming his work and regaining his notoriety. He's already signed a low-six-figure book deal with Farrar, Straus and Giroux for a combination memoir and manifesto. He's featured in a short documentary released today by director Alex Winter and production company Field of Vision, who filmed his release from prison. And foremost in Brown's post-prison plans, he's already plotting to launch a new and improved movement of online activists, one designed to pick up and expand his hacktivist muckraking from where he left off . . . All of that, it's worth noting, may for now be more of a solitary-confinement fantasy than a real roadmap.

Though Greenberg went on to remind readers that I was unusually experienced in recruiting people into such adventures, he was entirely correct about the scale of the problem. To do this properly, I would have to recruit software developers with specialized skills. It would be necessary to convince journalists, producers, and editors that such a project would enable them to conduct meaningful crowd-sourced research of a sort that would improve upon conventional practices, and get some of them to use the new system. I would need assistance from some of the more dynamic political organizations, particularly in Europe, and it would be necessary to establish partnerships with some of their local and national governing bodies. I'd have to conduct outreach to nonprofits and NGOs and make plans to assist existing organizations in using the platform to make better use of their supporters. Eventually, our own nonprofit would have to be established to oversee funding and handle the dozens of other matters that something on this scale would require; as such I'd need to recruit a board of directors and fill it with respected, nationally known figures representing a range of sectors. I'd need to recruit people to fly around the world to speak at conferences and meet with organizations and convince them to sign on: people to identify and apply for grant money, oversee donation drives, establish bank accounts; lawyers. The project would have to be floated in major news outlets so as to attract early support and volunteers; ongoing and staggered media exposure would be necessary as well, covering at least a year, so as to broaden the potential constituency for an effort that, being not only ambitious but also rather unconventional, would require extraordinary institutional support if it was to be taken seriously, and ultimately to prove successful.

The preparations described above were all finished within a year of my release. Pursuance would come to be overseen by a board of directors that included Alex Winter; the member of Iceland's parliament, poet, and Pirate Party stalwart Birgitta Jónsdóttir; the CIA whistleblower John Kiriakou; the novelist, U.S. intelligence critic, and former CIA Directorate of Operations covert asset Barry Eisler; the famed activist attorney Jay Leiderman; the Bard College professor Robert Tynes; and the former Courage Foundation executive director Naomi Colvin, whom I'd snatched up from Assange as previously related. Along with the inevitable network of other contacts and well-wishers such as the NSA whistleblower Thomas Drake and the DOJ whistleblower Jesselyn Radack, we were able to present the case for this effort sufficiently to formally recruit some 2,700 individuals and organizations who signed up to participate upon our launch and raised $48,000 to pay for an executive director and part-time lead developer, something we did in the course of a grueling Kickstarter campaign that entailed such things as me performing the entirety of Shakespeare's *Julius Caesar* via livestream using random objects on my desk as characters while I spoke all the lines on behalf of the highly senatorial stapler and the treacherous Nintendo Switch controller and so forth, reading from a bound copy off-camera. I supplemented this by going out to Minnesota to work for one of our donors on various ill-conceived projects in exchange for a couple of thousand dollars a month to be divided between myself and the nonprofit, plus a couple of thousand dollars more I kicked in from my first round of the book advance to help keep our mostly volunteer lead developer afloat as we got up and running throughout 2017.

The coverage my nonprofit and I had received regarding these efforts to bring something fundamental and good to the public through a decade of labor and sacrifice had this time been unblemished by the confusion and contradictions and outright disinformation that had so often mutated my associates and me into charlatans in the eyes of those dependent upon *The New York Times* or *Gawker* to tell them what they needed to know to secure their world. By the middle of 2018, I could link interested parties to a piece by *The New York Observer* that summed up our intent as follows:

> Small teams of journalists found some shocking behavior inside the ad-selling brains at Google and Facebook over the last couple days. Imagine how much more effectively these companies could be held

> accountable if hordes of people were brainstorming similar searches to check like the handful these reporters were able to do. That's the kind of activism the convicted activist journalist Barrett Brown wants to organize online, as the *Daily Dot* reported in August. Last night, he spoke to supporters of what he calls the Pursuance Project over YouTube, answering questions about his open source software project . . . Brown envisions his Pursuance Project as a task management scheme for groups of online activists. So using the example above, participants could log in whenever they want and start brainstorming new phrases to check. The system would already have a record of phrases that had already been checked, so no one would need to check the same phrase over . . . The project is accepting applications for its first cohort of online activists. It mainly wants to take on the police state and surveillance now. A big part of Pursuance's work looks like it will continue the kind of thing Brown liked before he went to prison: digging through piles of pilfered or uncovered data and looking for stories of power that has been abused . . . In the end, it doesn't matter how complicated Pursuance is inside, so long as it's easy to use. If Pursuance makes it simple for a new activist to have a rewarding experience of doing something and feeling like they nudged the ball forward, that will be enough . . . If Brown thinks he's got a solution, we'll withhold judgement and let him and his posse try.

It was difficult not to contrast this with the wave of strangely phrased and echo-prone coverage that hit me and

Project PM and the most effective elements of Anonymous in mid-2011—especially if, like me, you recently spent several years going back and reviewing the preponderance of such materials in the course of researching the life story that it has lately become your career to tell and retell.

I have run into vast difficulty in telling this part. What I have included by way of example, cumbersome as it is, constitutes a small fraction of a far larger total that I had become reflexively anxious to try to convey. I was deeply wounded by much of what I discovered about the last decade when it became my job to see all of this completely and accurately. Suffice it to say that the first draft of this book was written in a year and a half, whereas revisions to this last chapter have taken an additional three years, the great majority of which I spent avoiding the book altogether, for it had gradually become clear to me that the happy and triumphant ending I'd planned was no longer possible under the circumstances. Neither was the book itself. I'd seen too much of what had gone wrong in 2011 and 2012 to ignore the same processes and dynamics that had made the crushing of our movement so easy for the state and its partners the first time around; I'd seen too much of the consequences to regard this sickeningly familiar conduct as anything less than the same threat it had posed last time.

In February 2018, after several months of back-and-forth emails and a two-hour studio interview that I'd assumed would give us the best chance yet to raise the money we needed to get Pursuance built, NPR's *All Things Considered* broadcast a segment to the entire nation warning of the threat I posed to the United States itself.

The segment begins by helpfully defining the term "hacktivist" as "someone who breaks into computer systems to promote their cause" and then immediately defining me as "real-life hacktivist Barrett Brown." Just in case the transitive property does not make it sufficiently clear to everyone listening that I break into computer systems, it is further explained that our dear subject "served time for his role in the hack of a private security firm" and thereafter "spent years in a prison cell thinking about what he might do when he got out . . . And he says he is ready to change, so next time he gets involved in hacking a corporation he is able to inflict maximum damage." We also learn that I served as an inspiration for the protagonist of the program *Mr. Robot*; and when the show's creator, Sam Esmail, provides too benign a quote on the crucial function served by people like myself in a free society, the audience is promptly set straight: "But *Mr. Robot* is hardly a glowing portrait of hacktivists. Its hero, Elliot, is a drug addict who can't access his own emotions. Sound familiar? Elliot leads a group called fsociety that takes down the world's largest corporation—erasing everyone's debt. Chaos erupts."

But it's not just fictional oligarchies that are at risk from my emotional unavailability; real-life pseudo-democracies have already been impacted. "During the 2016 election," NPR's Laura Sydell explains, "Russian state-supported hackers used some of the same tools as Anonymous—hacking emails from the Democratic National Committee and posting them on WikiLeaks to embarrass Hillary Clinton. I wondered, is there really any difference between a foreign agent and hacktivists like Anonymous? They both aim to circumvent our democracy. Is Brown a hero or a villain?" But then I understand why people might be reluctant to trust me ever since a composite character based largely on my colleague Gregg Housh did a series of things that Sam Esmail made Christian Slater force him to engage in while I was in prison doing normal prison stuff and not bothering anybody in any of these other universes.

NPR listeners also got a preview of Pursuance, which everyone else had been fooled into believing had been designed for research campaigns and civic engagement, such that we'd already formed partnerships with journalistic entities and nongovernment organizations providing things like medical care in conflict zones and safer conditions for Arab reformers facing prison and torture. According to Sydell, the software we'd been building "will allow anyone with the program installed to recruit and lead a team to hack and expose corrupt governments and corporations."

In NPR's defense, they did eventually issue a correction to their claim that "Stratfor was involved in top-secret government missions like the killing of Osama bin Laden." As to how such a heroic view of Stratfor might have made its way into NPR's coverage, one can only guess. Perhaps the extensive correspondence between the national outlet's staffers and Stratfor itself that anyone may view for themselves via WikiLeaks can yield some clues, along with the fact that Stratfor analysts had been regular guests on NPR programming for years, a practice that continues to this day.

We carried on with our work nonetheless, raising money and recruiting software engineers and researching existing approaches to collaborative software and interviewing different types of target users ranging from well-funded European NGOs to at-risk democracy activists living under dictatorships. We sent our members to Berlin and Canada to do panels at relevant conferences.

Things were rocky from the start, even aside from the escalating dispute with Assange and his proxies that prompted rather dishonest attacks on my project from Assange on down, starting after my first public criticisms in late 2017. The lead developer who'd volunteered after reading the *Wired* piece turned out to be incapable of overseeing other coders, many of whom quit over his managerial style. Worse yet, the software he'd been putting together had little resemblance to the framework I'd envisioned and refined since 2009. A year or so after work on Pursuance had begun, a San Francisco outfit called Aspiration that assists promising nonprofits with advice and fiscal sponsorship and the like confirmed what several of us had come to suspect—that our only way forward was to fire the developer, pay him a small severance, and go back to square one.

While we put out feelers for a new developer and brought on more volunteers to help flesh out a more cohesive design for the Pursuance framework, we looked for ways by which to put our core volunteers to work on the same sort of information-centered collaborative activism we intended to facilitate en masse when the software was finally built. The most promising opportunity came when one of my old collaborators, Emma Best, founder of the leak distribution platform Distributed Denial of Secrets, asked me to assist in recruiting and organizing journalists to work on something with potentially massive impact. A few weeks later, I announced the project in *Counterpunch*:

> It is my cheerful duty to announce the acquisition of around 85 gigabytes of leaked emails, phone calls, faxes, and other documents originating from the London-based tax shelter firm Formations House, best known to the public for the assortment of often colorful scandals involving such figures as former Ukrainian president Viktor Yanukovych, and best known to the global kleptocracy as a cheap and discreet option by which to avoid taxes or steal them altogether . . . What makes this story unique is that the millions of pounds in assets pilfered with the help of a London "financial services" firm were ultimately recovered. If even one of the "400,000 companies, partnerships, and trusts" Formations notes having set up for its clients since the turn of the century are discovered to serve a similar function, and the stolen funds returned to the developing nation that can scarce afford to have lost them, this project will have served its purpose.

In the weeks to follow, I recruited some two dozen reporters from outlets as diverse as CNN, *The Guardian*, *The Washington Post*, and the *South China Morning Post*, briefed each of them as needed, and brought them into the Signal channel we'd created for the purpose, where Best and my two aides-de-camp of Pursuance—the executive director, Claire Peters, and the director of operations, Annalise Burkhart—would be on hand to facilitate access to the leaks and assist reporters. But it became clear early on that our two underfunded and makeshift orgs lacked the resources we would need to take full advantage of the situation, and so we were all quite pleased when the far more established Organized Crime and Corruption Reporting Project was brought on as well—especially me, as I was too busy staving off homelessness and emotional collapse to put as much energy into the project as I'd originally intended.

By the beginning of 2020 my own fortunes had ebbed so low that I'd ended up having to move in with my girlfriend's family in South Texas. I was still considering the future of Pursuance, and myself with it, when *Der Spiegel* came out with an article about how I'd spent my time since getting out of prison "spreading conspiracy theories and harassing women on Twitter"; although no specifics were provided even when I reached out to the reporter, it appeared likely that the latter charge stemmed from the *Quillette* editor Claire Lehman, who had accused me of "harassing women in tech" in response to my public request for information on the Peter Thiel protégée Riva Tez. Aside from her now-deleted past articles extolling the "human biodiversity movement"—summarized in a 2016 *Forward* piece on the subject as "the pseudoscientific racism of the alt-right"—Lehman is perhaps most notable for her regular articles praising Thiel, who has also contributed articles to *Quillette*, and her dinners with the Thiel Capital head Eric Weinstein.

The *Der Spiegel* article was the last straw, and I wrote a line-by-line rebuttal in a column for *Counterpunch* that ended with an announcement to that effect:

> As I've informed the board of directors of my nonprofit, Pursuance, I'm shutting down the project until such time as I have any reason to believe that it will

prove any less vulnerable to the whims and incompetence of the Western press corps than did Project PM, which was eventually denounced as a "criminal organization" by the DOJ as the FBI investigated dozens of people for nothing more than contributing to the wiki I maintained detailing misconduct by the military-intelligence community in both their public and privatized forms, or because they donated $50 to my legal fund.

Between this, my banning from Twitter that makes much of my work impossible, and effective ongoing suspensions from Facebook for undisclosed reasons on the eve of the publication of my memoirs that includes material on both firms; the $800,000 judgment the DOJ has actively been collecting from my publishers on behalf of Stratfor over its defrauding of its own customers in cooperation with the FBI; the bomb threat over my work and subsequent Dallas police cover-up and press silence after my public fight with cop union president Mike Mata and *Dallas Morning News* editor Mike Wilson over the Botham Jean shooting; and the Tarrant County DA office's recent surveillance of my Facebook page and comments made by its users over my role in publicizing Arlington PD bodycam footage of their officers watching Treshun [Miller] bleed to death in a parking lot—I simply don't see a viable way forward for any project associated with me until such time as the difficulties we already faced in creating a secure framework for large-scale civic engagement and crowd-sourced journalism are not further compounded by amoral mediocre yuppie media trash.

Over the next year, I continued organizing investigations and campaigns by activists, researchers, and journalists via the Signal groups that we'd come to favor as a means of providing a relatively secure collaborative environment to those who needed it. I also attended to a few necessary personal issues, such as going to rehab and then, in September 2020, leaving the country for good—arriving first in Antigua at the invitation of a wealthy supporter, and thereafter heading to the United Kingdom. Having put an ocean between myself and the United States, I felt safe for the first time in a decade. I was still naive.

A few weeks before the January 6, 2021, Capitol siege by the alt-right, FBI agents from New York and Houston arrived at the bureau's Los Angeles field office to ask Val Broeksmit for ongoing assistance in spying on the real threat to American democracy, which turned out to be me.

It's difficult to summarize Broeksmit's role in recent U.S. history other than to note that it has been both complex and largely covert, and also that it will never be widely understood. Even those aspects that have been reported in outlets like *The New York Times*, such as his work for the Fusion GPS founder Glenn Simpson during the latter's role in the Steele Dossier, have passed largely unnoticed. Indeed, his role in public affairs has been quite similar to my own, with the chief difference being his willingness to work with the feds.

Like the American centrist Establishment, Broeksmit saw the FBI as a potential partner in the fight against high-level corruption. Unlike the American centrist Establishment, Broeksmit knew enough about the FBI not to trust its agents, which is why he covertly recorded the entire four-hour meeting on his phone and provided a copy of what ensued to one of our mutual colleagues, the former *Vice* executive editor Rocco Castoro, before disappearing a few weeks thereafter. Castoro later passed them on to me.

As the audio begins, Val is introduced to Special Agent David Ko from the Houston office, Special Agent Boeing Shih of the local LA office, and an unidentified agent from the New York office. They proceed through the federal building's security checkpoints on the way up to the conference room where the interview is to be conducted.

The next hour and a half is given over largely to discussion of the matter Broeksmit wants help with in exchange for his cooperation—a custody battle and related court proceedings involving himself, his girlfriend, Marie Peter-Totz, and the child from her marriage to a prominent Australian novelist. The child had been taken from their care and returned to the father after the apparent death by overdose of a domestic worker at the home Broeskmit and Tolz shared in California.

Broeksmit follows up this narrative with a summary of the various major financial crimes of which he's become aware via his yearslong investigation into Deutsche Bank, where his father was an executive privy to matters concerning such clients as Trump before his apparent suicide a few years prior. He also talks of the organized disclosures of high-level financial fraud overseen by groups like Distributed Denial of Secrets, with which he'd been working closely in recent months.

Neither Special Agent Ko nor the other agents in attendance seem particularly interested in any of the crimes alleged to have occurred, whether perpetrated by Broeksmit himself or the financial institutions he had thoroughly investigated for the last several years.

> KO: What other . . . are you involved in any hacking groups? Do you know of any hacking groups? . . . There's a lot of these things and we like to see what's going on.
>
> BROEKSMIT: Yeah, you guys are in that Signal group, aren't you?
>
> KO: What Signal group?
>
> [*Laughter*]
>
> BROEKSMIT: There's more than one Signal group. And there's a group of people—they're not all hackers. It's a mix of very interesting people. Yeah. It's some of the greatest journalists, some of the greatest hackers, and some of the greatest activists—some of the greatest writers . . . And everyone's just having a conversation. But specifically a hacking group? No. But there's different variations of these Signal groups. And this one's Barrett's. When you said Houston, I said, fuck, he's after Barrett. Barrett Brown.
>
> KO: Barrett's on the radar. But you know that. He's been arrested already.
>
> BROEKSMIT: I know. He's in rehab right now.
>
> KO: So what's Barrett up to? You talk to him?
>
> BROEKSMIT: Yeah, I talk to him all the time . . . And I have reams and reams of texts with him. But he's a good guy. But he doesn't understand about computers. He's not a hacker.
>
> KO: He was part of Anonymous for a good bit of

time . . . Where is he right now? I mean where in rehab? Is he in Dallas, or . . .

BROEKSMIT: Mmmmmm . . . do you really want to know?

KO: I'm just curious. I mean, like . . .

BROEKSMIT: Like, what?

KO: If you don't want to tell, you don't have to tell.

BROEKSMIT: Like I told you before, I'm happy to help you, but I want to know what and why. Like if I'm going to take accountability for doing something to somebody that could get them in trouble or jail, I want to know who it is and why I'm doing it and what for.

KO: I get it. I'll tell you this right now—I can't tell you everything we do. Like I said, I'll be honest with you if you're going to be honest with me. I can't tell you the motivation behind every single question I ask. There are a lot of things we do, the FBI does. If we had an investigation into, whatever—call it Barrett Brown, for example—and you want to know why, and it's because we're going to arrest him tomorrow, and then—

BROEKSMIT: Right . . .

KO: —you go say, "Barrett, by the way, I think the FBI's going to bust you tomorrow"—that probably wouldn't go well for us, right?

BROEKSMIT: That would have to be my choice though, right?

KO: Everything you can tell us is totally up to you. I'm not forcing you to do anything.

BROEKSMIT: Well, I'm not going to give you Barrett Brown right now. If there's something that he's done, and you feel you want to know, or if this is a vendetta thing, then I don't want to be a part of a vendetta.

KO: Don't worry about that . . . I'm trying to assess what information you have, because he's up there, I'm in Houston.

BROEKSMIT: Yeah, I know Jeremy Hammond, Gregg Housh, all the guys.

KO: That's the other thing we need to assess too. If you're not willing to—

BROEKSMIT: Gregg worked with you. Gregg worked with you already. Gregg worked with you guys.

KO: Yeah, yeah. That's the thing, we're collecting a lot of information on a lot of different things. Part of it is, it's going to be a one-way street of information this way. I can't give you all the information today. I can't tell you everything we do, because you don't know me and I don't know you either . . .

BROEKSMIT: I don't expect you to tell me everything you do. If I'm going to be accountable for someone's life, I'd like to think it through.

The conversation meanders, mostly over the topic of my Signal groups and the nearly one hundred people working within them at the time. Ko asks Broeksmit how many of my people he could identify for certain, whether he's ever met me in the flesh, and asks about the identities of several key researchers, including TooManySecrets, offers info on several others, including a young woman who goes by the moniker of Doc Rocket and who exclusively researches far-right operatives. Broeksmit answers here and there, dodges elsewhere, and sometimes responds with a degree of pointless irrelevance that is irritating even to those of us who will later listen with anxiety over how much he gives them. Prompted to describe Joe Fionda, a Project PM vet and television actor with an encyclopedic knowledge of Ukrainian oligarchs and Trump co-conspirators and Weev's emergence as a major node of the neo-Nazi movement, Broeksmit notes that the New York native is fond of riding bikes.

As the interview proceeds, Broeksmit admits to what would appear to be crimes, as well as things that would definitely become so were it feasible to connect them to those of us the FBI has already deemed targets—which, as we've seen, it usually is. He talks about asking Emma Best for $100,000 in cryptocurrency that was put out as a bounty for hacking banks—one of the things he attested to having done. He talks about asking Best for assistance in conducting hacks—the basis of a criminal conspiracy when perpetrated by an FBI target, rather than an FBI collaborator.

> BROEKSMIT: I'm the only idiot who asks Emma Best, "Can you help me hack [*New York Times* editor-at-large] David Enrich?"

The Signal groups come up again and again. And again and again, Broeksmit explains that these are made up largely of journalists, whistleblowers, and activists, and involve no criminal activity of which he is aware.

I was idly staring out the window of the London canal boat that had come to serve as my home and headquarters when I first spotted the spotters. There were two of them, just as there had been that day in 2012 when a joint Dallas Police/FBI SWAT team had been suiting up to raid me come nightfall.

My fiancée, Sylvia Mann, had likewise clocked them as suspicious as she left the boat a few minutes prior. But both of us had let our guard down in the weeks that had passed since a *Sunday Times* article had appeared in which it was noted that my very presence in Britain, even aside from my activities since arriving from Antigua last November, constituted an "embarrassment for Priti Patel." Thus it was that I was actually surprised when the Metropolitan Police soon arrived to board our boat, seize my files, and book me into the Barking and Dagenham Custody Centre to be interviewed on the subject of whether I had been trying to incite the murder of British police.

Incidentally, I hadn't. But I had accompanied Sylvia and some friends to a demonstration in front of parliament the previous month. A couple of them had brought banners and asked me to help hold up one of them, which consisted of two segments, reading "Cops" and "Kill," respectively. As I drank rum out of a bottle being passed around, the guy who'd made the banner moved behind me and to my left such that "Cops Kill" became "Kill Cops," with me standing right in the middle. A photo began making the rounds on Twitter within the hour; within a day, the far-right operative Andy Ngo publicly identified me by name and made it known to the Metropolitan Police Federation that I was associated with "Antifa." He would later be listed in police filings as the "informant"—and, more dubiously, as a "journalist."

When I was brought to the booking desk, the station chief demanded to know why I was uncuffed. My Met captors mumbled something in response and then offered to put the handcuffs back on.

"Well, they're off now anyway," the chief concluded at last, with exquisite Britishness.

As the booking procedure continued, one of the officers present casually mentioned to the desk clerk that I was wanted by the FBI, and that this was known to him thus far only through the "unofficial channels."

Sylvia had long ago made me memorize several phrases and names to be intoned in case of assorted emergencies. In the case of this particular emergency, I evoked "ITN Solicitors." A few hours later, with an ITN lawyer supervising on speakerphone, I replied to several dozen questions with another sacred intonation: "No comment." After Officer Lee and I had completed the ritual, I was returned to my cell. The ceiling was adorned with the twenty-first-century Metropolitan Police equivalent of the Sistine Chapel's *Last Judgment*: a painted proclamation stating, "If you can read this, we have your DNA."

The Met granted me bail later that night, which didn't really matter, since the Home Office had already ordered my continued detention. The Immigration Office, I learned, was coming to interview me in the morning.

"What happens after I talk to immigration?" I asked another senior station official when he opened the door slot to advise me of my rights.

"After that they'll come and take you to a secure facility while you wait for extradition to the U.S., I reckon."

Like the Met officer who'd heard from the FBI back-channel, the station official knew the score.

In contrast, Home Office Immigration Officer Luke Spencer was still in the dark when he arrived the next morning for what he initially seemed to assume would be a routine and lawful immigration interview of an American citizen. "It's very likely you'll be given vow," he told me, in reference to the immigration department's version of bond, "which means you'd be released here and then required to report in to our office at a later date." I had only overstayed my six-month visa by a week, after all, falling well within the normal grace period, and was scheduled to get my second vaccine jab from the NHS in June, after which I planned to move on to Berlin to attend to some business while I waited for my fiancée to get her affairs in order vis-à-vis her ailing mother and then meet me in Europe to plan our life together. All I wanted to do, I told him, was to see Sylvia again before moving on—and to avoid whatever latest trap had been set for me in the United States, a country to which I could not safely return. He assured me again that I would probably be fine; he just had to call his boss to confirm and would be right back, he said as the cell door closed between us.

When Spencer returned an hour later, the door remained closed, his demeanor had shifted, and I was handed a series of documents through the horizontal door slot wherein was set forth the Home Office's official position: that I was "likely to abscond if granted immigration bail"; that my "removal from the UK is imminent"; and that I had "failed to give satisfactory or reliable answers to an Immigration Officer's enquiries." Spencer concluded by noting that the transport unit would arrive to take me to the immigrant relocation center in a few hours, then closed the hatch and left me to my fate. I would have objected, but I'd already noticed that the detention order claimed my six-month visa granted in November had expired five months later, in April, rather than six months later, in the current month of May, and I also knew that this was not the sort of thing that mattered any longer.

Forty-eight hours after first being taken into custody, I was finally permitted to contact Sylvia and inform her that I had been arrested and moved to a detainment center for immediate deportation to the United States, where I would apparently be handed over to the FBI.

It's a fine thing, then, that the head of a major London law firm's immigration division agreed to take on my case for asylum, prompting my release for the duration. The asylum process is long and complex; it has barely begun as of this writing in December 2021, and will likely be ongoing upon publication of these memoirs.

The Crown Prosecution Service dropped its most serious charge against me a few days before my brief trial, which itself resulted in me being found guilty on the lesser charge of having caused "alarm and distress" to unspecified UK police officers and ordered to pay a fine, rather than imprisoned for up to six months, which would have allowed for only a handful of prison columns. Presumably the CPS, the Met, and the Home Office had collectively paid close attention to the slow drip of revelations I began making upon emerging from the immigrant detention facility;

among the materials these agencies were eventually required to hand over were notes made by some other, even more unspecified police officer about a livestream interview Sylvia gave while I was still locked up, in which she "talks about how police must have done digging to locate him," "talks about her and BROWN's relationship," "confirms he is registered at their family doctors," and "claims that BROWN is recruiting people with the Detention Centre for his project." And as for the "comment [from a viewer asking] if the US can put him in prison if he gets deported," we may assume the answer to be yes. As for what specifically the FBI thinks it has on me, it's hard to say. But so long as I remain outside its direct reach, it's more to the point how much I have on them. In this case, you may presume the answer to be "far more than is included here."

These memoirs have no ending insofar as my own fate is concerned. And under the circumstances, I am not even at liberty to speak about my plans for the future, or how these may relate to the broader plans under which I've operated in the past. The best I can do is to conclude with a story that made a very strong impression on me as a child and came to inform my life to follow.

The first memory I have of any full narrative, or even much of anything at all, is that of an episode of *Alfred Hitchcock Presents* I saw when I was eight years old and recently tracked down again for the purpose of describing it in some detail here. The episode is titled "The Crooked Road."

It begins with a well-dressed man and woman driving down a rural highway. When a police car pulls in front of them, the man at the wheel understandably assumes he is expected to pass the officer, and so he accelerates to do so, still staying within the speed limit. The cop turns on his siren and forces the car off the road. The man demands an explanation but none is forthcoming; instead, the officer fixes him with a predatory gaze as he pulls the man's key out of the ignition and asks for his license and registration. As the situation grows more tense and the woman speaks up, the cop tells her to remain silent while the "men folk" talk, and then orders them to follow his squad car into town. But their car is now too damaged to drive. Rather than allow the man to replace the damaged tire with a spare, the cop insists that this won't work. The man insists this is false and that the cop himself knows it to be false. The woman cautions him to comply nonetheless. "Don't you see what he's trying to do?" she says. She understands the cop is trying to get him to react to this series of injustices and falsehoods in the way that any honorable person would, thus putting him in further legal jeopardy.

Just then a tow truck arrives on the scene, and the cop repeatedly notes what a lucky thing it is that the town's mechanic should show up at that moment. As the man insists that the mechanic should be the one to decide if a tow is really necessary, the tow truck's radio broadcasts from the local police band radio, which everyone can hear through the open window. The man observes that this is illegal, prompting a menacing reply from the cop, who then tells the mechanic that the car is too damaged to drive and will indeed require towing. The man responds that the mechanic and cop are obviously working in tandem. The cop punches him so hard that he crumples to the ground, and then turns to the mechanic, who states that he witnessed the man resisting arrest.

In front of the judge, the cop provides his concocted version of events. The man—now "the defendant"—repeatedly objects to individual falsehoods, until finally laying out the totality of the truth, which is that the cop and the mechanic are the actual criminals. The cop punches him in the stomach, and the judge proclaims that he was right to do so, as the defendant had made a "threatening gesture." He is charged with speeding, and pleads not guilty for the reasons he has already outlined. The judge tells him to appear in court the following Friday and post a hundred dollars' bond; otherwise he will spend the intervening time in jail. In the exchange that follows, the judge makes it clear that the defendant should simply plead "guilty." The defendant reluctantly agrees, at which point the judge piles on additional charges, fines, and court costs. When the defendant asks what "court costs" entails, the judge threatens to triple them.

Afterward the man and woman walk over to the body shop to pick up their car and pay another round of illicit fees to get it back after the needless repairs. When the man makes a quip about how well the mechanic, the cop, and the judge made out from their crooked dealings that day, the mechanic threatens him with a wrench and tells him to leave before the cop gets back and makes things worse for him.

In the last scene, the couple is back on the highway.

Woman: Charming community, wasn't it?

Man: One in a million. Well, I guess we've had enough, don't you think?

Woman: More than enough.

Man: You better check and make sure you got everything.

The woman nods and opens her purse, which turns out to contain a built-in tape recorder.

The United Kingdom's asylum process requires that I be

able to demonstrate certain things about the United States and its institutions if I am to avoid being sent back. I have no choice but to comply.

And so ends my story. The moral is that if you take lots of hard drugs and fuck with the government, everything will work out fine in the end.

ACKNOWLEDGMENTS

A tremendous number of people have assisted me in the course of this struggle. Many have come under unwanted scrutiny as a result, to such an extent that the FBI and DOJ were discovered to have sought to identify every single donor to my legal defense fund. Under the circumstances, the only responsible way to express thanks to those not mentioned in the book is to refrain from naming them at all.

A NOTE ABOUT THE AUTHOR

Barrett Brown is an award-winning journalist who has written for *Vanity Fair*, *The Daily Beast*, *The Guardian*, *Vice*, *The Intercept*, *Skeptic*, Al Jazeera, *The Huffington Post*, and other outlets. In 2016 he won the National Magazine Award in the category of columns and commentary. He was released from federal prison in November 2016 after serving four years. He applied for political asylum in 2021 in the United Kingdom, where his case is currently pending. He lives in London.